James Stark

The Lights of the North

Illustrating the Rise and Progress of Christianity in North-Eastern Scotland

James Stark

The Lights of the North
Illustrating the Rise and Progress of Christianity in North-Eastern Scotland

ISBN/EAN: 9783337252847

Printed in Europe, USA, Canada, Australia, Japan

Cover: Foto ©ninafisch / pixelio.de

More available books at **www.hansebooks.com**

The Lights of the North:

ILLUSTRATING THE

RISE AND PROGRESS OF CHRISTIANITY

IN NORTH-EASTERN SCOTLAND

BY

JAMES STARK, D.D.

AUTHOR OF
"JOHN MURKER OF BANFF"; "DR. KIDD OF ABERDEEN"; ETC.

ABERDEEN: D. WYLLIE & SON
MDCCCXCVI

PRINTED AT THE "FREE PRESS" OFFICE
ABERDEEN

To

Sir WILLIAM DUGUID GEDDES, LL.D.

PRINCIPAL OF THE UNIVERSITY OF
ABERDEEN

PREFACE.

EVER since I wrote the life of Dr. Kidd it has been my cherished desire, by an appeal to the records of the past, to show to the people of this part of Scotland, where I have spent almost the whole of my public life, how much they owe to that Evangel, which has been here for more than a thousand years, and still lies at the heart of the ministrations of all true churches of Christ. The hours of leisure which the cares of my pastorate allowed I have spent in trying to master this large subject in its successive historical enshrinements and various denominational phases, that the central and vital element in our common Christianity may be seen, especially by the young, to be to-day what it has ever been—the rock and bulwark of all that is most precious in our life. The method pursued has been to use biography as subservient to history; to seize the essential facts and salient features of the successive periods of the Church—Celtic,

Roman, and Protestant—and to group them around local figures of pre-eminent brilliancy and usefulness. There is no book that I know of which sets forth what is here attempted; but is it not well that some one should undertake the task?

The field is so wide, and the details, with their local colouring, so multiplied that it will be strange if no errors have crept in; but I have done my best to insure accuracy, and, above all, to maintain fairness and catholicity.

In the course of the narrative I acknowledge my indebtedness to various authors; it would be too long a list to print were I to name all the books I have consulted, and the many tracts and pamphlets which have yielded me fugitive gleanings.

One of the main advantages of a book such as this is that the information which is scattered and locked up in a literature that is miscellaneous and often not very accessible, is here knit together and presented as an organic and continuous whole.

Among the many friends who have been of great service to me in my work, I cannot refrain

PREFACE. ix.

from mentioning the names of George Walker, Aberdeen; P. J. Anderson, M.A., LL.B., of the University Library; and James MacDonald, F.S.A. Scot., The Farm, Huntly.

Through the kind permission of the Senatus of Aberdeen University and the Fine Art Institute of Glasgow, we have been able to reproduce in photogravure the portrait of Bishop Elphinstone which is in King's College.

J. S.

ABERDEEN, *November*, 1896.

CONTENTS.

CHAPTER.		PAGE.
I.	Columba—521-97 .	1
II.	Drostan	18
III.	Machar and Ternan	31
IV.	From the Celtic to the Roman Church —1069-93	46
V.	Archdeacon Barbour—1316-95	57
VI.	Bishop Elphinstone—1431-1514	65
VII.	The Religious Life of Pre-Reformation Times	75
VIII.	The Reformation—1560	87
IX.	John Craig—1512-1600	103
X.	Bishop Patrick Forbes—1564-1635	115
XI.	Samuel Rutherford in Aberdeen—1636-38	130
XII.	The Covenanting Struggle in Aberdeen —1638	145
XIII.	Andrew Cant—1584-1663	157
XIV.	The Quakers in Aberdeen—1662	170
XV.	Alexander Jaffray of Kingswells—1614-73	175
XVI.	Church Life in the Seventeenth Century	188
XVII.	The Seceders—1733	197
XVIII.	The Moderates	213

CONTENTS.

CHAPTER.		PAGE.
XIX.	Principal Campbell—1719-96	221
XX.	John Skinner of Linshart—1721-1807	232
XXI.	The Methodists—1747	245
XXII.	George Cowie of Huntly—1749-1806	255
XXIII.	The Independents—1797	264
XXIV.	Dr. Kidd—1793-1834	276
XXV.	Patrick Robertson of Craigdam—1777-1867	287
XXVI.	The Disruption of 1843	296
XXVII.	—The Revival in Aberdeen of 1858-60	308
XXVIII.	—The Christianity of the Present Day—1896	318
	APPENDIX	331
	INDEX	337

The Lights of the North.

CHAPTER I.

COLUMBA—521-97.

IT is a far cry from Aberdeen to Iona, but there is ground for the belief that our northern county owes its possession of the most precious and sacred things in life to the direct instrumentality of him whose name has invested the little green isle of the Western sea with an imperishable fame. Besides participating in the general indebtedness of the greater part of Scotland for the truly apostolic labours of the Irish missionary of soldier-like spirit, there is evidence that Columba, along with his disciple Drostan, landed on the shores of this district and traversed the north-eastern part of it, in the course of a pioneering tour.

The first distinct and documentary account we have of the evangelisation of Pictland, or that stretch of country which lay to the northeast of the Roman wall that was built between the Forth and the Clyde, is in the pages of the life of Columba written by Adamnan, who was born twenty-seven years after the Christian hero passed away, and was one of his successors in office. There were probably some fugitive glimmerings of the Christian light seen in the far north before that date. Tertullian, with the triumphant tone of a Christian apologist who sees the truth prevailing, maintained that the Cross had trophies in remote parts of Caledonia which were inaccessible to the Roman arms. While it would not be safe to attach much weight to that vague assertion, which may have been only a rhetorical flourish, yet it is not unlikely that some bold and enthusiastic converts to the Christian faith ventured into the unknown region of mountain, swamp, and forest, which lay like an island outside the boundaries of the world-empire, and preached the Gospel to its wild and hardy inhabitants, who might be conquered by the drilled legions of Rome, but were never subdued. There are numerous traces still discernible of the encampments and marches of the Imperial army north of the Forth, and it is not too much to assume that there were some Christian soldiers in its ranks who dropped the seed of the Kingdom by the way, more especially after the Emperor Constantine's conversion early in the fourth century, which brought the religion that had been persecuted with a Satanic fury among the things that now basked in the sunshine of popular favour. If Paul could speak in his day of saints in "Cæsar's household," there were surely some Christian military men from Rome who did not put their light under a bushel when marching through benighted Caledonia.

But, speaking generally, it may be affirmed that while Romanised Britain, to the south of the great wall, was more or less superficially familiar with the creed of Christianity by the fifth century, through the labours of Ninian in Galloway, along with other workers whose record is in heaven, all beyond the line of Roman conquest, with the exception of one or two favoured spots, such, perhaps, as Abernethy, in Perthshire, was an unbroken extent of unrelieved heathenism. To Columba belongs the honour of making it his special endeavour to bring that part of the world under the sway of Christ.

Columba was in every way eminently endowed and fitted for the herculean task to which he felt himself called, and to which he gave the whole-hearted devotion of the best part of a lifetime. He had a splendid capital of natural resource and social consequence at his command. He was of Royal descent, and was widely connected with the ruling families in Ireland. He himself was a born leader of men, the outward frame of uncommon height and strength corresponding with his inward force of character and ardour of spirit. He had a voice, too, of such penetrating power that, while in a building it did not impress the hearer as being much louder than that of others, yet, it is said, could be heard on the other side of the Sound of Mull, about a mile distant from Iona. He had much of that kind of greatness which could not but make itself felt among the savages whom he sought to tame in the name of Christ. He was by no means a saint of the orthodox monastic pattern—meek, mild, and inoffensive. He had a great deal of the "old man" in him, which to the end rubbed shoulders with the "new man," and occasionally over-mastered him; it is reported, for example, that he chased a wrong-doer into the sea till he was up to the knees in water, cursing him all the time.

But he had rough work to do, and sometimes his patience was sorely tried and his superabundant energy taxed. He addressed himself with a quenchless valour against the polygamy, the slavery, the brutal cruelty to women which then prevailed, for, as Professor Mackinnon tells us, in the regions where Columba laboured the female slave was the standard of value in fixing the price of an article, and women fought alongside men in battle.

Columba's occasional explosiveness was no more than his strong sense of justice outraged; it was the righteousness within him in an active and perhaps turbulent state. He had much of what is called an "impassioned uprightness." He was a Celt of the Celts, easily roused, but withal warm-hearted and generous; or, as an old composition written in praise of him says—" He was a harp without a base chord, a physician of the heart, a consolation to the poor, beloved of all." He had the heart of a poet, and was alive to the finer sentiments which give tenderness and beauty to life. In proof of his love of his native land, from which he had exiled himself, there is an old tradition that on coming to this country he landed first on the island of Oronsay, but because he could see Ireland from the hill, he must needs press still further north.

In fitting him for his work as the founder of the Celtic Church in what is now called Scotland, he had all the culture which Ireland, the principal seat of learning at the time in Europe, could give him. It is noticeable that the men whose personality is conspicuously marked in the great epochs of the world's history were usually well-equipped with all that the schools could furnish them at the time in which they lived. Moses, the Hebrew legislator, had the full benefit of the best education Egypt could afford; Paul sat at the feet of Gamaliel and had his mind stored with all the lore of his nation; Luther and Knox were well schooled in various ways before they began their career as Reformers; Columba was the flower of the culture and piety of the "Isle of Saints," and had founded many monasteries and churches in Ireland before, at the age of forty-two, he began the great Gospel enterprise of which Iona was to be the centre.

It is interesting to notice, as showing the strange changes and startling contrasts which time brings round, that more than fourteen hundred years ago Ireland was in many respects in advance of all other countries in Europe. Learning flourished and piety rooted itself in that island when the Continent was in the throes of a great transition state. It was a refuge to the scholar and a quiet sanctuary to the devout seeker after God amidst the commotion and upheaval caused by the breaking up of the empire, and the establishment of a new political order. Ireland, the original land of the Scots, did more for religion and general culture in those days than any other country in the world. What, too, is more remarkable still, no country was then so independent of the hierarchy in Rome, and, indeed, seems to have had little communication with it.

In leaving Ireland for missionary work in this land, Columba was doing no more than many of the best of his fellow-countrymen did, who, like Paul, felt they were debtors to the

Greek and barbarian; but more than one motive has been ascribed to this fiery son of Erin, for his action at the time. It would appear that a breach of cordial feeling between him and some of his friends had something to do with his departure. It arose in this wise:—Columba, who was a most industrious and expert transcriber, had copied a psalter which belonged to Finnian. That grasping Churchman meanly insisted that the copy which Columba had taken with his own hand should be handed over to him, as it could not have been in existence but for his psalter. The high-spirited Columba resisted such a demand, and the question having been referred to Dermod, King of Ireland, the decision was given which afterwards became a proverb in Ireland—" To every book belongs its son-book (or copy), as to every cow belongs her calf. Therefore the book you wrote, O Columba, belongs by right to Finnian." This incensed Columba, and the difference deepening and spreading among the rival tribes, actually led to war and bloodshed.

Thus constrained by a variety of motives, the loftiest of which, however, predominated, as his subsequent history showed, Columba turned his back upon Ireland, and with twelve companions (the same number as St. Patrick had when he went to Ireland) in his osier craft, in the year 563 A.D., he landed at Iona, near the region to which his compatriots, the Dalriad Scots, had migrated. The place was admirably chosen for the purpose he had in view, which was not only to provide for the ready dissemination of the truth, but also to secure a strong and compact centre of religious life. He wanted to establish a little Christian community that would be isolated from the contamination and strife of surrounding heathenism, and yet have ready access to it, with the remedial agencies of the gospel, just as in our own day the principal station for the evangelisation of one part of New Guinea was at first an adjoining islet. He wanted to show what could be done for a little bit of this world, when all its inhabitants were more or less obedient to the law of Christ, and to give an effective object-lesson to every beholder of the order, peace, and industry of which the whole country might become the scene. He wanted also to make this spot a rallying point—a kind of ecclesiastical metropolis — for the Christendom that was to be in these northern isles. That little rock-bound islet, often swept with tempests, which fittingly pourtrayed the unrest and strife that raged among the surrounding heathen, was to be a world in itself, a kingdom of heaven that was coming, if not come. Has not his own glowing prediction, uttered before his death, been fulfilled—" Small and mean though this place is, it shall yet be held in great and unusual honour, not only by Scotic kings and peoples, but also by the rulers of foreign and barbarous nations and by their subjects; the saints also even of other Churches shall regard it with no common reverence." As Dr. Johnson put it, in a passage that has now become classic—" We were now treading that illustrious island which was once the luminary of the Caledonian regions, where savage clans or roving barbarians derived the benefits of knowledge and the blessings of religion. . . . Far from me, and from my friends, be such frigid philosophy as may conduct us indifferent and unmoved over any ground which has been dignified by wisdom, bravery, or virtue. That man is little to be envied whose patriotism would not gain force upon the plain of Marathon, or whose piety would not grow warmer among the ruins of Iona."

From hints dropped by Adamnan in his biography, it would appear that Columba had skill in teaching men how to make the best of this world as well as the next. Whatever else Iona was, it must have been the model farm of the day. Never were stinted natural resources more thoroughly developed than they were on that island under the direction and inspiration of this man of big brain and heart, as well as big body. The little patches of corn-land and pasture, notwithstanding tearful skies and fierce winds, yielded as much as maintained a hundred and fifty persons, besides a ceaseless stream of visitors. Those saints of ancient days, including Columba himself, put their hand to any kind of work that had to be done, not excepting what is usually reserved for the other sex.

It is sometimes stated that celibacy was not enforced, even in the early days of the Celtic Church, but there is no evidence of its clergy being married when Columba was alive, or for many years afterwards. The "Island of the Women," which is near Iona, was probably the place where female members of pilgrimage parties were detained. Like the inmates of the other monasteries of those days, before they became luxurious and corrupt, the members of that commonwealth became adepts at all kinds of handicraft, and their homestead was a very hive of industry.

The Celtic genius, minute and patient, excelled in finish of artistic workmanship, and there are illuminated manuscripts still extant, the admiration of all beholders, which are said to be the product of that place.

The county of Aberdeen has the distinction of possessing what is supposed to be the most ancient symbol of the veneration in which Columba was held by our ancestors. One of the treasures of Monymusk House is the famous

Brecbannoch*, a small casket which had probably at one time contained some fragments of the bones of the saint. If it be the Brecbannoch mentioned in authentic charters, in looking upon it we see what was carried as a holy shrine round Bruce's army before Bannockburn was fought.†

There is a romance in the picture which Adamnan, by the incidental allusions he makes, permits our imagination to draw of the high-souled life that was lived there in the days of Columba. It is like a realised Utopia—one of the isles of the blest—even when we omit the miracles and the fabulous exaggerations of the credulous and fanciful narrator. It was in some respects a departure from the normal order of things, and, therefore, contained within itself the elements of its own coming dissolution; but there was Christ-like purpose in it, and it survived for centuries and for part of that time proved itself indeed to be an enterprise of heaven. What an ideal alternation of the manual and the intellectual, the secular and the spiritual, in the daily routine of those Celtic worthies! The island was a farm, a school of learning, a church, a missionary society. Columba and his coadjutors passed from the plough and the spade, the grinding of corn and the baking

* "Church and Priory of Monymusk," pp. 3, 4, 5.
† See Appendix.

of bread, to the transcription and illumination of copies of the Scriptures; they went from private devotion and public worship to the entertainment of strangers and the teaching of those who came from afar to be instructed, or launching one of their fleet of boats for a missionary expedition to a distant part of the coast, where the Crucified One had not as yet been lifted up.

One man under God was the moving, moulding spirit of the whole. What an almost unexampled position of trust and responsibility was that which Columba erected for himself in Iona. No king that ever sat on Scotland's throne wielded such power. There has been much controversy about the ecclesiastical order which prevailed in Iona and in the Celtic Church to which the society there gave birth; but practically the polity was summed up in one word— Columba. He was a Presbyter abbot, like the head of similar institutions in Ireland, but he was above all things himself under authority to Christ, and such a strong and noble personality could not fail to give effect to itself while it was a living presence.

Part of the secret of the spell which he exerted upon others lay in the personal application of the example of Him who, though the greatest of all, was yet the servant of all. Columba said to his followers "Come" rather than "Go." Where high and perilous service was needed he was at hand. Adamnan says he could not spend the space of even one hour without study or prayer or writing or some other holy occupation. There can be no doubt he was a man of prodigious industry as well as colossal force. There is a tradition that in every church he planted (and he planted hundreds) he deposited a copy of the Gospels which he had copied with his own hand.

He was original on the active rather than the reflective side of his nature; the hero, not the thinker; the herald rather than the theologian. Yet he knew how to feed the flame of piety by prayer and meditation. Like Bernard he preserved a due balance of force between the inward and outward in his life. The "three fifties," as he called the Book of Psalms, and the other parts of Scripture committed to memory and frequently recited, kept alive in his character those elements which were the sure basis of his sainthood and soldiership. Spiritual song, with some sort of accompaniment, was also extensively used in quickening the inward life.

But we must now hasten to deal with Columba's work in our own part of the world. Adamnan makes no mention of it, though he names several of the churches and monasteries which the Abbot of Iona had founded in other parts of the land. He tells us also that two or three years after the great missionary crusade was begun, Columba crossed the border of the Pictish kingdom, travelling through Breadalbane, Atholl, and the Grampians until he reached the Ness, beside which, and not far from the site of Inverness, was the fortress and palace of King Brude, son of Malcolm, where a good stroke of work was done for the cause which was so much at heart. Although the pages of Adamnan are silent concerning any visit paid to the north-east coast, there have been persistent traditions clinging to certain localities in that region which point to close association with Columba. Among these, Aberdour, near which there are traces of a considerable population belonging to prehistoric times, and Old Deer have conspicuously made their mark on the popular memory, which is shown in the names given to wells and other places associated with the saint; and in the discovery of the "Book of Deer" in Cambridge University in 1860, a remarkable witness has risen up in confirmation of tradition. This manuscript consists of the Gospel of John and parts of the other three Evangelists in Latin, along with the Apostles' Creed and a fragment of an office for the visitation of the sick. The name of the writer is not given, but he asks for the prayers of the reader. Dr. Stuart gives us some interesting information regarding this MS. In 1697 the "Book of Deer" formed part of the collection of MSS. of John

Moore, then Bishop of Norwich. It came into the possession of the University of Cambridge in 1715, the Bishop having died in 1714, and his library, bought by King George I., was presented to Cambridge University. The rare value of this MS. lies in the entries—in the vernacular—of grants of land made to the monastery and inserted in the eleventh and twelth centuries. These memoranda give us glimpses of the patriarchal polity which still existed, but was soon to give way to a feudal kingdom. We give what is of importance to our purpose as Dr. Stuart translates it *:—

"Columcille and Drostan, son of Cosgrach, his pupil, came from Hy, or Iona, as God hath shown to them, to Abberdoboir, or Aberdour, and Bede, the Cruithnech or Pict, was mormaer of Buchan before them, and it was he that gave them that cathair or town in freedom for ever from mormaer and toisech. They came after that to the other town, and it was pleasing to Columcille, because it was full of God's grace, and he asked of the mormaer—viz., Bede—that he should give it him, and he did not give it; and a son of his took an illness after refusing the clerics, and he was nearly dead. Then the mormaer went to entreat the clerics that they should make prayer for the son, that health should come to him, and he gave an offering to them from Cloch in tipart to Cloch pette meic Garnait. They made the prayer,

* The "Book of Deer," p. 48 in preface.

and health came to him. Then Columcille gave to Drostan that cathair, and blessed it, and left as his word—'Whosoever should come against it, let him not be many-yeared [or] victorious.' Drostan's tears came on parting with Columcille. Said Columcille—'Let Deer be its name henceforward.'"

There have been many shiftings since Columba's time, and Iona is no longer a centre and focus of missionary activity, but just as Nature, which still keeps Iona's grass green and flows in the tides which wash her rocky shores every day, is as fresh and vigorous as ever, so the truth, of which the island in its history is a witness and a symbol, is Scotland's glory and security to-day. There is not a visible thing bearing the trace of man's hand in Iona now that can with certainty be identified with Columba. Six times did the marauding Norsemen reduce the monastery to ashes. There is not, of course, the slightest vestige of the turf-walled or wattled structures in which the monks lived and worshipped; the stone edifices reared in a much later age are now in ruins. The Celtic Church, which sprang from his labours, was merged in the Roman Church six centuries ago; that again was discarded by the nation at the time of the Reformation. Yet Columba lives in the hearts of all Scotsmen who know Christ; for that stalwart figure of far away times can never be effaced from the memory as long as we appreciate the labours of those who did most to bring the races from which we sprang into the possession of the unfading glories and undying hopes which cluster around the Cross.

CHAPTER II.

DROSTAN.

LET us, by the use of available sources of information, obtain as vivid an idea as possible of the state of this part of the country at the time of Columba's arrival. The Romans had long ago taken their departure from the other side of the rampart between the Forth and the Clyde which had with difficulty held back the untamed races of the north. The Imperial people, who for so many centuries had been invaders, were in turn invaded, and to concentrate their forces at home, where they were urgently needed, had to withdraw entirely from Britain in 410 A.D., shortly after Ninian had built his stone church—Candida Casa—on the Solway Firth. The inglorious fall which came at last after such a splendid career, which has been written in ineffaceable characters in the history of the world, brought unsettlement and confusion to the greater part of Europe.

The hardy Picts of the North, scarcely touched by the refining but enfeebling civilisation of Rome, which held possession of the greater part of Britain for nearly five hundred years, now made short work of the wall, and were a source of terror to their neighbours on the other side. The nearness of a common foe so powerful as Rome, whom they had resisted to the death, had doubtless tended to the consolidation of the various independent tribes that peopled the northern part of the land. By the time that Columba paid his first visit to Buchan with Drostan and founded the Monastery at Deer, what now bears the name of Scotland was divided into four parts—Northumbria and Strathclyde on the south-east and south-west, Pictland and Scotia on the north-east and north-west. The latter part was inhabited by an Irish colony, the Dalriads or Scots, who had migrated from the mother-country to Argyle and adjacent parts in the fifth or sixth century, and who by their aggressive energy succeeded eventually in mastering and giving their name to the whole land, "Scotland" by the eleventh century no longer being the sister isle, but our own native Caledonia.

The native Picts, to a large extent mixed with other races, Celtic, Saxon, and Norse, were the ancestors of the inhabitants of this part of the country. Before Christianity was introduced the civilisation of our ancestors was not greater than that of many heathen districts in Africa as they may be seen in the present day. The numerous spear-heads and battle-axes of stone and the arrow-heads of flint which the plough and the spade have unearthed in our fields tell their own tale of the time. The chief occupation of those Picts when not fighting with each other or their neighbours was hunting and fishing, by which they obtained most of their food supplies. To a large extent the land was a wilderness of forest and swamp, where the deer, the wolf, and the boar abounded, the patches of ground that were cultivated being generally on the slopes of the hills. Our savage ancestors navigated lake and sea in canoes made out of hollow trees, such as are still occasionally dug up out of the morasses, or in boats made of wicker-work covered with skins of animals.

While we are left to a great extent to speculation and guess-work in trying to ascertain the origin and use of such "vitrified forts" as Dunideer and Tap o' Noth, which "stands sentinel over the upper waters of the Bogie," yet the highest authorities lean to the conclusion that they were strongholds in which the people of the district we are describing could shelter themselves when hard pressed by dangerous neighbours, or, at a later period, by the more dreaded invading and marauding Norsemen, as the beacon fires were kindled. How much do those remains suggest, and yet how much do they veil, of the period to which they belong. There is a pathetic vagueness in the utterance of their testimony which reminds us that oblivion claims so much more than history of the movements of the succeeding races of mankind.

The religion of the ancient Picts, it would appear, was little better than fetichism—a vague deification of the objects and forces of Nature; in the absence of light from above, it was an unconscious projection of their own wayward ideas and fierce passions into space, so that which they really worshipped was a reflection of themselves. There has been endless controversy about the Druids, who have been described as the high priests of the native religion, a learned and sacred caste somewhat like the Magi of Persia, but our identification of them with the religion of this part of the world may be attributed to reasonable conjecture rather than to actual knowledge. It has been sarcastically said by agnostic historians that Druid is a word that has been invented to conceal our ignorance. It is certainly difficult for the human mind to reconcile itself to a state of avowed vacancy, and when knowledge fails we are frequently not unwilling to allow fancy to take its place. For a long time we connected what Julius Cæsar said of the Druids as he saw them in Gaul with the ancient monoliths and stone circles, popularly called "Temples," more or less complete, which are found in this as in other parts of the country. As the result, however, of deepening research, we have learned to be more cautious, and are beginning to admit that we really have no evidence for any very definite conclusion as to the use to which the enclosure within those huge weather-beaten stones was put. So far as we know there is no mention made of those stone circles by Roman writers, and, as they were very particular in the information they gave of our country as observed by them, we may fairly assume that those huge stones were not put up till after the Roman period.

Human remains have been found beside those rude survivals of a remote past, but that proves little, as it was not uncommon in ancient times to bury the dead beside any remarkable or historic place. The general consensus of opinion amongst those who by special study are entitled to be heard is that those circles were places of assembly and of justice, and probably also of worship and interment. They were the "high places," the "forum," of the tribes, and when the people themselves lived in caves, in mud or wattled houses, there would be, in their eyes, something exalted in the circles, taking in old heathen times the place that the cathedrals did at a later and Christian period. As has been well said, "the church, market, court, and sepulchre represent ideas and facts which ever tend to group themselves among all nations, especially among ourselves;" and the stone circles probably answered all those ends.

Some of the relics of the heathen life of those remote times are with us, lurking in the customs and words still in use. There are superstitious practices stealthily clung to which are just the remote past keeping its foot in the present. Yule, All-Hallow E'en, the very days of the week, such as Wednesday and Thursday, called after the Saxon deities Woden and Thor, are survivals of the heathenism which once had a place in this land. Less than two hundred years ago it was not so very uncommon in the more benighted parts of Aberdeenshire, to leave a portion of the farm untilled, "the guid man's craft," as a gift of propitiation to the "auld man" to keep him from "shakin' the corn."

That superstition dies hard, that the ancient and buried layer of heathenism has succeeded in keeping itself in view down to our own century, we have proof of in a "Book of Power" lying in the Aberdeen Free Church College library. It belongs to the museum that was bequeathed by the late Mr. Thomson of Banchory to the above-named institution. Up till about the middle of this century it was used by a wizard or "wise man" to enable him to have power over the people of the island of Lewis. It stands now in a more useful place, with the black and white yarns enclosing it, and the key that had to be put within certain pages before the charm could work!

What may be regarded as the last utterance of Celtic heathenism known to us is found in the Book of the Dean of Lismore, where the bard—perhaps of Ossian's time—is represented as addressing one of the Christian missionaries who was regarded as being oblivious in his saintliness of Nature's charm—" Patrick of the solemn psalms, how great your love must be since you do not close your book and listen to the voice of the blackbird. Sweet blackbird, high on yon bending bough, how soothing is your song! Although you never heard mass said by priests, how delightfully you whistle!" It is so difficult for men to realise that there is nothing incompatible between the psalms and the "song of the blackbird!"

Before closing this chapter, we must dwell for a little upon the life and work of one who has left his mark upon our country—Drostan, the nephew of Columba. The little information we have about him is almost all legendary, but, as we have seen, his name is mentioned in the "Book of Deer" as having accompanied Columba when he came to Aberdour and passed over to what is now called Old Deer. Like many more of Columba's distinguished associates and followers, Drostan is said to have been of Royal descent. There is evidence that just as in the early days of the Reformed Church in Scotland men of high social position devoted themselves to the work of the ministry, so in the spring-time of the Celtic Church many of noble birth abandoned the pursuits of war and became soldiers of the Prince of Peace. That may partly account for the easy access the missionaries of those days had to chieftains and kings, and for the successful efforts they made to bring such into the Christian fold. When the religion of the Cross was first planted, her adherents were chiefly the poor and the obscure. Christianity, as it came to be increasingly a force in society, gradually rose socially till the Emperor himself, Constantine, identified himself with it. But in the sixth century we find that the order was reversed by the Irish evangelists, and their first aim was to win over the head of a tribe, and all the members of it gradually, at least in name, followed his example. That made the work of the time very superficial, more rapid than thorough, and accounted for Paganism lingering in our land as a feeling and factor long after Christianity, by general profession, held the field. In proof of this it may be mentioned that when pestilence or other appalling calamity came it was attributed, sometimes, to the change in religion which had taken place, and a bad harvest often drove the people to seek help from their idols.

The legend tells us that when Columba left Drostan in charge of the Deer Monastery, tears came into the eyes of the pupil at parting with his beloved master. So Columba said, "Let Deer (from the Gaelic word meaning "tears") be its name henceforward." Celtic scholars, perhaps, are nearer the mark in suggesting that the real derivation of Deer is from *dair*, an oak. The country then abounded in oaks, as is shown by their remains in mosses, and the names of such places in the neighbourhood as Aikie-hill and Aikie-brae.

After doing service for a considerable number of years at Deer, we are told that when age came upon him, Drostan retired to Glenesk, where he lived as a hermit and founded a church by the side of Lochlee, where his name still lingers. The church in Insch also was dedicated to Drostan. There is a "Dustan" fair held at Deer and at Insch, and one also near Wick. Thus the name has travelled down all the centuries and is still with us to testify to the deep and enduring impression the man who bore it has produced upon this part of Scotland. Tradition says he was buried at his own request at Aberdour. His day in the calendar is 15th December.

As a matter of policy as well as of sentiment, Christian pioneers in our own land did not obliterate, but Christianised heathen institutions and associations. There is a curiously-wrought stone with a cross upon it within the domains of Aboyne Castle that was originally set up on the site of the ancient *Al* at Kinnord.* There are few things more interesting in human history than the tenacity with which tradition and custom cling to certain spots made sacred and familiar long ago by worship. A hermit sets up a cell or oratory, a missionary rears his humble chapel of reeds, a "creel house," often in a place where heathen religion had held its festivals and offered its sacrifices, and for ever afterwards there is a difference between it and other parts. It is a centre, a rallying point, a place of concourse; building displaces building, in the course of ages, each in its structure and style partaking in the advancement that comes with the years; it may be long after every vestige of man's hand is gone, not one stone being left upon another, and the place has ceased to be a chapel for the worshipper or a shrine for the pious pilgrim, yet the name remains of the saint who by his devotion to duty had hallowed the spot. Men still unconsciously do homage to his memory by meeting periodically for business at a fair or market on the spot to which sacred tradition and custom cling, like the rowan tree or stunted rosebush we see in a Highland glen, which tells us of clearances and dismantled human abodes, and of field and garden now merged in the wide wilderness.

* Michie's "History of Loch Kinnord," p. 43.

Those Celtic evangelists had a strange blending in their lives of roving enterprise and ascetic solitariness. They were Christian explorers, pioneers, missionaries, and they were recluses. They isolated themselves from the heathenism that was around them, and yet they daringly invaded and penetrated it with their aggressive evangelism. They had the retreats belonging to the community of which they were members— the *familia*—where they devoted themselves to prayer and industrial pursuits, and yet, unlike most of the monks of Roman Catholic times, they had their periodic incursions into the world with a view to its subjugation. There is evidence that the Orkneys, the Faroe Isles, Iceland, and other parts of the far north were visited and so far reclaimed by those daring Columban evangelists. There are distinct traces of them in France, Germany, Italy, and Austria. Columbanus, twenty-seven years after Columba landed in Iona, crossed over to the Continent, and his companions and followers founded new houses, and carried with them light and enthusiasm wherever they went. The books which those Scotic missionaries used were written in their own hand in Latin and freely glossed in Gaelic. Some of them are still preserved in the libraries of St. Gall, Milan, Turin, and other towns in Europe.

The intensity of their Celtic nature made

them equally at home in the oratory and the coracle. We read of Cormac sailing out in the North Sea for fourteen days in one of those frail and tiny vessels which placed nothing between the voyager and the great deep but a framework of wood with hides stretched upon it. On lonely islets and in other solitary places in the West Highlands, where Nature's Sabbatic quiet is almost as much undisturbed to-day as it was in those far-off times, we see the remains of rude structures of uncemented stone where they meditated and worshipped; and in the names still clinging to parishes where men have dwelt since the dawn of history we see evidence of their practical activity, which was as pronounced as their love of seclusion. A place of retreat for prayer and meditation was called a "desert," and the name Dysart, in Fife, is traceable to that circumstance.

Let us try to picture to ourselves their manner of life. Each monastery, such as Mortlach, Monymusk, or Deer, which was a kind of "military base of operations against the powers of heathenism," following the Apostolic tradition, had its college of twelve monks, with the prior as their head. Each monk had his separate cell, or hut of wattles thatched with reeds. The inner court or citadel of the community was the church, which was often of hewn oak, there being no trace of stone buildings till about the eighth century.

Truly the noblest period of many institutions is often the meanest to the eye. Around the whole was a turf embankment for protection. The dress of the clergy was severely plain, consisting of a tunic, over which was a cloak " with a hood of rough texture made of wool of the natural undyed colour," and shoes of hide. While in residence they were called to united prayer three times during the day and three times during the night. From their beds of straw they could soon rise and respond to the midnight bell, as they slept in their ordinary clothes.

In going forth as evangelistic pilgrims, like the Seventy, they went two and two, each carrying a long walking-stick and a leathern wallet. They would spend weeks or months in preaching in the open air to the heathen tribes, exposed to privation and danger, and then return to the monastic house to be recruited in body and refreshed in spirit by fellowship with the other members of the fraternity.

CHAPTER III.

MACHAR AND TERNAN.

IN the Aberdeen Breviary compiled by Bishop Elphinstone, we have brief summaries of the lives and labours of some of the more prominent preachers of the early Celtic Church. But that and such-like books were not written for a strictly scientific and—shall we say?—sceptical age as the present. John Hill Burton says:—
"Perhaps the life of a saint in the middle ages was not, after all, intended to be taken as an accurate biography even by a credulous person. . . . It was a kind of rhapsody or written ecstasy displaying to the best of the artist's power the idea of a poor human creature achieving all but perfection in devotion to the Deity, and obedience to the moral law, and humble observance of the duties towards fellow-mortals."*

Perhaps the eminent historian from whom we have quoted may be regarded as the very antipodes of the "credulous person," he having gone as far in the direction of the other extreme as it was possible for an able and honest narrator

* Burton's "History of Scotland," vol. i., p. 266.

to go; but the suggestion is not one to be dismissed without respectful consideration, that the "Lives of the Saints" are to a large extent ideal biographies, the facts, handed down by tradition, being viewed through the colouring medium of a vivid imagination and fervid admiration. In order to stimulate faith and spur to emulation by the loftiest possible examples, the men whose characters they depict went through a transfiguring process in their minds as they wrote, and we know from patent evidence that the supernatural was brought in lavishly as an auxiliary to invest them in the eyes of a superstitious age with an added importance.

How different, we may say by the way, from the accounts of men the Scriptures bring before our notice. There are no "faultless monsters" in the pages of the Bible. Men of our own flesh and blood, subject to our numerous infirmities, come before us as they really were and lived—good men, but not angels. It is wonderful how at once sublime and sober is the narrative of the Acts of the Apostles compared with the pious tales of the early and middle ages. In the New Testament you have the supernatural coming in, but not in a way that is gratuitous and obtrusive. There is much of the wonderful, little of the marvellous, nothing of the childish. But the "Lives of the Saints," in their exuberance of an unpruned fancy, and the trivial use which they make of the miraculous, remind the reader more of the "apocryphal" gospels.

All that we know of our own Machar, who has indelibly stamped his name upon this part of the country, is that he was said to be the son of an Irish Prince, that he was a disciple of Columba, and that he founded a church where Oldmachar Cathedral stands. There is a beautiful legend that he was instructed to choose as a site for a church in this neighbourhood a part near the bank of a river, where in its winding it made a figure not unlike that of a pastoral staff. Anyone who stands on the north side of the Cathedral, and looks down upon the Don in the valley, cannot fail to see what, to some extent, answers to that description.

The church that Machar founded on or near the spot where the Cathedral now stands was certainly very different from that solid granite edifice, impressive by its very simplicity. The original church would be a wooden or wattled erection, and more than one structure probably occupied the place before Bishop Elphinstone and others who preceded him built Oldmachar Church, which gave Aberdeen its most imposing feature. Spots chosen for worship, as we have already remarked, were generally for ever afterwards held sacred for that purpose. Men might come and go, buildings might be burned or crumble into dust and be replaced by others, but the same part of mother earth was clung to in congregating for religious observances; and we can, therefore, without any great stretch of imagination, picture to ourselves our forefathers for more than a thousand years meeting under some roof or other on the same part of the bank above the winding Don. There are two parishes that bear Machar's name in Aberdeenshire, and in Kildrummy there is a "Macharshaugh."

St. Wollok is associated with the parish of Glass, where there are two "baths" or pools* in the Deveron bearing his name, which were long ago supposed to have healing virtue in them to bathers, and the scanty ruins of a church. St. Devenick, said to be contemporary with St. Machar, has two churches—Nether-Banchory and Methlick—dedicated to him. St. Ternan and St. Fergus, too, are among the men whose hallowed memories are embalmed in the names which cling to localities in our neighbourhood.

Ternan, sometimes called " Archbishop of the Picts," is said to have had the book of the Gospels in four volumes, cased in covers wrought with silver and gold, and which up to the time of the Reformation were in the Church of Banchory. A church and well in Findon, Banchory-Devenick, have the name of Ternan.

* Dr. Robertson's " Scottish Abbeys," p. 99.

One of many wonders related of this saint was that a friend sent to beg some seed corn from him, and Ternan having given it all away in charity, filled the sacks with sand. His friend, having unlimited faith in the power of the saint, sowed the sand, which produced an admirable crop of corn!

Those saints' names which we unthinkingly repeat in our ordinary intercourse as mere local landmarks have noble histories behind them, better known to heaven than to earth. Even in the most thoughtful moods such names stir our fancy more than they enrich our intelligence, but there is nothing in our local nomenclature more worthy of respect. Tradition has handed down to us those names as almost the only memorials we have of men who by their self-denying lives and patient labours turned the horrible heathenism of the distant past into a Christianity that grew in depth and breadth with the ages. Their cells or monastic settlements dotted over the land were fortresses in which they stormed heaven with their prayers, and from which they sallied, not with hostile intent, but as emissaries of the Prince of Peace, and preachers of glad tidings.

It is to be noted that the good men of the early Christian ages whose apostolic labours have given a hallowed savour to names which still cling to chapels, parishes, and market *stances* were strangers to this country. They were of Irish birth, and it is remarkable that the piety of intervening ages did not bring to the surface and keep there some names with similar associations to be added to the popular calendar. It is quite to be understood how the first missionaries should have impressed the popular imagination more than their successors, who were merely building upon other men's foundations; but it is inexplicable that there should have been such a dearth of "saints" during all the centuries that followed — unless we make the unflattering assumption, as some do, that saintliness in those days in our land was to a large extent imported, and that the altar fire, though not allowed to go out, yet burned low, soon after the first few generations of zealots of Irish extraction passed away.

There can be no doubt that the type and form of Christianity set up in our own land were largely determined by what prevailed in Ireland. In other parts of Europe Christianity, gradually following in the line of the Roman conquests, was to a large extent modelled on the constitution of the Empire. Diocesan Episcopacy, which led up to the acknowledgment of the supremacy of the Bishop of Rome, was the evident reflection of the vast system of civil government which crumbled to pieces as Christianity rose to power; and thus the Roman

Church has been well called the ghost of the Roman Empire. But Ireland was never occupied by Ancient Rome, and the Christianity which found its way to that island organized itself on the tribal basis. The larger part of Scotland, also, being completely uninfluenced by Rome, and being mainly indebted to Ireland through Columba and others for the introduction of the religion of Jesus, naturally took the form of church government which was favoured in the sister isle.

The ravages of plundering hordes of Norsemen and the disturbances of the Reformation period are responsible for the loss of records that would have shed light upon many points that are now wrapt in total darkness, which is relieved only by the questionable lights of conjecture or speculation. We have no original document in Scotland that goes farther back than eight hundred years. From the period of Adamnan, who wrote the life of Columba, to the reign of Margaret, of saintly memory, with Malcolm Canmore — for nearly five hundred years—the history of the Church in Scotland is almost a total blank. It is remarkable that we should know less of our own country as it was a thousand years ago than we do of Egypt as it was more than four times farther back. From the side glances which the more abundant records of the less-disturbed monasteries of Ireland afford, we can realise how Christianity in our land at that period was like a stream which flows from the open and the sunlight into a subterraneous passage, from which by-and-bye it emerges.

The "sculptured stones," of which we have a large number in north-eastern Scotland, and which are supposed to belong to the period referred to, do not help us much, except that the cross which is often to be seen on one side of many of them tells where the faith of the men of that day lay. There is a touching helplessness about most of those ancient monuments—such as the Newton Stone or the Maiden Stone, near Pitcaple—which were quarried, polished, and decorated to tell us of the past, but which are so very old as to speak in a language that we have a difficulty in making out. Imagination, cunning workmanship that delighted in its exercise, are lavished upon some of those moss-encrusted memorials of a bygone age, but it is only scholars and specialists who can decipher what is chiselled; and even they are puzzled, or are far from agreeing in the interpretation of many of the symbols used, such as the comb and the mirror, which some think were old heathen emblems taken over by the new religion, but it is more probable they are representations of ornaments that indicated the rank and dignity of the deceased who is commemorated.

It is interesting to find that many of those

"sculptured stones" have a curious Celtic ornamentation, the endless knot, similar to, if not almost identical with, what is to be found in illuminated MSS. which are treasured in the archives of Trinity College, Dublin. The runic stone standing in the churchyard of Rosemarkie is a good example of that class. It has also to be gratefully noticed that while on the few Roman remains which have been unearthed traces of designed indecency can be seen, not a single sculptured stone of what is believed to be the Christian period has anything improper delineated upon its surface. Such things and the cross were instinctively felt to be incompatible. That symbol of the cross, worn with age and weather, though engraven on hard stone, is a meek but efficacious testimony to the fact that in those remote and barbarous times men had discovered the glory and felt the power of Christ in their hearts as one who could tame and purify, or at least begin to do so.

While notions and practices had crept into the Church, in Scotland as in other parts of the world, which in some instances were a serious departure from Apostolic simplicity, and which in others invested little things with an importance inconsistent with the spirit and genius of Christianity, yet there is evidence that the followers of Columba were resolute in the maintenance of their spiritual independence, and in doctrine and belief were more in agreement with New Testament purity than what was to be found generally in those ages on the Continent of Europe. For example, in Adamnan's life of Columba there is no mention of worship of the Virgin, of invocation of saints, nor of purgatory. Columba and his followers made so much of the Scriptures that they may be presumed to have been more evangelical than the Church generally on the Continent, into which many of the corruptions of sacerdotalism had by this time crept.

Some of the ways in which the Celtic Church claimed the right to exercise its liberty, such as in the choice of the correct shape of the tonsure (it being not a circular shaven area on the crown of the head, but a crescent-like stripe from ear to ear), or the proper time for the observance of Easter, may appear to us to be trivial, but they were sufficient to exhibit its individuality, and to make clear the fact that the perfect uniformity crowned by Rome was the creation, or rather the dream, of a later age. In the main, the methods of the Celtic Church in its purest days were those of the earliest times which followed Pentecost, the preaching of the Word, the chanting or singing of psalms, the inculcation by precept and example of the Christian virtues, and self-denying devotion to the interests of the people round about them. In celebrating the rites of the Church the native Gaelic was used, and not Latin, which was the language of the Church generally at that time.

Much controversy that has generally radiated more heat than light, has arisen in connection with the constitution of the early Celtic Church. The modern denominationalist who tries to father the church polity he favours upon the arrangement which prevailed in the Columban Church undertakes a fruitless task. It must be owned by the enlightened and unbiased student that the connection and resemblance are more easily traced by fervid imagination than by historical research. Whether the inquirer has the bias of Episcopalian, Presbyterian, or Congregationalist, he must candidly own, if facts and not zeal are to enthral him, that the organisation of the primitive Church of Scotland was greatly different from anything of the kind now existing in the land.

Available records give no evidence of diocesan Episcopacy, and while there are allusions to something approaching Presbyterian parity, a kind of missionary monasticism would more fitly describe the form which the Church took, each new establishment being modelled after Iona, and belonging to the "family of Iona." Yet it was different from the monasticism Rome favoured. It was freer, less secluded, more active, less hampered by artificial rules and imposed vows. Indeed, the

Columban Church in its palmy days was eminently practical, and ever subordinated means to ends, outward equipment to the functions which had to be discharged. As an ecclesiastical type, it lay somewhere between the purity of the Apostolic Church and the full-blown Romanism which came in course of years. There was in it not a little of the naked directness of aim which characterised the first century, and yet it had in it elements of error and superstition, and departures from original and authorised standards, which brought their own developments. The one thing of which we can speak with certainty is the fact that the Columban Church was not in subjection to the See of Rome. Like the Irish Church from which it originally sprang, it remained for centuries in a state of comparative isolation from the rest of Europe, where by the sixth or seventh century something like a consistent and symmetrical system of church organisation was established, headed by Rome.

The identification of the Columban or Celtic Church with the Culdees in Scotland is an error that recent research has slain, but it would be going beyond the facts to affirm that we know clearly and definitely who the Culdees were. There is no term in the whole range of ecclesiastical nomenclature more elusive and tantalising than that of the Culdees. It is the will-o'-the wisp of Scottish archæology, and the energy which many have eagerly expended upon the chase of it has been but ill rewarded. So far as available sources of information afford any basis of judgment, the last word on the subject has probably been spoken by Dr. Reeves. His faculty of worming himself into the heart of things as they were long ago, and piecing together scattered fragments so as to make them bear the weight of what may be accepted as a reasonable explanation, has made him the benefactor of weary antiquarians, who are glad at last to have some solid result to point to which releases them from further obligation to pursue the interminable subject.

It appears from the scanty evidence that the first mention of the Culdees in Scotland was contemporaneous with the attempt which Nectan made about 710 to induce the old Columban clergy in Pictland to submit to Rome. It is evident that the term was used in a loose, popular sense to designate those Celtic monks who adhered to the old order, and were therefore regarded by the representatives of Catholicity as obsolete schismatics, or at least as men who could not be classified according to the prescribed rules of general Christendom — they were "Keledei," Culdees, irregular worshippers or servants of God. Skene, it must be mentioned, however, thinks that the Culdees were an order within the Celtic Church, the term being generally confined to men who adopted the severer order of asceticism and lived in solitude.

We cannot do better than sum up all that is known of the Culdees in the language of Dr. Reeves :—" In fact, during the range of time in which the term is on record, we discover the greatest diversity in its application—sometimes borne by hermit, sometimes by conventuals; in one situation implying the condition of celibacy, in another understood of married men; here denoting regulars, there seculars; some of the name bound by obligations of poverty, others free to accumulate property; at one period high in honour as implying self-denial, at another regarded with contempt as the designation of the loose and worldly-minded. . . . When at last 'Célé Dé' does become a distinctive term, it is only so as contrasting those who clung to the old conventual observances of the country with those who adopted the better organised and more systematic institutions of mediæval introduction; in fact, as denoting an old-fashioned Scotic monk. . . . The generality of monasteries both in Scotland and Ireland were in a state of decrepitude at the beginning of the twelfth century, and those which survived for any length of time owed the continuation of their existence either to the super-addition of a bishop and chapter or their reconstruction on a new model. Most of the old religious communities were 'Keledei' (or Culdees) till the changes last mentioned took place, and then the name became limited for their brief future to those institutions which adhered to the original discipline as contra-distinguished from those which were re-modelled or erected in the new."

CHAPTER IV.

FROM THE CELTIC TO THE ROMAN CHURCH—1069-93.

THE transition from the Celtic to the Roman Church was hastened, if not completed, under the long reign of Malcolm Canmore. A variety of circumstances known to history, in which the big, bold warrior-king had little direct personal part, contributed to that result.

In the first place, by that time the glory of the Columban Church had passed away as a witnessing body for Christ, consecrated with a martyr-like steadfastness to the promulgation of saving truth; the fire of devotion had almost expired, leaving little but ashes and the altar on which it had burned. The traditions and tenets to which the successors of Columba still clung were simpler, and in some respects more in accordance with the teaching of the New Testament than the doctrine, the elaborate organisation and ceremonial of proud, aggressive Rome, but by the time of which we are writing they were almost emptied of life and power. Iona was a name and a memory, a hallowed place where great men were buried, but did not live. The process took effect in the ancient British Church as it has done in almost all religious societies which history brings under our notice—"They got renown for piety; that renown brought its showers of wealth, which in due time undermined its piety."

Nine years after Malcolm ascended the throne, William of Normandy invaded England and became its king. The iron rule of the strong, stern "Conqueror" drove many of the high-born Anglo-Saxon families to Scotland, and they brought with them some of the elements of the higher civilisation which England possessed. Among the refugees who arrived seeking Malcolm's protection were the displaced prince Edgar Atheling and his mother and sisters. One of the sisters—Margaret—who was beautiful in person and enthusiastic in temperament, captured the heart of the rough but vigorous and chivalrous Malcolm.

To the influence which Margaret, a pious woman and a devoted daughter of the Church, gained and kept over her consort, King Malcolm, is mainly due the great ecclesiastical change and revival of interest in religion which took place at that time. While she could not restrain her husband's warlike propensities, she was allowed full liberty to introduce what measures she approved for the moral amelioration and spiritual advancement of the nation. Her chaplain and biographer, Turgot, tells us that while Malcolm could not read his wife's missals and books of devotion, he kissed them in token of reverence, and caused them to be richly bound and ornamented with gold and jewels.

Coming from England, where, in common with the most of Europe, the spiritual supremacy of Rome was acknowledged, she naturally identified the Church of Christ with Roman Catholicism, and regarded the old Scotic functionaries, with their rude symbols of worship and effete institutions, as schismatics and mongrel priests, who could do nothing better for their country than give place to the new order of things, which would bring Scotland into accredited union and fellowship with the rest of Christendom.

Remembering what an influence Mary Stuart at a later period wielded by the fascination of her person and manners, even when her character was held in doubt and her policy was not generally approved, we can quite understand how Margaret, who had everything in her favour, should have been a signal power at this crisis in the internal development of the Scottish nation. Although what is rooted in the past and sanctioned by long usage has always many stalwart champions, yet the poor Celtic ministers, who exhibited at the time stubborn tenacity in their attitude rather than lofty enthusiasm, must have felt that they were more than matched when they had the Queen, the Pope, and, above all, the forces and tendencies of the times against them. Still, the old Celtic Church was not so much extruded as absorbed.

We cannot forget that almost all we know of the Celtic Churchmen is drawn from the records of their Roman opponents and successors, and we should, therefore, in justice to those whose case is not stated by themselves, be prepared to receive with caution the indictment that is made. Still, all the evidence available points to the conclusion that the Church in Scotland as Margaret found it was dead and worldly, if not as corrupt as it became three centuries afterwards. The Church lands were to a large extent secularised, celibacy was held as an ideal but often departed from, the priesthood had become very much a hereditary caste, the Lord's Supper was seldom observed, the Sabbath was neglected and had become very much as other days. There can be no doubt that the ardent and energetic Queen— the most imposing historical figure in Scotland since the death of Columba—had ample material for discussion for the three-days' conference she had with the representatives of the old order. She may have been somewhat demonstrative in her piety, but her enthusiasm sprang from the heart and ever kept the life and practice in keeping with itself, and in what she did for Scotland she has, through residence, reflected a lustre on

Dunfermline second only to that which belongs to Iona.

One of the most convincing proofs that could be adduced of the genuineness of the revival of religion and manners inaugurated by Queen Margaret and her three sons who succeeded her was the readiness evinced generally to part with money and lands for the maintenance of the ministers and institutions of the Church. James I., standing by King David's tomb in Dunfermline, is reported to have complained that "he was ane sair sanct for the Croon," but if the intelligence, the enterprise, the self-sacrificing devotion to the higher interests of the people and the glory of God of Queen Margaret and her co-adjutors and successors in the twelfth century had been carried into the fifteenth, the complaint would probably never have been made, or would have had no sting to keep it in remembrance. That was a glorious outburst of energy and consecration to high ends, of which many of our cathedrals and abbeys, now in ruins, with their magnificence of design and unapproached finish of workmanship are the standing witnesses and worthy memorials. A Protestantism that is enlightened and broad is guilty of no disloyalty to its own cherished principles when it goes out in unstinted admiration to men and women who, according to the light they had and the ideas of their age, honoured their God and served their day and generation with a lavish expenditure of time and thought. The sloth, ignorance, and debauchery of later days in the Roman Church cannot hide from us the splendour of the twelfth and thirteenth centuries, that was able to conceive and to execute such great undertakings, the remains of which are still with us. Better far a faith that is alive and operative, though it should have mixed with it much error and superstition, than one that is correct but cold as an icicle and as destitute of inspiration and power as a string of propositions that are divorced from life. Error is not to be condoned nor truth despised, but if the little truth that is in a man's creed is alive, it will do more for him than a confession of faith as true as Scripture itself if the intellect is the only part of him by which it is held. The Churchmen of that distant epoch had a faith that is not ours in many important particulars, but such as it was it gave birth to visions of sublime aspiration which they tried to embody in those Gothic structures that bear witness to the fact that the genius, and art, and handicraft of the age, found their highest employment in the service of God.

It is a little thing, but it means much as showing what spirit the builders of those Cathedrals were of, and how the glory of God, and not their own glory, was the object they had in view—there is no name on those magnificent structures. Mr. Gladstone says:—"It has been observed as a circumstance full of meaning that no man knows the name of the architects of our cathedrals. They left no record of themselves upon the fabrics, as if they would have nothing there that could suggest any other idea than the glory of that God to whom the edifices were devoted for perpetual and solemn worship."

The Scottish Church was now to a large extent remodelled and fired with an inspiration such as it had not felt for centuries. The old simplicity, which had degenerated into stiffened and uncouth baldness, was displaced by a system that was elaborate, many-sided, and palpitating with new life. The Celtic Church in its administration, as we have seen, was not parochial but monastic. A monastery was planted in a district, which became the headquarters of religion, and besides being the point of departure for fresh pioneering incursions, was in many instances responsible for the maintenance of religious ordinances in churches or stations grouped at varying distances around it.

Saxon Margaret and her sons introduced the parochial system. The country was divided into parishes, tithes being taken from the land for the support of the church that was built in it, and which became the principal feature within its bounds. At first the manor was frequently the parish, and if it was large it was eventually subdivided, each part being in course of time raised to the status of an ecclesiastical centre, with full parochial rights.

Diocesan Episcopacy, such as prevailed in the rest of Christendom, was also introduced into Scotland. The Abbot now gave place to the Bishop. The Bishopric of Aberdeen extended from the Dee to the Spey, rivers and other dividing lines of nature being often used in defining the boundaries of a diocese. The old Columban monasteries of the district, Mortlach and others, furnished part of its endowment. The cathedral constitutions were borrowed from the more advanced country on the other side of the border, Lincoln being the model for Aberdeen. Owing mainly to the jealousy of England, and its desire to keep Scotland in a position of inferiority, no metropolitan or primate was appointed for a considerable time. At length, after much contention, the Scotch Church was authoritatively declared to be independent of English control, and sometime later the Pope erected St. Andrews into an archbishopric, with the other twelve bishops as the primate's suffragans.

The old Celtic monasteries, too, had to give way to the Roman orders, with their more strict rule and fuller, fresher life—the Cistercians and the canons of St. Augustine, numerous and powerful, establishing themselves all over the land. The monastic orders in our town have left their mark in our street nomenclature. The Carmelites and friars, black and grey, are still with us in the names which they have imprinted upon localities that are as familiar to us as household words. William the Lion, who favoured Aberdeen as a place of residence, gifted his palace and garden to Trinity Friars. Alexander II., his son, had a house on the north side of the Schoolhill, on what are now the grounds of Robert Gordon's College, which became the abode of the Black Friars. When a foundation was dug for the Art Gallery, a great many bones were found, which were supposed to be those of the old monks, and they were re-deposited in a vault prepared for them.

We are not to judge of those monasteries by the corrupt condition in which they were found at the time of the Reformation and long before that date. They were to a large extent founded on wrong principles, and sooner or later were bound to breed what is not wholesome, but at first they were in many cases the embodiment of pure and lofty aspiration. They were also in many ways useful to the society of the time. They were schools of learning, centres of varied industry, sanctuaries in time of confusion and peril, places where men were of account as creatures of God, the oppressed being championed, the poor fed, the ignorant instructed. Little record of the good they did has come down to us, but we have to remember that the work which goes deepest down and is most enduring is often noiseless, and is chronicled only in the results which in after days stare us in the face. Sir Walter Scott, who more than any other man that ever lived stood abreast of Scotland's past and tried to make it live, observes, when writing of a later period, that castles have many more traditions clinging to them than monasteries or other religious houses. He explains this by reminding us that the stirring events and striking scenes connected with the warfare in which the old strongholds figured, made a deeper impression upon the popular imagination than the quiet and often unnoticed deeds of institutions whose business is more with the inward than with the outward—more with the soul than what appeals to the senses. The dashing cataract draws more attention to itself than the quiet-flowing stream, though it nourishes a district. So those old saintly men, who spent their lives in a work of spiritual instruction, are not so well remembered as the rough warriors who by their frequently wielded swords, carved a name for themselves in the records of the land.

The importance of the city of Aberdeen in those early days may be gauged by the footing which ecclesiastical authorities sought within its borders. As Cosmo Innes reminds us, "long before Edinburgh had acquired the precedency of a capital, or even a first place among the four burghs of Scotland, while Glasgow was yet an insignificant dependency on its bishop, Aberdeen had taken its place as a great and independent royal burgh, and a port of extensive foreign trade."

CHAPTER V.

ARCHDEACON BARBOUR—1316-95.

BARBOUR'S name is the only one among the local ecclesiastics of the fourteenth century that rises up claiming special notice, but it is one that Aberdeen cannot allow to die. It is no small distinction belonging to our city to have been the home and sphere, and probably the birthplace of one who, besides ministering in holy things amongst us, was our "Scottish Chaucer," the "father of Scottish poetry."

In perusing annals such as these we cannot be too often reminded that the work of true ministers of Christ's Church is generally of such a nature that it is not likely to be recorded in any book on earth; and men may have rendered service of the very highest order to their fellows that has no place in accessible chronicles. Statistics cannot be furnished, and it is beyond the power of literature to give any exhaustive account of the spiritual effect of prayer in secret, the word spoken in season in the privacy of home, or the faithful, though otherwise unremarkable, discourse that has gone into a congregation as light into a flower or a shower upon the mown grass.

We may be assured that Aberdeen in the thirteenth and fourteenth centuries, during which the impulse given by Queen Margaret would still be felt throughout the land, had many earnest-hearted ministers who served their day and generation with all fidelity, though, like the minor mountains of a range, their name is lost to posterity in such an outstanding one as that of John Barbour.

But the memory even of Barbour has been preserved not on account of anything he did in the line of what strictly belonged to his own high calling, but owing to his distinction in the field of literature. If it had not been for his "Brus," he would in all probability have had no place in the recollection of men, and this part of the earth that knew him once would have known him no longer; but, as the poet of the struggle for national independence, which really made Scotland what it is, he is not likely ever to be forgotten.

Because of the name he has made for himself and the service he has rendered to letters, to history, and to patriotism, diligent search has been made in the fugitive records of the past, by no one more than by our own Dr. Joseph Robertson, with the view of ascertaining as many facts as can be ferreted out regarding him. We have no known official record as an authority for saying he was born in Aberdeen, but as we know that he was Archdeacon of the church here as early at least as 1357, and held that office till his death, and as also there are contemporaneous notices of families of that name in the town, we may fairly assume, until something is brought out that proves the contrary, that Aberdeen was his birthplace. The scanty and scattered notices of him that have been unearthed reveal that in his own age he was esteemed to be a man of learning and worth. When his career does rise to the surface of history it is always as a person of weight who was trusted and honoured. There is reason to believe that he studied at Oxford and Paris. Oxford was then the centre and rallying point of the new world of letters in Britain; and we are informed that in 1357 and 1364 he travelled into England, accompanied by scholars, for the purpose of studying at that seat of learning. In 1365 he obtained a passport to travel through England with six companions on horseback towards St. Denis and other sacred places. In 1368 he again received permission to travel through England with two servants and two horses on his way for scholarly purposes in France.

It is abundantly evident that he was one of those Churchmen who saw much that lay beyond the narrow round of the sanctimonious observances of the priests of that day. His numerous offices show him perhaps too much on the secular side of life. He was a travelled Scot who appreciated the advantages of the highest culture of the time and fellowship with kindred spirits who had received it into their minds. The scholars who accompanied him in those journeys were probably the sons of the nobility in the north.

The higher clergy of that day received an education such as was not desired generally by the nobles, who thought the sword befitted men of their rank more than the pen; and they had often to be the lawyers and statesmen of the time as well as its religious functionaries. So we find that in 1373 Barbour was Clerk of Audit of the household of King Robert II., and one of the auditors of Exchequer. It appears that in the discharge of his duties he gave great satisfaction to his royal master, for we learn that in 1377 he had a gratuity of ten pounds from King Robert, and, in the following year, he received from the same prince the high compliment of a perpetual annuity of twenty shillings. It throws some light upon the character and sincere piety, as it then expressed itself, of the Archdeacon, that he bequeathed this annuity to the dean and chapter of Aberdeen upon the condition that they should sing a yearly mass for the rest of his soul.

But Barbour's great claim to the appreciation of posterity lies in his "Brus."* We are all the

* "The Brus." Edited for the Spalding Club by Cosmo Innes.

more disposed to make the most of him as an author as Scotland compares most unfavourably with England in the literature of that early period.

Owing to the unsettled state of affairs in our country for many years, and the want of facilities for the cultivation of learning, such as libraries and scholarly fellowship, most of the intellectual life of Scotland went to England or to the Continent, John Duns Scot, or Scotus, being an eminent example of that class. By the frequent and exhausting wars with England, and the consequent distraction and unrest, Scotland could have had little attraction then for the quiet student. He may be able to cultivate literature on a little oatmeal, but if he is not sure where even that is to come from, or if it may be stolen by the marauder from his barn, it is not unlikely that he may consider the advantages of an abode in another land. We are, therefore, all the more thankful for Barbour, who has redeemed his country from the reproach of being without a literature in the fourteenth century, and has turned the ample materials at his hand connected with a national crisis and hero into an epic which, take it all in all, is worthy of both.

That voice which sounds out clear and bold over the centuries may have an old-world accent that is strange to our ears, yet there is something within us which leads us to recognise and hail him as a true Scot as he exclaims in the famous lines—generally acknowledged to be one of the best, if not, indeed, the finest, apostrophe of freedom ever uttered:—

> "A! fredome is a nobill thing!
> Fredome mayss man to haiff liking!
> Fredome all solace to man giffis:
> He levys at ess that frely levys!
> A noble hart may haiff nane ess,
> Na ellys nocht that may him pless,
> Gyff fredome failythe; for fre liking
> Is yearnt our all othir thing.
> Na he that ay hase levyt fre
> May nocht know weill the propyrte,
> The augyr, na the wrechyt dome,
> That is cowplyt to foule thyrldome.
> Bot gyff he had assayit it,
> Than all perquer he suld it wyt,
> And suld think fredome mar to pryss
> Than all the gold in warld that is."

If Barbour, while keeping by a basis of fact in his "Brus," which historians of the period, such as Tytler, follow, being "nought bot suthfast thing," yet allowed imagination to shape his material, so as to make it effective to the reader, he certainly takes still greater latitude in his other two works. His "Brute," which is a genealogical history of the kings of Scotland, and his book of the legends of the saints, where he gives us

> "Storyss of sere haly men,
> That to pless God vs may kene,"

deal with things farther removed than the days

of that Scottish chivalry of which Bruce was the glorified knight, and his treatment of them is less dependent upon fact and reality.

It should also be mentioned, in giving a summary of the deeds of Barbour, that as the Cathedral of St. Machar was begun in 1366 and it is on record that the dean and chapter taxed themselves for the fabric in sixty pounds annually for ten years, he must have been one of the original contributors to the erection of the edifice which Aberdeen justly regards as what largely contributed to give it consequence and dignity.

Dr. Joseph Robertson thus describes the subsequent stages in the progress of the erection of our Cathedral:—" The Pope, in 1380, made a liberal grant of indulgences to all the faithful who should stretch forth a helping arm to the work. But all these appliances availed only to raise the foundations of the nave a few feet above ground. Forty years passed before Bishop Henry Leighton (1422-40) reared the two western towers, completed the wall of the nave, and founded the northern transept. His successor, Bishop Lindsay (1441-59) paved and roofed the edifice. It was glazed by Bishop Spens (1459-80)."* Then he goes on to tell of the very important part that Bishops Elphinstone and Dunbar took in the work, to which we make reference in other parts of this book.

* Dr. Robertson's " Scottish Abbeys," p. 75.

John of Fordoun, supposed to have been so called because he was born at Fordoun, in Kincardineshire, was a contemporary of Barbour and a canon of the Cathedral. He, in his "Scotichronicon," has given us a prose narrative of the course of events in Scotland down to the twelfth century, which has been an invaluable quarry to all the historians who succeeded him. He seems to have had a passion and a conscious call to put in writing all that by painstaking research could be learned regarding the past of his country, for he travelled on foot over Scotland and Ireland, gleaning information at the various churches and monasteries he visited. Like many other authors with large designs, he died before his work was finished. He brought the chronicle down to 1153, leaving material which was used by others for the story of the next two centuries. Is it not remarkable that the principal historians of Scotland, both of ancient and modern times, had a more or less close connection with Aberdeen?

CHAPTER VI.

BISHOP ELPHINSTONE—1431-1514.

IT is a leap from the period of which we have been writing to the fifteenth century; but William Elphinstone, who was born in Glasgow in 1431, and became Bishop of Aberdeen in 1484, was really in many respects more a man of the former than of the latter date. In consideration of his unsullied character, many-sided activity, public spirit, and unstinted devotion to all that tended to the advantage of the people belonging to his diocese, he may be regarded as one of the best examples of the best period of the Scottish Catholic Church. He certainly cannot be taken as a representative Churchman of the age in which he lived. Amidst general degeneracy and corruption, as Cosmo Innes testifies, "with manners and temperance in his own person befitting the primitive ages of Christianity, he threw around his cathedral and palace the taste and splendour that may adorn religion." Or, as another writer puts it, "his morals were a pattern and a reproach to his country and order."

He had something to contend with from the very day of his birth, for his father was one bound by solemn vows to celibacy, being rector of Kirkmichael and archdeacon of Teviotdale. He was educated at the school and University of Glasgow, took his degree when twenty-four years of age, studied canon law and practised as an advocate at the Church courts; in short, his natural gifts, which were far above the average, were cultivated to the very utmost, and he acquired all the various branches of learning which his country could give to fit him for the many spheres of public duty he was destined to fill.

In addition to all that, he was sent abroad at an uncle's expense, and in France and other parts came into contact with the choice spirits and cultured intellects of the day, acquiring that urbanity and polish which added grace to his strength, and enabled him to take his place and act his part in Court or Cabinet, with scholars and men of the world as well as with ecclesiastics.

When appointed to the See of Aberdeen, his refined taste and love of learning drew around him men who had something else to live for than the pleasure of the moment; and the literary reputation which Archdeacon Barbour and Fordoun had won for Aberdeen was enhanced by Elphinstone and those associated with him. One of the ways in which human greatness shews itself is in the quick discovery and frank acknowledgment of whatever excellence may be at hand.

Moreover, there is generally a desire on the part of persons like Elphinstone to bring able men from afar if they should not be near. The highest peak has usually other elevations around it, and a man of power can attract and turn to advantage ability of various kinds. To remind the clerics of his diocese and the whole nation of better days in the Church, and teach them by nobler examples than what could easily be found at the time, he wrote a series of sketches of the lives of the Scottish saints. He also gave of his means to finish Oldmachar Cathedral, the great central tower, now gone, which was seen far out at sea, having been completed at his expense. He furnished it with fourteen bells, and had proceeded with the choir, but there was only a small part of the work done when he died.

Amongst the good deeds of Bishop Elphinstone, it cannot be forgotten, whatever else relating to him should lapse from the memory, that he was the founder of King's College, which he framed after the model of Paris University, where he had studied and also taught. The requisition that was sent to the Pope, stating reasons why such an undertaking as the erection of a University in Aberdeen should have the Papal sanction, is an interesting document. A most doleful account is given of the country, as "intersected with mountains and arms of the sea," "the roads so dangerous," "youth had not access to the benefits of education." Yet the advantages of the situation were also pointed out —"excellent temperature of air," "conveniency of habitation," etc.

In justice to the old Roman Church, it should ever be remembered to her credit that chiefly to her devoted sons is due the honour of conceiving and giving effect to one of the grandest and most fruitful ideas since the introduction of Christianity—the establishment of the University, where knowledge was to be propagated, and the utmost reaches of intellectual attainment made possible to anyone, whatever his birth or rank, who hated darkness and loved the light.

It may be said that the existence of those seminaries of learning on an extensive scale was mainly owing to the pressure of the intellectual forces of the times, which scholars generated more than Churchmen. The revival of learning, an outburst of fresh interest in classical studies, and a growing desire for the emancipation of the intellect from the thraldom of dry and barren scholasticism, had perhaps more to do with the erection of those venerable piles sacred to the pursuits of the mind than any deep anxiety on the part of the College of Cardinals at Rome for the furtherance of the enlightenment of the world. That may be true, but it is also true that, from whatever source the idea came, it was cordially taken up by the leading Churchmen of the land, and by none more so than by Bishop Elphinstone. Little did they know how, in some Universities, if not in the Aberdeen one, influences were to radiate that should favour the great Protestant movement which was to overturn the ecclesiastical system they had most at heart; but to found those institutions came to them as the duty of the hour, and they did it.

It cannot be denied that those ancient institutions, which were never more prized than they are to-day, sprang from the Church and were rooted in religion. Dr. Walter C. Smith, in singing of the old University town between the Don and the Dee, puts it thus:—

> "O'er the College Chapel a grey stone crown
> Lightsomely soars above tree and town,
> Lightsomely fronts the minster towers,
> Lightsomely chimes out the passing hours,
>   To the solemn knell
>   Of their deep-toned bell;
> *Kirk and College keeping time,*
> *Faith and Learning, chime for chime.*" *

Theology at first overshadowed all other branches of learning. Those schools of learning represented the Catholic Church on its intellectual side, and had much of its catholicity—universality of scope in their constitution and aim. It is interesting to notice how the Parisian University has stamped itself legibly unto this day upon our school of

---

* "Selections from the Poems of Walter C. Smith," p. 86.

letters, as is shown in such terms still in use as Bejeant.

King's College was very much an expansion of smaller educational institutions in our city. Long before the Reformation, Aberdeen, like some of the other towns in Scotland, had its Grammar School. John Vaus is named as rector of the school, and commended by Hector Boece, the learned Principal of the University, for his knowledge of the Latin tongue.

But Elphinstone had an eye to progress in things that are usually considered to be beyond the ken and interest of Churchmen. He was eminently practical, and was willing to spend his time and money on material projects that were needed for the convenience of the people and the amenity of the district. He began to build the Bridge of Dee, and, when he died, left a sum of money for its completion.

The Bishop was a born ruler of men, and an ardent lover of order and right. While benevolent and considerate, he was yet a severe judge, keeping in his mind, we are told, the adage—"He hurts the good who spares the bad." His firmness and sagacity were often brought into requisition in affairs of State, in the Privy Council at home, and on embassies in France. It is said that he was against the war which led to Flodden; but he went with his King and countrymen to the fatal field, and after returning

home was never seen to smile again. He died*
on 25th October, 1514, and was buried in King's
College Chapel. It is said that when he was
laid in his grave his pastoral staff of silver
clove in twain, and one portion fell into his
last resting-place, when a voice said—" With
thee, William, the mitre shall be buried!" Not
quite yet was that to be. Gavin Dunbar entered
into the vacant bishopric, and after him for a
short time, William Gordon, one who, during his

* In Boece's "Bishops of Aberdeen" (p. 106), edited and translated by Dr. Moir, of the Aberdeen Grammar School, we have the following account of the death of this revered man :—

"He [Bishop Elphinstone] returned to Aberdeen to devote the rest of his days to the construction of the bridge and the choir of the Cathedral, as well as to other pious works. It was the wish of our worthy father (had his destiny so allowed) to end his days at Aberdeen, the scene of his first settlement, in that holy tranquillity and quiet which he had so well deserved by his many labours. But being recalled to meet the nobles, because dissensions had broken out amongst them which could not be settled except by his presence, he gave up his design. His friends dissuaded him from going, for he was now ill, but he replied that he was born not for himself only, but for his country, and that he owed more to the State than to his own safety ; and would not be prevented by the state of his health nor any one's persuasions from undertaking the journey.

"Accordingly, setting out in poor health, about half-way on his journey his fever increased, and he stopped at Dunfermline. After he had been confined to bed there for some days he made his will, leaving all his gold and silver and whatever furniture he had to complete his College and bridge, and not forgetting his poorer friends. The Bishop at that time had ten thousand pounds in his coffers, besides much personal effects. Then he proceeded to Edinburgh. On the sixth day after he came to the capital the fever increased so that he could get no rest. . . . On the day before his death he entered the chapel as usual. He discoursed long with piety and learning on the religion of Christ, pointing out its truth and the great rewards which it held out to its faithful followers. Feeling too weak, in spite of his zeal, to finish the service, he brief tenure of office, signalised his occupancy of it in a way so different from that which is expected of a bishop that the Roman Church may well disown him.

In this connection we must also take notice of the first Principal of King's College, Hector Boece, whom the Bishop succeeded in securing as the head of the new College, and who held the office for more than thirty years, having proved himself to be eminently qualified for its duties. He was born in Dundee in 1465, educated in Paris, and the intimate friend of some of the most learned men of his age, such as Erasmus. The general use of the Latin language and the love of learning gave a cosmopolitan feeling to men of high education at that time, such as has never to the same degree been seen since. The objects that were of weight to men like Boece

_{ordered the Holy Body of Christ to be brought to him, which he received prostrate on the ground, with eyes streaming with tears and hands outstretched to heaven. When he had finished his accustomed prayer before the image of the crucified Saviour, he was led to his bedchamber, where he lay down and slept a brief space in hopes that sleep might give a respite from pain. In the evening he supped with some of the nobility who had come to comfort him. . . .}

_{"In the morning, feeling a choking sensation from the accumulation of phlegm in his throat, he calls for his chamberlain with such strength of voice as he possesses. His friends hasten to his side, and find they are called to his death-bed. Some weep, some pray, others exhort him to be of good courage and not prove unworthy of himself, for soon he will be past danger. Then he, for a brief space, raising his eyelids and gazing on his weeping friends, said—'I thought you would have given me better advice: the health I hope for is eternal. Henceforth the cares of this transitory life shall not affect me. Be it yours each to help his neighbour.'"}

and Erasmus were such as the cultured of all parts of Europe had in common; and the attractions of the guild of knowledge, in not a few instances, became more than the ties of nation and kindred.

We are told, and are not surprised, that it was not without some hesitation that Boece consented to quit the cultured society of Paris for what must have appeared to him to be a barbarous region. Money was not the attraction, for his salary was forty merks, or about £2 4s. 6d. sterling. He became canon of Aberdeen and rector of Tyrie, and, in addition to the multifarious duties connected with his position, clerical and academic, he found time to write the lives of the Bishops of Aberdeen and the history of Scotland, in which works he showed more learning and imagination than judgment. Soon after the publication of his History he got his degree of D.D., when the magistrates, according to an entry in Town Council Records of Aberdeen, under date 1528, voted him a present of a tun of new wine when the new wines should arrive, or a sum of money to purchase a new bonnet!

Not any of the bishops of the Roman Church who succeeded Elphinstone need be mentioned here except Dunbar, who was a real benefactor to the diocese, and a man who, by his private virtues and public spirit, deserves to be held in honourable remembrance. He made it his great endeavour to carry on and complete what Elphinstone and others had undertaken. King's College buildings were extended and the Bridge of Dee finished under his direction and as the result of his munificence. He also did much in carrying out the designs of his predecessor for the Cathedral of Oldmachar.

CHAPTER VII.

THE RELIGIOUS LIFE OF PRE-REFORMATION TIMES.

"ORATE pro anima Radulfi Sacerdotis"—
"Pray for the soul of Radulf the priest"
—is the meek appeal inscribed on one of the most ancient gravestones in Scotland, standing against the gable wall of the old church in Insch. Among two thousand inscriptions that have been collected from the graveyards of the north-eastern districts of Scotland, it is believed by experts, such as Jervise, to be the oldest, and is assigned to the twelfth century. As the ecclesiastical revenues of the parish of Insch had been gifted to the Abbey of Lindores, on the south side of the Tay, it is probable that this priest was the stipendiary vicar of that powerful and flourishing monastery, which had no fewer than twenty-two parish churches belonging to it.

It is not unlikely that a desire by others for the same kind of devout remembrance, as was expressed on Radulf's tombstone, had something to do with his lot, as a priest, being cast in that part. Sometimes, in passing from this world, local magnates felt that they had much need of prayer to put them in a better position before their Maker than the one that their past deeds would entitle them to, and having a superstitious veneration for the efficacy of the prayers of monks, upon their death-bed, if not before, they granted property in lands and teinds to favourite monasteries on condition that prayers should be made regularly on their behalf. The consequence was that often the greater part of the temporal provision which had been made for the maintenance of religious ordinances in a parish went to increase the bloated revenues of a "house" that was on the road to moral ruin through overflowing coffers and abounding luxury, and a pittance was given to some poor priest who went his round of duties as their vicar or substitute.

It is calculated that for many years before the Reformation, by far the greater part of the wealth which had been accumulated and held in trust for the religious welfare of the land was alienated from the various parishes and concentrated in a few priories and abbeys, the heads of which had the lion's share of the spoil. There was, indeed, ground for Dunbar's complaint:—

> "I knaw nocht how the Kirk is gydit,
> Bot benefices are nocht leil devydit;
> Sum men hes seven, and I nocht ane,
> Quilk to considder is ane pane."

In that excellent work, "Monymusk: Its Church and Priory," we glean local information, much of which is taken from original documents

bearing on this point. In it the author says:—
"We learn that after the Reformation one minister living at Keig had actually 'under his charge' all the four parishes whose teinds, &c., had been payable to our priory—Keig, Alford, Leochel, and far distant Braemar; and in this rent roll that tells how Lord Forbes had appropriated its lands as well as its teinds, he himself using the first person—'hes it off me for xij. Lib.'—hands down what was the magnificent allowance for which he farmed out the vicarage or lesser teinds to the poor minister. One wonders that the minister was able to travel even once a quarter to Braemar, and we are able to judge how dependent the parishes were upon 'Readers.'"*

From all the evidence that is before us, however, it would appear that most of the priests got as much as they were worth. The parish priests, or secular clergy, as they were called, lost their good name even before the monks. Their energies were certainly not overtaxed in preaching. In the General Provincial Council summoned by Archbishop Hamilton at Edinburgh in 1559 to arrest the Reformation movement by bringing about a reform from within, a friendly remonstrance was presented, in which, among other things, it was requested that "they provide for preachings and declarings of God's Word sincerely and truly to be made in every parish kirk of our realm

* "Church and Priory of Monymusk," p. 205.

upon all Sundays and other holidays, at the least on Yule, Pasche, Whitsunday, and every third or fourth Sunday."* It comes out incidentally that what had been previously enjoined was a sermon only four times a year! There is no evidence that in Scotland pre-Reformation preaching was of much account at any time. Sir David Lindsay of the Mount often flouted the higher clergy for their unwillingness or inability to preach :—

> "Great pleasure were to hear one bishop preach,
> One dean or doctor in divinity,
> One abbot who could well his convent teach,
> One person flowing in philosophy ;
> I tyne my time to wish what will not be."

Knox, in his history, gives us a specimen of the kind of discourse the people were accustomed to in church. He represents a priest as saying :— "Ane has tynt a spurtill; there is ane flaill stolen from them beyound the burn; the goodwife of the other side of the gait has tynt a horn spoon : God's malison and mine I give to them that knows of this gear and restores it not."

Let us try to have a full and clear view of the religious institutions in Aberdeen before the Reformation. Dr. Joseph Robertson, in his "History of the Reformation in Aberdeen," gives us interesting particulars :—

"The extent of the ecclesiastical establishment in this quarter at the era of the Reformation is

---

* "A Discourse on the Scottish Reformation," by Bishop Wordsworth, p. 58.

deserving of prominent notice. At the head of it was the Cathedral of St. Machar, with no fewer than twenty-nine prebendaries. The building of this edifice had been expedited by a Papal Bull, by which all persons who aided the work were generously absolved from penance for the precise space of twelve months and forty days. Next in importance was the Collegiate Church of St. Nicholas, consisting of sixteen chaplains, though in the previous century the number was much greater. To these are to be added the Chapel of St. Clement, at Futtie; the Chapel of St. Ninian, on the Castlehill; the Chapel of the Virgin Mary, at the Bridge of Dee; a Chapel at the Bridge of Don; the Chapel of St. Katherine, on the hill of the same name; the Chapel of Mary Magdalen, or 'The Vault of our Ladye of Pity,' under St. Nicholas Church; and the Parish Church of Old Aberdeen, called the Snow Kirk, from its dedication to Maria ad Nives, or ex Nivibus, so called from a superstition not more blasphemous than indecent. We pass, in this enumeration, the Collegiate Chapel of King's College; but there remain to be taken into account the Church and Monastery of the Trinity Friars, on the shore; the Church and Monastery of the Carmelite Friars, in the Green; the Church and Monastery of the Black Friars, on the Schoolhill; and the Church and Monastery of the Grey Friars, in the Broadgate. Of the precise number of the members of these monastic institutions there is no record; but from the ascertained dimensions of their buildings and other circumstances, the number in each may be estimated, with great safety, at fifteen or twenty. It will thus be seen that within the city there were thirteen places of worship, and a body of endowed clergy, of one or other of the classes, numbering certainly not less than one hundred and ten, and probably approaching nearer to one hundred and fifty."*

At death even the weighty and oppressive hand of the Church was felt. The "corpse present"† was exacted, though not due by any law or canon of the Church in Scotland. It was something over and above what was required by the priest in connection with the interment of the body and the deliverance of the soul from purgatory. The perquisite consisted of the best cow of the deceased, the "cors-presant kow," the uppermost cloth or covering of his bed, or the uppermost of his body clothes. Sir David Lindsay, the poet, alludes to this exaction :—

> "And als the vicar as I trow
> He will nocht fail to tak ane kow
> And upmaist claith."

When the Papal establishment was abolished this went with many other abuses. It was decreed, as the First Book of Discipline informs us, that "the uppermost claith, corps-present, etc., etc., can neither be required nor received of good conseience."

* Dr. Robertson's "History of the Reformation in Aberdeen," pp. 5, 6, 7.

† M'Crie's "Life of Knox," p. 386.

PRE-REFORMATION TIMES.

There is evidence from the burgh records and incidental allusions in the writings of the time that the Sabbath, which is one of the main bulwarks of the religious life, was observed very much as it is now in Roman Catholic countries on the Continent of Europe, with this difference—that attendance at public worship was then much more general. But after being at church, the people betook themselves to sport and pleasure, to archery and other forms of amusement. About the middle of the fifteenth century, butts were ordered to be erected at every parish church by Act of Parliament, that the young men, at this place of concourse, might exercise themselves in archery, with the view of insuring their proficiency in time of war.

Religion was intimately associated, after a fashion, with the festivities, the processions, and the social life generally of the people. Each guild of craftsmen had its patron saint, its chapel, and altar, and in the pageants of the time pride in the craft and zeal for the Church were strangely blended. In 1531, the Town Council of our city enacted:—" According to the lovable custom and rite of this burgh and of the noble burgh of Edinburgh, of which rite and custom the Provost has gotten a copy; that is to say, that, in the name of God and the blessed Virgin Mary, the craftsmen of this burgh, in their best array, keep and decorate the procession as on Corpus Christi day and Candlemas day, as honourable as they can, every craft with their own banner, with the arms of their craft thereon, and they shall pass, each craft by themselves, two and two, in this order—First, the fleshers, and next the barbers; next the skinners and furriers together; next the shoemakers; next the tailors; after them weavers and listers together; next them the bakers; and, last of all, nearest to the Sacrament, passes all the hammermen—namely, smiths, wrights, masons, coopers, slaters, goldsmiths, and armourers. And every one of the said crafts in the Candlemas procession shall furnish their pageants according to the old statute of the year of God 1510."*

It would appear that on those high occasions at Candlemas, or when their patron saint's day, St. Nicholas, came round, attendance was compulsory, for John Mackintosh, in his "History of Civilisation in Scotland," points out that a man named John Pitt, a tailor in Aberdeen, was punished for refusing to take his proper place, with the signs of his craft, in the procession. He had to appear "the next Sunday bare-headed and bare-footed in the church, in the time of High Mass, with a wax candle in his hand to offer it to their patron saint, St. Nicholas. He was also bound to have the usual token of his craft on his breast—that is, a pair of shears; and

* See original extract from the Burgh Records in Appendix.

then to go down humbly on his knees and beseech the Provost to remit his fault."

Religion, also, had its place in dramatic representation in those days. Aberdeen had its "Abbot and Prior of Bon-Accord," "two young citizens, probably sons or connections of the magistrates," as Kennedy in his "Annals" conjectures, who had charge of those exhibitions, which were supposed to be for the edification as well as amusement of the people. Those "mysteries," or "miracle plays," with which every reader of mediæval history is familiar, that were at first intended to popularise spiritual things, degenerated, as they could not well fail to do, into scenes of profanity and buffoonery. In that respect, Aberdeen was no exception, for it is recorded that they were afterwards restricted to certain days of the year.

In 1511, Margaret, Queen of James IV., paid a visit to Aberdeen, and, after the pageant connected with that visit, Dunbar, the national poet, sang thus:—

> "Blyth Aberdene, thow beriall of all tounis,
>   The lamp of bewtie, bounty, and blythness,
> Unto the heaven (ascendit) thy renown is
>   Of vertew, wisdome, and of worthiness."

There were festivities in the month of May, in the "greenwood," to welcome the advent of summer, that were accompanied with such licentiousness that they had to be repressed.

Again and again we come across entries in burgh records showing what difficulty magistrates and ministers of religion had in suppressing those celebrations that were so demoralising. Besides setting up the Maypole on the first Sunday of May, garlanded with flowers, round which they danced, many went on that day to St. Fithalk's Well, on the south side of the Bay of Nigg, and in drinking of its water invoked the protection of its saint, always, before leaving, putting a bit of clothing on some bush near the spot.

The life of those days had many picturesque touches. However much some parts of human nature were neglected, certainly the imagination had its due. Every Monday prayers were made for the souls of the dead, and a priest went through the streets of Aberdeen announcing the service by the ringing of a bell, one of the bells of the church being also rung at noon and at six o'clock "for all Christian souls."

One can quite understand what pride the people took in their church. What a place must a noble Gothic stone edifice have been in the eyes of those who lived in houses that were little better than huts or wooden sheds! To cross its threshold must have been to pass into what was the nearest approach upon the earth to heaven, so far as it can be figured by material things. When the choir of St. Nicholas, their parish church, was needing repair, the people not able to give money bound themselves to pay so much in kind. "Alexander Reid, Alderman, and Alexander Chalmers each gave a barrel of salmon," others gave barrels of grilse, a quarter hundred lamb-skins, etc. "Andrew Litster gave ane cow."

Money was scarce, as the above account shows. Yet "games of chance" found a place at that date among the amusements of the people. But, seeing the pernicious effect of gambling, the Magistrates made several bold attempts to repress it. "In the year 1444, William White, sutor, was tried before the baillies, and convicted by a jury composed of fifteen citizens, for permitting players of cards and dice and other unlawful games to frequent his house."

What the people required at this time was a fresh spiritual impulse. They needed something done for them from within. They for the most part reverenced divine things, and took part in religious performances with decency and devotedness. What was wanted to a much greater extent than existed at that time was a New Testament faith, a personal acquaintance with God, such as Luther struggled for and attained. The ministers of those days were to a great extent ecclesiastical and moral police rather than spiritual guides. The best of them went little further than the presentation of the intellectual and moral side of religion. They were patrons of learning and lovers of virtue, and did good service as heralds of the coming Reformation, which, as we learn from the history of Martin Luther, had inward personal renovation at its root.

CHAPTER VIII.

THE REFORMATION—1560.

NO Church in any part of the world ever owned such a large proportion of the wealth of the country as did the Romish Church in Scotland for many years before the Reformation, and no Church was ever less worthy of such possessions. About one-half of the land, it is computed by careful and reliable writers, was held by the various monasteries and other religious establishments, and that at a time when they, speaking generally, were centres of worldliness, and many of them sunk in shameless corruption. Unfortunately, the public policy which most of the kings of Scotland deemed it expedient to pursue in the circumstances of the country tended so far to bring about, or at least aggravate, that unhappy state of affairs. The Crown, being unable to cope with some of the strongest and most turbulent of the barons, and feeling itself powerless before any widespread combination among those proud and self-willed magnates, was obliged for its own protection to favour the pretensions and growing power of the Church, which, from its connection with Rome and the influence that accompanied its large worldly estate, was a force not to be despised.

The Church, being exceptionally strong as a thing of the earth, offered powerful inducements to the younger sons of nobles and others to enter its service, who had no piety in their hearts and often not even decency in their lives. Thus the Church sank lower and lower, until it became a by-word and a reproach. There were honest and pious men in it, such as Bishop Elphinstone, who, amidst incentives to the opposite, lived an irreproachable life, and proved himself to be a far-seeing and large-minded lover of his country. There were also men of simple faith and, for the time, wonderfully sound evangelical sentiments, such as Bishop Brown, of Dunkeld, who, in dying, threw himself "entirely on the mercy rather than on the justice of God, and expressed a firm trust in his salvation, not for his own merits, but through the passion of Christ"; but the great majority of the ecclesiastics of that age were so different from what their vocation required them to be as to be a scandal to their contemporaries. William Dunbar, Sir David Lindsay of the Mount, and other writers of the day, did not spare the priests, who, by their cynical disregard of even appearances, laid themselves open to the most biting satire.

Ninian Wingate, or Winzet, a priest and schoolmaster of Linlithgow, and a strong opponent of John Knox, may be accepted as an unprejudiced witness in speaking of the Romish Church at the time of the Reformation. Here is his testimony, which came out in a tractate addressed to the "Queen, pastors, and nobility":—

"Your dumb doctrine in exalting ceremonies only, keeping in silence the true word of God necessary to all men's salvation, and not resisting manifest errors, to the world is known. What part of the true religion by your slothful dominion and princely estate is not corrupted or obscured ? Have not many, through lack of teachment, in mad ignorance misknown the duty which we all owe to our Lord God, and so in their perfect belief have sorely stammered ? Were not the Sacraments of Christ Jesus profaned by ignorants and wicked persons neither able to persuade to godliness by learning nor by living ? Of the which number we confess the most part of us of the ecclesiastical state to have been, in our ignorant and inexpert youth, unworthily by you admitted to the ministration thereof. Were ye commanded in vain of God by the mouths of His prophets and apostles to watch attently and continually upon your flock and know diligently the same by face ? Or gave the princes of the earth yearly rents (as the disciples in the beginning sold their lands and gave the prices thereof unto the apostles) to the end that every one of you might spend the same upon his dame Dalila and bastard brows ? And albeit it chance oft to the infirmity of man that he fall asleep when he should most wake, and be given to pastime when he should most diligently labour—but yet, oh, merciful God! what deadly sleep is this that has oppressed you, that in so great uproar, tumult, and terrible clamour, ye wake not forth of your dream? Awake! awake! we say, and put to your hand stoutly to save Peter's ship."

The condition of the Church in Aberdeen may be inferred from an extract which we give from an address to William Gordon, the last Bishop of Aberdeen, by the Dean and Chapter, dated 5th January, 1558:—

"Imprimis, that my Lord Bishop cause the kirkmen within his diocie to reform themselves in all their slanderous manner of living, and to remove their open concubines, as well great as small. Secundo, that his Lordship will be so good as to show edificative example—in special in removing and discharging himself of the company of the gentlewoman by whom he is greatly slandered, without the which be done, diverse that are partners say they cannot accept counsel and correction of him which will not correct himself."

Scotland was the scene of religious awakenings before the time of the Reformation. The "Lollards," or wandering disciples of Wickliffe, by their secret meetings for breaking the word and for prayer for some years before the Reformation, were as evanescent flashes of light in the darkness, not prolonged nor widespread enough to have any perceptible or immediate effect in its

THE REFORMATION.

dispersion. But when the great Reformation in Germany began to draw the attention of Europe, not a few in Scotland, longing and praying for a better state of things at home, were kept acquainted with its progress and principles. All along the east coast, from Edinburgh to Aberdeen in particular, the truth was quietly disseminated. The many ships which came over from the Continent brought tidings and statements of the new doctrine, which were handed about. In a letter engrossed in the burgh records of Aberdeen, which James V. sent to the clergy of the diocese in 1525, there is a reference to "syndry strangers ande otheris w^{t}in his diocesy of Aberdene, has bukys of that heretick luthyr, and favors his errorys and fals opinionys, incontrar our act of parliament laitlie mayd in o^r last parliament."

At first, the persons specially interested were of the learned class—observant, thoughtful men who had correspondence with the big world outside of Scotland, and who, after much groping, like Luther himself, had found the pearl of great price, which was not known to the mass of the people. But the martyrdom of Patrick Hamilton, and still more that of George Wishart, seemed to send home the conviction to the nation at large that a great work was begun within their borders; the flame of those burnings was as the candle of the Lord, and the truth of the testimony which was put to the proof at the stake, silently and in a way unknown to ecclesiastics and statesmen, was taking root and gradually supplanting the old discredited system.

Nor were suitable leaders lacking for the movement in Scotland. The special service which John Knox and his coadjutors rendered to Scotland lay in their unselfish and unfaltering adherence to the truth which was essential to the higher life of the nation. Like an old Hebrew prophet—a Scottish Elijah—he stood there, firm as a rock, with no other message than—"Thus saith the Lord." Doubtless he was rough, but he had rough work to do. You cannot fell a tree with a lance, but with the sturdy blows of an axe. Remember Carlyle's sentence—"It was not a smooth business; but it was welcome surely, and cheap at that price, had it been far rougher." Knox was not a courtier of the most approved pattern. He had a rigid inflexibility which Courts are not accustomed to, and which was highly inconvenient to a Queen who hoped, by her blandishments and tact, to win the nation back to Rome. He of all men of the day, with his piercing penetration, saw, and was steadily fighting against the policy of the Palace.

We know we are approaching dangerous ground when we even hint at an impeachment of Queen Mary. Her personal beauty, romantic career, and tragic end have thrown a spell over many writers, and made them incapable of dealing with facts relating to her in a rational and sober way. Feeling and imagination come in with their colouring and idealising effects, and, say what you may, "Ephraim is joined to his idols."

But men who revere truth more than Mary feel bound to admit that, among the many interests which conflicting parties kept well in view, to John Knox above all others belongs the signal honour of urging his countrymen, in season and out of season, to seek first the Kingdom of God and His righteousness. The most of the nobles were deaf to all considerations but the aggrandisement of their patrimonial estates, bearing out what John Knox, with more point than refinement, said—"The belly has no ears;" the Court was playing its part for a time with consummate address, wearing the silken glove on the iron hand; the Church had its scholarly champions, who were ready to enter the lists against the new doctrines, and, when they had the power, were eager to burn those who propounded them. Against all those, John Knox, with the simplicity and courage of true faith, put his confidence in the Word of God.

In the echoes of that critical and exciting period which have come down to us, we often hear mention of the Scriptures. When Thomas

Forret pulled from his sleeve his New Testament that he might cite a passage in his defence, his accuser exclaimed, as he looked upon it—"This is the book that makes all the din and pley in the kirk." He gauged the situation exactly. The neglect of the teaching of that book had led to the declension of religion, and revival was due to the prayerful study of its contents. The invention of printing, which had not been turned to much account for the dissemination of sacred knowledge by the Romish Church, was one of the most serviceable auxiliaries of the Reformation. Copies of Tyndale's translation of the New Testament were brought over from the Low Countries by the Scottish traders, and were distributed on the north-east coast, some of them reaching Aberdeen. Some of the bishops of the day, in passing sentence upon men whose only crime was that they circulated the Scriptures and preached from them, boasted that they knew nothing of them.

The fundamental principle of the Reformation was the paramount authority of Scripture. As has been well said, "At one bound the Church leaped over ten centuries, and came back to the Scriptures." In the first Confession of Faith drawn up by the Reformers, their reverent regard for the Scriptures is strikingly shown in the following extract from the preface:—" We conjure you if any man will note in this our

Confession any article or sentence repugnant to God's Holy Word, that it would please him of his gentleness and for Christian charity's sake, to admonish us of the same in writing, and we upon our honour and fidelity do promise him satisfaction from the Holy Scriptures, or due reformation of that which he shall prove to be amiss." The one thing which the Scottish Reforming party placed against the authority of Pope, Bishops, and Cardinals was the Word of God. In that respect the Reformation in England was different. It was the Crown that, in the first instance at least, was brought prominently forward there, and Henry VIII. and his Ministers arrayed themselves against the Pope. In Scotland it was the people, led by the preachers, who were in opposition to the hierarchy, and that accounts for the more radical and thorough-going character of the work that was done. In our country the Reformation was less the outcome of State-craft, and was more due to the simple-hearted and resolute action of men who knew no higher rule or test in things religious than the word of God.

It is simple matter of history, patent to every attentive reader, that during the last four centuries Scotland owes more to her preachers than to any other class of men for the preservation of her civil and religious liberties. When her other natural leaders were generally thinking

chiefly of the interests of their own order and
family, the ministers of those days, with the
narrowest possible margin of worldly means—
which, as compared with the bloated estates of
their ecclesiastical predecessors, were as the
crumbs which fell from the rich man's table—
fought the battle of the people. They have their
reward now, for Scotland's greatest men,
honoured and cherished in the hearts of the
people, include in their ranks not a few whose
distinction it is that they gained and maintained
an influence such as has been wielded in very few
parts of the world by the simple preaching of
the Word. Buckle says:—" When the Scotch
Kirk was at the height of its power, we may
search history in vain for any institution which
can compete with it except the Spanish Inquisition." By such a sentence as that Buckle does
harm only to himself, by failing to distinguish
between the power that is in the hands of the
agents of a huge system of hierarchal despotism
and the moral weight of men who have nothing
behind them but the Word of God and the
religious sentiment of a free people. The exiles,
confessors, and martyrs of the Reformation
period, whose blood was the seed of the Church,
were for the most part ministers of religion,
many of them men of good birth as well as of
high education. Among the more distinguished
of those priests of the old order, who were the

self-sacrificing heralds of the new, was Patrick Hamilton.

The spectacle of that man of gentle blood and still gentler spirit, Patrick Hamilton, passing away from this world amidst piles of slowly-burning faggots near the sea-cliffs of St. Andrews is indelibly imprinted upon the national heart. The wood for the sacrifice was green, unskilful hands tended the fire, a tempestuous east wind was like to blow it out, and for six hours did he endure the agonies of consciousness —"roasted at last rather than burnt," as a spectator remarked. One of the articles for which he was condemned to this death was his belief—" that a man is not justified by works but by faith; that faith, hope, and charity are so linked together that he who hath one of them hath all, and he that lacketh one lacketh all; and that good works make not a good man, but a good man doeth good works." As he was patiently enduring the tortures which cruel men were inflicting upon him in the name of Christ, a solitary voice out of the awe-struck crowd asked him to give a sign of his steadfastness to the faith. Whereupon three fingers of his scorched, half-consumed hand were held up. Soon after that, and before expiring, he said—
" How long shall darkness overwhelm this realm? How long wilt Thou suffer the tyranny of men? Lord Jesus, receive my spirit."

It came to be a common saying in Scotland that "the reek of Patrick Hamilton infected all on whom it blew." How suicidal was the policy of the ecclesiastics of the day! The only effect of their diabolical rage was to convince the nation of the reality and power of a cause that could enable men so to live and die. George Wishart also, who was educated at King's College, Aberdeen, by his life, and still more by his death, hastened on the work of the Reformation. An Angus man, he frequented Dundee, and his Gospel ministrations met with such success in that town that it gained the name of the "Scottish Geneva," being at that time the chief centre of light in Scotland; its "gude and godly ballates, changed out of prophaine sanges for avoyding of sinne and harlotrie," by the brothers Wedderburn, rendered great service to the whole country.

It is quite true there were multitudes in Scotland then with little spiritual sympathy who went in strongly for the Reformation. There were many who had no mind for divine doctrine, and no experience of its power in their heart and life, who were quite able and willing to join the crusade against an oppressive and licentious priesthood. Criticism and assault are always easier and more popular than moral reconstruction, and the ranks of the Reforming party were therefore thronged with men who, to a large extent, were strangers to divine grace, but were the subjects of a natural indignation against the scandalous condition of the Church.

There was a great deal of protesting before the famous formal protest was uttered, and that, too, sometimes by men who did not have behind their critical and destructive attitude those deep spiritual convictions which were Luther's starting point as an ecclesiastical reformer. Men of letters, like Erasmus of European fame, and poets, like our own Dunbar and Sir David Lindsay, satirised with merciless lash the vices of the clergy and the gross corruptions into which the Church had fallen. Clear-sighted and bold men of all countries and ranks rendered splendid service to the cause of the Reformation by putting in strong and vivid colours the degeneracy which had overtaken the institutions that bore the name of Christ.

Ambitious statesmen, also, and greedy territorial magnates, who saw in the lands from which the Church was about to be displaced an opportunity of enlarging their estates, had much to do with the rapid course of striking events we call the Reformation. As has been well said, "the soul of the Reformation was encased in a body of fleshly elements." With the honourable exceptions of Argyll, Moray, Glencairn, and a few more, the members of the Scottish aristocracy who espoused the popular cause showed only too plainly, in their subsequent career, that worldly wisdom and selfish aggrandisement played a more important part in their public action than the disinterested love of truth. It is always so; in all noble movements there are ignoble elements; there are those who are not of the truth, but who see in the general overturning an opportunity of serving their own ends. When the advancing tide comes up against heaps of rubbish upon the shore, it is inevitable that its waters should be defiled and should for a time carry on their bosom what they have touched.

The power, however, which carried the movement forward and gave it a place in history came from higher sources. The Reformation had the soul for its starting point. In its real inception it was not a mere thing of criticism and ecclesiastical reform, but of spiritual experience. It was inward life, throbbing, expanding, and demanding that first right of all life—freedom to be. It was life as before God, seeking that the environment which was to minister to its wellbeing and growth should correspond with its own innermost principles and distinctive aims. There was the work of receiving the divine gift and nourishing the divine life in secret, which led to the public repudiation of the artificial trammels that would suppress or cramp its outgoing energies. No was said to the Pope, because Yes had been previously said to the soul's true Lord.

The negation and destruction were in order to, or rather in consequence of, sublime affirmations. That is a sufficient answer to Roman Catholic writers who jeer at the term Protestant as if it were the mere offspring of irresponsible criticism without anything more valid behind. The Protestantism was only the resisting power of Evangelicalism. The essence of what goes under the name of Protestantism was not mere dissatisfaction with the imposition of the Papal hierarchy. It went far deeper down. It sprang from satisfaction with Christ and consequent submission to his authority. It was in no fit of scornful scepticism that Knox, when a galley slave, asked to do reverence to an image of the Virgin Mary, flung it into the water as so much "painted bredd," that was fitter to swim than to be worshipped. It was reverence for God which made it impossible he could do honour to a piece of painted wood as "the Mother of God." Luther was not so much setting himself against the representatives of Christendom as putting himself into rightful subjection to God, when in the Diet of Worms he wound up his declaration with the memorable words—" Here I am. I cannot do otherwise. God help me. Amen." The protesting part of the Reformation was no more than the work of men who, in preparing for a launch, strike away the wedges and bolts which detain the vessel from its native element.

What tended to confirm the leading Reformers of Scotland in their Protestantism was the horrible outrage perpetrated in France on St. Bartholemew's day twelve years after Popery had been formally unseated by our Parliament. Such was the effect of the massacre of the Huguenots upon the mind of Europe that the principal perpetrators of that foul deed were not long in discovering that, besides being guilty of an atrocious crime, they had allowed passion to hurry them into a stupid blunder. What was the Reforming party in Scotland to think of the Church, the responsible heads of which ordered a medal to be struck to perpetuate the memory of the butchery of Protestants. Roman Catholic writers have denied the existence of such a medal, but in the museum bequeathed by Mr. Thomson of Banchory to the Free Church College, Aberdeen, this witness against the Roman Church can be seen any day, with the image of Pope Gregory XIII. on the one side, and on the other a soldier with a sword in the act of killing Huguenots.

CHAPTER IX.

JOHN CRAIG—1512-1600.

THE struggle which had been going on for more than half a century, with varying fortunes to both sides, at last came to a head, though not to an end, in 1560, when the ritual of the Romish Church was declared to be illegal, and all Papal jurisdiction was abolished by the Scottish Parliament. Such a complete overthrow of the most ancient institution in the world, which appealed to the deepest and most sacred feelings of the human heart, and was sanctioned by the usage and supported by the power of the greater part of Europe, is—next to the introduction of Christianity itself—the most remarkable event which has happened in the whole history of Scotland. It will not be deemed an unprofitable task to endeavour to discover the forces which contributed to such a striking result.

Foremost among them must be placed internal disorder and decay. The Church's worst enemies were those of its own household. If the Romish Church had continued to be even moderately loyal to the truth which it professed to hold, the error that was embedded in its doctrine and ritual might probably have been allowed to sleep for centuries. But it has to be remembered, on the other hand, that the corruptions which scandalised the nation often sprang from what was in the system itself, such as the enforced celibacy of the clergy.

The church perished by its own hand, as that institution is doomed whose responsible guardians are grossly indifferent to its fundamental principles and aims; and for "holy Mother Church" to have passed away in such circumstances was not to die, but to be murdered. The indictment which history brings against the churchmen of the fifteenth and sixteenth centuries is that, with a few noble exceptions, they were guilty of spiritual matricide. Alert enough to pounce upon heresy or anything that tended to subvert their own order, the Kingdom of God, which is not meat and drink, but righteousness, peace, and joy in the Holy Ghost, was not only neglected by most of the men entrusted with its interests, but was trampled upon and profaned. So that the typical man of the period was not Bishop Elphinstone, but that masterpiece and mirror of his age, that brilliant embodiment of its ideas and aspirations, that consummate piece of strenuous and polished worldliness—Cardinal Beaton. Dr. Forbes Leith, who wrote the "Narratives of Scottish Catholics," in lamenting the death of the Cardinal, calls him the "mainstay of religion" in Scotland. In view of his private life, the facts of which are notorious and matter of public record, one is inclined to ask what kind of religion was that of which Cardinal Beaton was the "mainstay." Was it the religion of Christ and the Apostles, the religion that was inaugurated by the Sermon on the Mount, and of which lowliness and chastity were among the common characteristics? Were his example and influence the "mainstay" of such a religion? Ah! it is only when a mere ecclesiastical system, shaped after the ideas of a lapsed world, is substituted for the Kingdom of God and His righteousness, and the Christian name and its symbols of worship are prostituted for the furtherance of objects as far away from the mind of Christ and the examples of the Apostolic Church as Ancient Rome of the first century was from the little company who waited in an upper room for the outpouring of the Divine Spirit—it is only when the Church has become a mere thing of the earth, the creature of priest-craft and the tool of ambition, that such a man as Cardinal Beaton can be called its "mainstay."

In addition to greed, jealousy was also at work in the breasts of the nobles, constraining them to identify themselves with the policy of destruction, though most of them were sufficiently backward when reconstruction was begun. They were envious of the political influence that was wielded by the dignified clergy who held the chief offices of State, as being "the best scholars, the most capable statesmen, the most accomplished diplomatists, and the profoundest and acutest lawyers."

In enumerating the forces which operated in favour of the Reformation, mention must also be made of the spirit of inquiry and criticism that began to manifest itself in the fifteenth century. It is possible to make too much of the "revival of letters," in which Erasmus and others before him took a conspicuous part, as an auxiliary in the regeneration of the Church. For countries much nearer the centre of this revived interest in literature, such as Austria and Spain, were content to remain in the shackles of Rome, notwithstanding the light that came streaming around them from the reopened classics of Greece and Rome.

Still, it cannot be doubted that it was, in a general way, a great gain to the cause of truth and progress to have the dull, dead monotony of the Middle Ages broken, and stagnant thought stirred by questions other than the stale scholastic ones which had occupied rather than exercised the mind for so many years. The budding literature of Scotland, of which William Dunbar and Sir David Lindsay of the Mount were the chief ornaments, took its share in this work of opening men's minds to the facts which were around them.

They lashed the Churchmen of the day with their scornful effusions, and by their satire, more biting than delicate, helped to prepare the way for the Reformation, by enabling the people to realise that there was need for it.

The population of the city of Aberdeen at the time of the transition from the Romish to the Protestant faith was only about 4,000, and the inhabitants of the whole of Scotland did not number half a million—less than what the city of Glasgow now has within its boundaries. Yet, for that small number of people in our town, it is calculated that there were more men set apart to the offices of religion in church and monastery than what we have to meet the wants of the present population!

Owing to the distance of Aberdeen from the large centres, where the new currents of thought and feeling were at work, and the want of leading men with the reforming spirit to take the initiative, little of the stir of the times reached our city. It has been humorously said that in those far-away times an Act of Parliament was out of breath by the time it reached Aberdeen, and thus many influences at work in the central parts of the land were faintly felt in this remote region. The men in the University and the priests of the Church evinced no desire to espouse the "heretical" notions that were abroad. The Earl of Huntly and other feudal lords of the neighbourhood, who were thick-and-thin supporters of the old order, overawed the burgesses, and made the native caution doubly strong. It was true then that "the Gordons hae the guiding o' 't." It is very much owing to the same cause that there are considerable belts of land in the north, such as Glenlivet and Glengairn, which are still largely inhabited by Roman Catholics. The feudal heads of the people of those districts did not sever their connection with the Roman Church at the time of the Reformation, and that had its effects upon their retainers. Some of the leading proprietors in those regions did eventually pass over to the Protestant side; but, there being no general movement at the time, many of the people continued to adhere to the ancient faith.

It was left to John Marshall, rector of the Grammar School, to take the Protestant position and vindicate freedom of thought in religious matters. He was brought before the Magistrates on a charge of heresy, and, whilst he valiantly stood out for two years, at last confessed his error and made peace with the powers that be. What a pity John Marshall did not hold out to the bitter end, if for no other reason than to redeem Aberdeen from the reproach of never having had a martyr within its borders! The martyr's pile was never kindled in our northern region, though, as we shall learn by-and-bye, its canny inhabitants had their share of suffering arising from the religious controversies of the period.

But the excitement that was seething in the southern part of Scotland made itself felt at last in the north. A band of men full of reforming zeal, which too frequently assumed the form of destructive violence, came to our city and defaced and spoiled some of the religious houses, and would have done serious damage to buildings which are the pride of Aberdonians, had they not been restrained. Aberdeen, without seeking the Reformation, had to accept it. It had to take its place as part of a nation that had abjured the Romish Church. Adam Heriot, the first Protestant minister, is supposed to have sprung from a branch of the family to which belonged the celebrated George Heriot, who was jeweller to King James VI., and founder of the hospital in Edinburgh bearing his name. On a small tablet erected to the wife of Adam Heriot, there is an inscription in Latin in which he is designated—" Preacher of the merits of Jesus Christ at Aberdeen." The official entry of his death in the town records is—" Maister Adam Heriot, fyrst minister of the trew word of God, departitt the 28th day of August, 1574 years." It is not surprising that he became prematurely old, and died when he was sixty years of age, for, with the University professors and most of the gentry hostile, and the people generally lukewarm, he must have had a hard battle to fight.

The next foremost figure associated with that period in this locality was John Craig, Heriot's successor. The life of this man, so full of rapidly-shifting scenes, hairbreadth escapes, and courageous endeavour, which never flinched from its lofty object, whether fortune smiled or frowned, reads like a romance. Providence had done much to fit him for high place and distinguished service in the Church of Christ. He was born in 1512 of "honest and substantial parents," known as the Craigs of Craig Fintray, now Craigston, of the county of Aberdeen. A year after his birth, his father was killed at Flodden, which reduced the family to great straits. For some reason that is unknown, he studied, not at his native University, King's College, which was at that time famous and attracting students from all parts, but at St. Andrews, where he graduated with approbation. After serving for two years as tutor to the sons of Lord Dacres, he returned to St. Andrews, entered the Church, and became a monk of the order of St. Dominic. Being of an inquiring turn of mind, and not afraid to avow his convictions, he was suspected of heresy, and had to leave the country. We find him as a fugitive in England, France, and latterly in Rome, where he made the acquaintance of Cardinal Pole, who secured for him, when he was quite a young man, an introduction to the Dominicans at Bologna.

His career there was one of rapid promotion. After having approved himself as instructor of novices, he was actually made rector of the Dominican Academy at Bologna. This position gave him ready access to the Library, where he became acquainted with Calvin's "Institutes," a perusal of which ended in his conversion to the Protestant faith.

When the change in his religious opinions became known to the Inquisition at Rome, he was removed to that city and immured in a gloomy vault, where—Rowe reports—the prisoners had to stand twice a day up to their waists in water by the admission of the tides! He was condemned to be burned for his opinions on the 19th May, 1559, but managed to escape. After resorting to many hidings and shifts, he, in his toilsome wanderings, reached Vienna. To the end of his days he was accustomed to relate with solemn feeling an incident that occurred to him on the road, when his fortunes were at a low ebb, and he was like to lose heart. As he sat by the side of a brook, a dog, with a purse between his teeth, came fawning and lay down beside him. The gold that was in it helped him out of his difficulties, and greatly encouraged his heart.

From Vienna he eventually found his way to Scotland, where his return was hailed with delight in "the morning of the Reformation," the cause that Knox fought for having just received legal recognition and establishment. On his return to Edinburgh he preached for some time to the "learned in Latine" in Magdalen Chapel. When he recovered the use of his native tongue—which, by long absence from Scotland, he had almost lost—he preached for some time at Holyrood House, and shortly after was appointed colleague to John Knox as minister of St. Giles' Church. For ten years he did valiant service in that capacity, and proved himself to be a most valuable coadjutor to the man who was practically the ruler as well as bishop of Scotland.

In 1572 he was translated to Montrose. In about two years after that date he was sent further north "to illuminate those dark places in Mar, Buchan, and Aberdeen, and to teach the youth of the college there." He came to Aberdeen to relieve, and afterwards to succeed, worthy Adam Heriot, just as James Lawson, sub-principal of our University, had shortly before been called to be Knox's colleague and successor in Edinburgh. Craig's income was, as records show, £16 13s. 4d. for at least one year. Such was the pittance that was allowed for the man who was doing the work which "a bishop, a fully-equipped cathedral, and a noble parish church filled with well-paid priests had done."

The leading men of the "Congregation" in Edinburgh, as the Protestant party were called, knew what they were about when they sent a man of such ample resources and versatile talent to Aberdeen, where Protestantism had a stiffer battle to fight than in any other part of the kingdom. The scholarship, the landed interest, the social influence generally, of Aberdeen were with the old order, and the common people were not burning with desire to be emancipated from the Roman fetters.

During his stay in Aberdeen, Craig took an active part in the preparation of the Second Book of Discipline and the Catechism, of which he says " to the professores of Christ's Evangel in Newe Aberdene: that it was for their sakes chiefly that he took paines first to gather this brieff summe." He was Moderator, also, of the General Assembly for the second time on October 24, 1576, and served the Church over an extensive district beyond Aberdeen as commissioner or superintendent.

Having laboured in Aberdeen for about six years, he left it on 14th September, 1579, to be chaplain to James VI. It surely must have been an enemy, or a friend embittered by the enforced separation, who leaves it on record:—" On the 18th day of Sept., the year of God 1579, Maister

John Craig, sometyme minister of Aberdene, departed with his wyfe and bairns and haill housiel out of ye said burght, and left his floick unprovidit of ane minister: To be preacher to the King's grace: As he allegit."

He died on 12th December, 1600, leaving no portrait of himself except what can be found in his noble record of work and his unfaltering steadfastness as a champion of the truth. A cultured and travelled Scot, his chequered experience abroad, added to the excellent training he got in his own country, fitted him for the succession of difficult positions he had to occupy in the later years of his life.

CHAPTER X.

BISHOP PATRICK FORBES—1564-1635.

THE battle of the Reformation was fought on the question of doctrine rather than upon that of Church government. Knox and his co-adjutors had to contend for what lay at the very core of Christianity, the right of every man to have personal dealings with God in the great matter of salvation through faith in Christ as the only mediator. All available energy was used in the persistent and successful championship of that truth. Church government was a secondary question that could wait. Consequently, the Church in Scotland for some time after the Reformation was not very clearly defined as to its type of structure. It was partly Episcopal and partly Presbyterian, with a strong leaning to the popular form of government. Like sensible men, the Reformers took the government which the circumstances admitted of, as they were engaged in deep foundation work.

Largely owing to the strong personality of Andrew Melville, as the consolidation of the Scottish Church went on, the Presbyterianism that was in it became more pronounced, and assumed a definite and more permanent form.

Presbyterianism was not only established by law: it was in course of years nationalised in the deeper sense of being identified with the religious life of the people. But the Court and all under its influence did not like it, and were determined that the form of Church polity which England favoured should suffice for Scotland. So the battle between the Crown and the people went on for more than a hundred years, neither side showing any disposition to give way, even when the fortunes of war went against it. In 1610 Episcopacy came in, as King James would have it so.

It has often been a matter of surprise to some students of Scottish history, more impressionable than profound, that there should have been such strenuous feeling imported into the controversy between the advocates of the rival systems of Episcopacy and Presbyterianism. Why make so much ado about a question of government? The difference between the two polities and forms of worship was much less then than now. This is how the difference is minimised by an Episcopalian of the period. In "The Case of the Present Afflicted Clergy in Scotland Truly Represented," published in 1690, we find the following comparison between the worship of both Churches made:—

"As to the worship, it's exactly the same both in the Church and Conventicle; in the Church there are no ceremonies at all injoyned or practised, only some persons more reverent, think fit to be uncovered, which our Presbyterians do but by halves even in the time of prayer; we have no liturgy nor form of prayer, no not in the Cathedrals, the only difference in this point is, our clergy are not so overbold nor fulsome in their extemporary expressions as the others are, nor use so many vain repetitions, and we generally conclude one of our prayers with that which our Saviour taught and commanded, which the other party decry as superstitious and formal; Amen, too, gives great offence, though neither the clerk nor people use it, only the minister sometimes shuts up his prayer with it. The sacraments are administered after the same way and manner by both; neither so much as kneeling at the prayers, or when they receive the elements at the Lord's Supper, but all sitting together at a long table, in the body of the church or chancel. In baptism neither party use the cross, nor are any godfathers or godmothers required, the father only promising for his child. The only difference in this sacrament is, the Presbyterians make the father swear to breed up his child in the faith and belief of the Covenant or Solemn League, whereas the Orthodox cause the father repeat the Apostles' Creed, and promise to breed up the child in that faith which himself then possesses."*

M‘Crie also, who represents the other ecclesiastical side, in his "Sketches of Scottish Church

* "The Case of the Present Afflicted Clergy in Scotland Truly Represented," p. 3 of Preface.

History," writes thus of the period immediately preceding the Revolution of 1688 :—

"It is a curious fact that during all this time no attempt was made to introduce the ceremonies of the English churches. The form of worship differed very little from that practised by the Presbyterians. Our prelatic clergy had no liturgy, no ceremonies, no surplice, no altars, no crossing in baptism. What is more remarkable, they had no Confession of Faith, no standard of doctrine or discipline, no rule to guide their practice, except the will of the bishops, which, again, was regulated by the will of the king."*

If, then, Presbyterianism had the repetition of the Lord's Prayer, the Ten Commandments, and the Doxology as part of the Church service on Sabbath up to the times of the Covenant, and Episcopacy had no liturgy as late as the middle of the eighteenth century, why create so much disturbance and involve the nation in the horrors of civil war about the comparatively trivial difference as to whether Presbyters or Bishops should rule the Church?

In reply to this, it has to be called to remembrance, in the first place, that Episcopacy was imposed. That form of Church life was not the free choice of the people. In the circumstances of the country at the time the acceptance of Episcopacy meant the undue enlargement of the

* M'Crie's "Sketches of Scottish Church History," Vol. II., p. 236.

royal prerogative and the loss to the Scottish Church of spiritual independence. There can be no doubt that one reason for the passionate love of Episcopacy which found a place in the breast of the Stuart dynasty was the fact that it was supposed to lend itself more readily to their supreme aim, fondly cherished by each succeeding occupant of the throne from the time of Mary, which was to secure as near an approach to Absolutism, personal rule, as was possible in a free country. Presbyterianism was, in courtly eyes, an unknown and, therefore, dangerous quantity, with a decided leaning towards democracy, and it was feared that if there were no bishop there might by-and-bye be no king. The people were as determined to have their rights secured as the Stuarts were eager to hedge round their unconstitutional prerogative—hence the Civil War.

Besides, Episcopacy was more like the system which had been rejected at the Reformation, and Presbyterianism was deemed to be more consonant with the simplicity of Christianity as unfolded in the New Testament Scriptures, which the people had begun to study with great eagerness. While there is no necessary connection between sacerdotalism and government by bishops, yet as a matter of fact they often have been connected. In their rebound from priestcraft, therefore, in all its forms, and in their anxiety to secure an unoccupied place between the soul and God, the Scottish people turned away from that system which in their eyes, rightly or wrongly, had a proclivity for those things which impaired the freedom of the individual Christian, and marred the simplicity of the Gospel.

That untold multitudes of pious souls have been nourished within the communion of the Episcopal Church, and that character noble and strong has been formed by its ministrations, it would be downright folly as well as sheer bigotry to deny; but a prejudice has been excited against it in Scotland because many of its sons attach an importance to distinctive ecclesiastical order which it is found difficult to reconcile with the mandate of Scripture and also with the conditions of a true and enlightened catholicity. The adherents of almost all other forms of Church government and worship can hold their respective convictions as to what the outward structure of the Church ought to be, and yet feel that they stand equally on the common ground of an unimpaired and catholic Christianity; but some, and these the most pronounced Episcopalians, bring in things of which they as such claim to have a monopoly, which tend to subordinate the spiritual to the ecclesiastical, and make catholicity a much narrower thing than did Christ and the Apostles.

What helped also to draw the great majority of the Scottish people from an Episcopacy which readily identified itself with sacerdotalism was the fact that the men who took a leading part in opening the eyes of the nation to the grand verities of Gospel salvation put the chief stress and weight of their thought upon spiritual doctrine rather than upon ecclesiastical ritual. The religious awakening of Scotland could be traced to evangelical teaching, not to sacramental acts—to the exaltation of Christ before individual souls, not to the enthronement of any officials of the Church as depositaries of heavenly grace. The Reformers such as Wishart, Knox, and Patrick Hamilton, like Luther, brought the people face to face with their Saviour; and while they believed in the Church, it was only as a fellowship and means of edification for men who had met Christ for themselves. In short, the ecclesiastical was viewed by the men who by God's help have made Scotland what it is as nothing unless it was preceded by the spiritual and the experimental in the soul's own dealings with God. No doubt there were fanatical Presbyterians who thought their system should be set up over the whole world, but the recognised leaders and exponents of Scottish religious life introduced Presbyterianism not because it was the only channel of grace for men, but because they thought it was Scriptural, and it was the form of government which the Reformers on the Continent, such as Calvin, with whom they had close communication, favoured.

But there were Episcopalians then, as there are now, whose Episcopacy was little more to their Evangelicalism than the accident is to the essence—than the porch is to the palace. They accepted Christ as the only Saviour of men, and faith in him as the only condition of salvation. Such was Archbishop Leighton, that saintly and seraphic man, whose sermons lift you far above all consideration of ritual or Church order into the holy of holies of a pure spirituality and heavenly serenity, and make you feel indeed that "the pure in heart shall see God, not only in some future and far-off scene, but wherever they turn their eyes." Leighton's piety, so unmistakably sincere, as far redeemed from self and the world as is possible on this side of the grave; his penetrating insight into the meaning of Scripture; the spontaneous flow of his original thought, like the welling forth of a perennial spring; the rare glow and sparkle of an imagination that was at home amongst the things of God; the chaste beauty of his diction—all make you think, not of the Episcopalian, but of the Christian who has learned to look upon questions of Church order as little more than garments, to be put off or on according as they fit. Such, on a smaller scale, was Scougal, of Aberdeen, the author of the "Life of God in the Soul of Man." Such also, with a difference, was Bishop Patrick Forbes, whose portrait is in Marischal College. He was born in 1564, the eldest son of William Forbes of Corse and Kincardine O'Neil. His father gave him the best education which could be had, sending him to the Grammar School of Stirling, then under the charge of Thomas Buchanan, a nephew of the famous George Buchanan, the Latin historian and poet. From Stirling he went to Glasgow University, where he studied under the care of his relative, Andrew Melville. He kept company with Melville for some years after leaving the University of Glasgow, and pursued theological studies in St. Andrews with such success that he was offered a Divinity chair. This he refused, as his father wanted him to settle down on the family property of Corse after his own decease.

A tradition still lingers in Corse which shows us Mr. Patrick Forbes had a sense of humour which he did not repress:—An old woman came to him one day in great distress about her cow that seemed to be very ill. Mr. Forbes said he did not think he could do anything for it; but her anxiety being so great, he went, at her urgent request, to see it. The woman had great faith in his powers, and he felt that, to satisfy her, he must *do* something; so, happening to see a riddle (sieve) hanging on the wall of the byre, he took it down and shook it over the cow, saying, in a loud voice—" Gin ye live, ye live, and gin ye dee, ye dee!" To the old woman's great delight the cow recovered.

Some time after Mr. Forbes became very ill with quinsy, and was not expected to recover. When he was at his worst the woman came to the door and demanded to see him. The servant would not listen to her request, and said Mr. Forbes was "juist deein'"; but she would take no refusal. "There's the mair need for me to win in, than," said she, and forcing her way into the room with the aforesaid riddle, she shook it over the laird's head with the words—" Gin ye live, ye live, and gin ye dee, ye dee!" which caused him to burst into a fit of laughter, with the result that the quinsy broke and he was relieved!

That Patrick Forbes, a country gentleman, should have cultivated tastes and engaged in pursuits that are too often in these days regarded as the preserve of the professional clergymen, was not at all a circumstance to be specially noted at that period. All classes then, especially the gentry and smaller proprietors—not as a rule the nobles—in most parts of Scotland made religion, if not indeed theology, one of the special interests of life. As can be gathered from the extensive correspondence carried on by Rutherford, piety was an honoured guest in the mansion as well as in the cottage, there being a freshness of interest in the study of Scripture in those early days of the Reformation period, as of the opening up of the land of Beulah.

With his well-furnished mind and deep spiritual earnestness, it was not to be expected that Patrick Forbes should be allowed to remain long idle when there was such scarcity of Gospel ministrations in the land. He, soon after settling down in the paternal estate, was pressed into service as a preacher in the neighbouring parish church. In a simple, straightforward manner, he thus explains, in a letter to King James VI., how he was led to take up public work of the kind, though, owing to "the difficulties of the times," he did not see his way formally to enter the ministry:—

". . . Being cast in these parts where, within the precinct of two Presbyteries, at least twenty and one churches lay unplanted, whereby our state were little from heathenisme, I began in simple and private manners (necessity enforcing it on my conscience) to catechise my own family. Thereafter the Churchmen of that province dealing earnestlie with me to accept of some publick charge in the ministrie of the Church, which, upon divers respectfull considerations, I could not, as then, yield to, they next with all instance requested that at least, for the gude of others, I would be content to transfer my domestic paines to ane void church, now joining to my house; whairto having for a space condescendit, they afterward, by thair commissioners from thair Synod, directed to me for that effect, yet more earnestly entreated that I would still hold on that course which (as they judged) had been in some degree fruitful."

But a summary prohibition was put upon those preachings by Archbishop Gladstanes. It was not denied that Forbes was eminently qualified for the work he undertook, and that good results were flowing from it, but the one fatal objection to it was its irregularity—he was not in "orders." Rather than that a man should preach who had not had the hands of a bishop placed upon him, though it was clear he had every qualification for it, the people must be allowed spiritually to starve.

At length, after considerable hesitation, he was induced to yield to the pressure of many friends, and he formally entered the ministry. The circumstances under which he took this step were tragic and harrowing. John Chalmers, minister of the parish of Keith, having fallen into a morbid state of mind, laid violent hands upon himself by attempting to cut his throat. No sooner had he done the deed—which proved ultimately, though not immediately, fatal—than, struck with the deepest remorse and penitence, he bitterly repented of the criminal surrender to the melancholy which was brooding over his spirit. He sent for the laird of Corse, whose soothing sympathy and comforting yet faithful words, brought the unhappy man back to a healthy state of mind. He was deeply concerned lest the cause of religion should suffer by one of its ministers behaving in such an unworthy fashion, and he strongly urged Mr. Forbes to help to undo the mischief by coming himself to Keith and carrying on the Gospel work, for which, by his training and habits, he was so well fitted. The parishioners and the neighbouring clergy having urgently joined in this request, Forbes at last consented. He was ordained in 1612, in the forty-seventh year of his age, and for six years was minister of the parish of Keith.

In 1618 Patrick Forbes was asked to become Bishop of Aberdeen, as the man above all others in the north worthy of this place of responsibility and dignity. It would appear that he did not at all covet the post, and, in view of the unsettled state of ecclesiastical affairs, he was reluctant to take a position which would require him to enforce conformity on the part of Presbyterian ministers whom he in other respects could not but honour.

Like Archbishop Leighton, he was in the anomalous and highly uncomfortable position of being in his doctrine and spiritual affinities quite at home with those of the Presbyterian fold; but he did not see his way to join them—as his brother

John, of Alford, did—in their attitude of determined antagonism to the Church polity which was favoured by royalty and was by law established. He was of a strongly conservative turn of mind, a stickler for legality and order, with a constitutional dislike to anything that savoured of revolution and disloyalty. Dr. Grub, in his "Ecclesiastical History of Scotland," says of him:—"Retaining his strong attachment to the Protestant doctrines, he was disposed, like many other good men of that time, to acquiesce in the Sovereign's claims to regulate the external polity of the Church." But it cannot be doubted by every unbiased student of history that Scotland would have been a very different place to-day if that "acquiescence" had been general. It is not meant as any disparagement to his Christian character and spiritual earnestness when it is said that, from a failure in clear-sightedness or courage, he cannot claim the credit of having strengthened the hands of those with whom at heart he had so much in common, and who, at great cost to themselves, were fighting for the liberties we now enjoy.

But there can be as little doubt that as a bishop he was without reproach. His heart was in spiritual work, and he was no mere ecclesiastical magnate who delighted in pomp and show, and who, instead of being the servant of servants, lorded it over God's heritage. It was his great aim, and the burning desire of his heart, to secure efficiency and usefulness in his diocese. Without giving any notice he would go to a parish on Saturday evening, take a private lodging, and give the officiating minister next morning a surprise by presenting himself as an unexpected hearer and spectator. But while he was watchful and resolute in keeping others to their duty, he was quite as hard upon himself, and often requested his brother ministers to point out any fault or defect they saw in his character or his deportment as a public servant.

Bishop Forbes exercised his authority with great discrimination in his selection of men for the principal offices of the ministry in Aberdeen. He gathered about him a number of men—Barron, Scroggie, Guild, and others—the "Doctors" who by their learning and their dialectic skill, shed lustre upon the city. With Raban as printer, Aberdeen in Bishop Forbes's time became quite a literary centre. The "Funerals" of Bishop Forbes are a curious contribution to the literature of their kind. They are a collection of the funeral sermons and other effusions which were written on the lamented death of the Bishop, and show how much he was revered by his contemporaries.

CHAPTER XI.

SAMUEL RUTHERFORD IN ABERDEEN—1636-38.

SAMUEL RUTHERFORD stands alongside the very greatest men of the stirring period which we have now reached. He was not so much at home in the management of public affairs as Alexander Henderson, and did not have his calm, broad, tolerant, statesmanlike spirit; but for sheer intellectual force, kindling power, luxuriance of fancy, and that kind of originality we call genius, he was more than the equal of the noble-hearted man who was to be the leader of the Presbyterian Church at a troublous and critical time. Certainly, no one of all the stalwart heroes who fought for the liberty and spirituality of the Scottish Church has been more venerated and beloved by the godly of the land for the last two hundred years than Samuel Rutherford.

He brings a contribution of his own to the religious life and literature of Scotland. He has supplied an element of fervid spiritual emotion which is certainly not over-abundant in this land. He is our Scottish seraph, and is to the other theologians of the land and the time what John was to the rest of the twelve. Like John, he, too, could be a son of thunder when in a controversial mood.* As a polemic no one could be more inflexible and implacable, striking sturdy blows for the cause which his conscience approved, and giving no quarter to those whom he deemed to be on the wrong track; but he never was in his native and congenial sphere till he was expatiating on the loveliness and all-sufficiency of Christ with a rapturous exuberance which evidently was inspired by the experimental possession of that which was described.

He was the son of a respectable farmer, born in the parish of Crailing, some time in the year 1600. The ruin of the house in which he was born still stood at the beginning of the present century, and it is said that the then Marquis of Lothian, in token of respect, never passed it without lifting his hat. He went to the Grammar School of Jedburgh, which was four miles distant, then occupying a part of the ancient abbey, and from that circumstance called Latiners Alley. He had a quick apprehension and a fervid spirit, along with a tenacious grasp of what he had acquired, which do much in making the scholar; and his father, persuaded by the schoolmaster, sent his

---

* Spalding's "Memorialls of the Trubles" (Vol. I., p. 312) exhibits him in that mood one Sabbath day when he was in our town :—" Thair wes also ane minister called Rutherford, who hapnit to be wardit in Aberdein at King James' command. He, hearing Doctor Sibbald at that time preiche, stude up and accusit him of Arminianisme."

son to Edinburgh University, where he graduated in 1621. Soon after he was appointed Regent or Professor of Humanity, which office, however, he demitted after being in it for four years, and in 1627 he became the minister of the parish of Anwoth. In that lovely spot, near the Solway, he began a pastoral work, the story of which, so full of tender solicitude for the people committed to his care, and consuming devotion to their highest interests, has made the name Anwoth fragrant with a holy fame, and made it also a scene of highest inspiration to ministers all over the land.

It was, however, during his enforced retirement in Aberdeen, banished for his nonconformity by the High Commission Court, that he was destined to do the most memorable and effective work of his life. How often he complained while he was a "prisoner" in the northern city that he was not allowed to open his mouth in public, and by preaching exercise the one gift which he valued above all others. Little did he know that by the letters which he was compelled to write, as the only means of communication between him and his flock and other friends, he was thereby, in the "Lord's palace," as he called his lodging in Aberdeen, to address an audience throughout Christendom such as no man could number, and one which is not yet, nor is likely to be, dismissed as long as the world stands.

How often Providence so orders events that what appears to be a grievous hindrance to the onward movement of the good cause becomes a most valuable aid. Paul shut up in a Roman prison was not to human vision a very propitious circumstance for the infant churches which so much needed his fostering care; but by the epistles written during that confinement, how much more did the apostle do by his pen than could have been done by his voice, and what an inexhaustible treasury of precious thought has the Church thereby acquired for all time. There can be no doubt that Milton's blindness and consequent retirement from public life after the Restoration, had something to do with the composition of "Paradise Lost." The immortal dreamer, Bunyan, would not probably have had time for his great allegory, the "Pilgrim's Progress," if he had not been forcibly detached for a season from pastoral responsibilities, and immured in Bedford Gaol. As the most of "Rutherford's letters" were composed while the writer was a "banished minister" in Aberdeen, we can easily judge how much posterity owes to the banishment.

How ill-fitted, too, are the most earnest workers sometimes to form a correct judgment of the respective value of the several parts of their work. Rutherford regarded "Lex Rex" as the masterpiece of his mind, and, against the advice of some of his friends, persisted in publishing it.* The "letters" were effusions thrown off at a heat, as many as thirteen having been written in one day in Aberdeen, with no thought of publication; and yet "Lex Rex" lies now in the back shelves of a few libraries, and the "letters" are on the table of the cottager, and are the spiritual aliment of to-day.

Any judgment that is formed of the contents and style of those letters, to be fair and charitable, is bound to take into account the circumstances of their composition. It is not just to compare them with books of devotion that were carefully written, revised, and published during the lifetime of the author. Rutherford's letters were the outpourings of a heart opening itself in the intimacies of Christian friendship, with no thought of their being cast further abroad into the world than the narrow circles to which they were immediately addressed. A great deal would have been done to mitigate adverse criticism if the letters had been pruned and abridged; but the very love which men had for Rutherford and his writings on experimental religion caused them greedily to seize and, against his will, put into print all that came

* In it, and other similar publications, Gordon, the shrewd, but rather snappish, parson of Rothiemay, says "he shewes his talent in coyning new distinctions, ill to be understood for the most part."

from his facile pen, which has been against his reputation among critics. Just as there are moments when no one would care to have his portrait taken unawares, so in certain moods the best regulated mind may dash off upon paper what might have been repressed if the severe censorship of the printed page and the general reading public had been in prospect.

There are few things in literature more curious than the diametrically opposite estimates that have been taken of those letters; but it is noticeable that the admirers and detractors, speaking generally, belong to different camps in theology or ecclesiastical connection, and stand apart on many other things besides Rutherford. "Hold off the Bible, such a work the world never saw," says the famous Baxter, of those letters. "Disgusting ravings, not the less loathsome that they are under the mask of religion," says one of another school of theology. It is to be regretted, let it be frankly admitted, that the letters should be marred here and there by an extravagance of expression and the too frequent presentation of Christ under the figure of the nuptial relationship, for which indeed there is Scriptural authority, but which is carried too far by Rutherford.

But there are some men so very reserved in the expression of their religious feelings, whatever they may be with regard to other feelings, that David and Paul in certain exalted moods must in their eyes be guilty of fanatical extravagance, though they would not like to say it so freely of them as of Rutherford. "Whom have I in the heavens but Thee, and there is none upon the earth I desire besides Thee," or "I count all things but loss for the excellency of the knowledge of Christ Jesus, my Lord," are sentences which, if found in any other book than the Bible, would doubtless be regarded by those critics as lacking in sobriety. Would they not also take objection to such a sentence as this from Thomas à Kempis—"O my beloved Spouse, Jesus Christ, most pure lover of all creation, who will give me the wings of true liberty to fly and repose in Thee!"

There are some men who can keep their religious intelligence apart from their feeling, and their natures are like modern ships, with their watertight compartments, by which all communication can be shut off from one another. Their religion is kept in the sphere of intellect or sentiment; they do not admit it into the possession of the whole man, commanding and stirring the affections as well as linking itself to the thought. Such men who make religion a code of rules, a moral principle, or a sacramental ritual may be shocked by the ardour of Rutherford's love for Christ; but when a man who is naturally of deep emotional susceptibility brings it up to the contemplation of the adorable self-sacrifice, the marvellous condescension, the matchless beauty and unfaltering faithfulness of Christ, how can he do other than speak as one who is inspired and occasionally lifted into rapture that has in it more of heaven than of earth?

Those letters are to be read as we would do hymns; they are the poetry of religious experience. Bernard's attitude of mind in singing of the glories of the heavenly Jerusalem is essentially that of Rutherford in expatiating on the loveliness of Christ—he has given himself up to the contemplation of his theme, and is lost in wonder, love, and praise; as he muses, the fire burns. All true poetry is seeking after the ideal, and rejoicing in what it finds by the way. Rutherford found his ideal in Christ, and he gives us his impressions produced in language that is poetry in everything but the art of versification. If the soul is to be kindled by the sublimity of nature and enthralled by its beauty, why should not the surpassing excellency of Jesus Christ, as the brightness of God's glory and the express image of His person, thrill the heart and attune the lips of the believer? Is the altar fire to burn low when the fuel is supplied by the supernatural intervention of Christ? Is there to be impassioned song about the clouds and the sky and the hills, which are only so much vapour and dross, while He who is the substance of which they are the shadows, the glorious reality up to which they were intended to lead, is to have no rapturous song, but only the cold, dry assent of the understanding? Nay; he that keeps company with the Divine One as Rutherford did cannot be silent. If the clay has a sweet scent because it has been with the rose, no one can dwell in the presence of his Lord without being moved out of his cold, measured devotion.

There are in all three hundred and sixty-five of Rutherford's letters published, two hundred and twenty of these having been written during his sojourn in Aberdeen, which dated from September, 1636, till February, 1638. There are several allusions in his letters which cannot but be interesting to those now dwelling in the city. It appears that a deputation of his congregation from Anwoth came with him as far as the place to which he was banished, who "all wept sore" when parting with their beloved pastor. The change to the "dry kindness" which he received from the inhabitants of Aberdeen must have been felt acutely by such a susceptible nature. He was reluctant to go north, though willing enough to suffer in his Master's service. Writing from Edinburgh on his way, he said—" Neither care I much to go from the south of Scotland to the north, and to be Christ's prisoner amongst unco faces in a place of this kingdom which I have little reason to be in love with "*—alluding to the well-known spiritual lukewarmness of the place at that time. In the next letter he alludes pathetically to its distance from Anwoth— "eight score miles from thence to Aberdeen."† In the first letter he wrote after he arrived at Aberdeen he says—"I am, by God's mercy, come now to Aberdeen, the place of my confinement, and settled in an honest man's house. I find the townsmen cold, general, and dry in their kindness, yet I find a lodging in the heart of many strangers."‡ In another letter written on 13th November, 1636, he owns that "at my first coming here I found great heaviness, especially because it had pleased the prelates to add this gentle cruelty to my former sufferings (for it is gentle to them) to inhibit the ministers of the town to give me the liberty of a pulpit."§ "Madam," he says, addressing the Viscountess of Kenmure, "I find folks here kind to me; but in the night and under their breath. My Master's cause may not come to the crown of the causeway. Others are kind according to their fashion. Many think me a strange man, and my cause not good."‖ But he adds, "I know Christ shall

* Dr. Andrew A. Bonar's edition of the "Letters of Samuel Rutherford"—Letter lxii.

† Letter lxiii.   § Letter lxviii.
‡ Letter lxvi.   ‖ Letter lxix.

make Aberdeen my garden of delight." It seems that some of the good people were indignant because Rutherford was not allowed to preach—"Some people affect me, for the which cause I hear the preachers purpose to have my confinement changed to another place; so cold is northern love; but Christ and I will bear it."* "For myself I am here a prisoner confined to Aberdeen, threatened to be removed to Caithness because I desire to edify in this town; and am openly preached against in the pulpits in my hearing, and tempted with disputations by the doctors, especially by Dr. B."† "I am here assaulted with the doctors' guns; but I bless the Father of lights that they draw not blood of truth."‡ A few weeks later he says—"I am in no better neighbourhood with the ministers here than before; they cannot endure that any speak of me or to me. Thus I am in the meantime silent, which is my greatest grief. Dr. Barron hath often disputed with me, especially about Arminian controversies, and for the ceremonies. Three yokings laid him by; and I have not been troubled with him since. Now, he hath appointed a dispute before witnesses; I trust that Christ and truth will do for themselves."§

Not long after that he says—"I hope in God to leave some of my rust and superfluities in

* Letter lxix. ‡ Letter ccix.
† Letter lxxxix. § Letter cxvii.

Aberdeen. I cannot get a house in this town wherein to leave drink-silver in my Master's name save one only. There is no sale for Christ in the north. He is like to lie long in my hand ere any accept Him."*

But he had his joyous seasons in Aberdeen. In a letter written 13th March, 1637, he reports: —"I am in Christ's tutoring here. He hath made me content with a borrowed fireside, and it casteth as much heat as mine own. I want nothing but real possession of Christ, and He hath given me a pawn of that also, which I hope to keep till He come Himself to loose the pawn. I cannot get help to praise His high name. He hath made king over my losses, imprisonment, banishment; and only my dumb Sabbaths stick in my throat."† How touching are his longings, so frequently expressed, for liberty to preach! " Pray for me that the Lord would give me house-room again to hold a candle to this dark world."‡ " I am well every way, all praise to Him, in whose books I must stand for ever as His debtor! Only my silence paineth me. I had one joy out of heaven, next to Christ my Lord, and that was to preach to this faithless generation; and they have taken that from me. It was to me as the poor man's one eye, and they have put out that eye."§ " My trials are heavy

* Letter cxix.   ‡ Letter cciii.
† Letter cxxxix.   § Letter ccviii.

because of my sad Sabbaths; but I know that they are less than my high provocations. I seek no more than that Christ may be the gainer and I the loser; that He may be raised and heightened, and I cried down, and my worth made dust before His glory. Oh! that Scotland, all with one shout, would cry up Christ, and that His name were high in the land."* With what a spirit of pure and noble patriotism he was animated—" O Lord, cast not water on Scotland's smoking coal." †

During the latter part of Rutherford's detention in Aberdeen, stirring and decisive events were occurring in the Scottish metropolis, the tidings of which must have gladdened the soul of the "prisoner," and made him feel that the time of release was at hand. Jenny Geddes's stool and other signs of the times were so reassuring that, without any formal permission, he returned to his beloved Anwoth. A few weeks after that he preached a characteristic "Sermon to the Times," in which his pent-up energy was as a stream when the flood-gates are opened. In the famous Assembly of that year—1638—he was asked to return to Aberdeen and take the Chair of Divinity in the University of that city, which he refused to do. Lest, however, our civic vanity should be unduly wounded by such a refusal, it is well to mention that it was only by great

* Letter cclv. † Letter cclxxvii.

pressure he could be induced to take a professorship in St. Andrews, as it was preaching for which he had a passion and regarded as the special vocation of his life.

The ascension of Charles II. in the course of years to the throne brought another turn in public affairs, and several of the leading Covenanters were arrested and sentenced to death. It was not to be expected that Rutherford of all men should remain unmolested, and he was summoned to appear before Parliament on a charge of high treason when he was on his death-bed. "Tell them," he said to those who brought the summons, "I have to appear before a superior Judge and Judicatory; and ere your day arrive I will be where few kings or great folks come." It was actually discussed in Parliament whether he should be allowed to die in the college, and it was decided that such a privilege could not be granted. "Ye have voted," said Lord Burleigh, with just indignation, "that honest man out of the college, but ye cannot vote him out of heaven." Some of them remarked—"He will never win there; hell is too good for him." "I wish I were as sure of heaven as he is," replied Burleigh; "I would think myself happy to *get a grip of his sleeve to haul me in.*"

After all that has come and gone, it is pleasing to be able to give the following extract from the burgh records:—"23 May, 1644. The said

Provost furthurforme declair it to the nichtbors of toun that the Council of this burghe hade maide nomination and election of Mr. Samuell Rutherford, and failieing of him, of Mr. Robert Bailie, and failieing of him, Mr. Dauvid Dick, for supplieing the vacant roume of Mr. David Barron, last professor of divinitie within the new colledge of Aberdeen, and for preaching twyse ilk Sabbath day in the Colledge Kirk of the said burghe."

The house in which Rutherford at first lodged in Aberdeen is said to have stood on the left-hand side of Burn Court, 44 Upperkirkgate.

CHAPTER XII.

THE COVENANTING STRUGGLE IN ABERDEEN—1638.

ABERDEEN received more than its proportionate share of attention from both of the contending parties of the period of the Covenant. This was owing, not to superabundance of interest in the struggle, but rather to lukewarmness, if not positive hostility, to the popular side. The members of this northern community, dominated by neighbouring territorial magnates, conservative professors and "doctors," would gladly have jogged on as in former days, and allowed the controversy which was setting on fire the southern part of the land to exhaust itself. They had no irrepressible desire to interfere in any way, either in adding fuel to the flame or going out of their way to take part in its extinction.

But unfortunately for their Gallio frame of mind, they were imperiously called upon to take sides. The equanimity of their neutral position was ever being broken in upon. The King's party delighted to visit and utilise the resources of the loyal "northern men." The Covenanters were just as anxious to come to Bon-Accord to concuss, if they could not convert, the cautious and sure-going Aberdonians. Between the two rival parties, one coming not unfrequently as soon as the other had gone, the chronic unrest they created, and the heavy exactions they levied, Aberdeen soon became like the ground round a well on a country road, so trodden down by cattle from all parts that it was anything but a delightful place to dwell in. So deep was their dejection at one point in the struggle, that they actually begged for permission to remove themselves, their families, and property from their "devoted toune."* No sooner were they slapped on one cheek than the Aberdeen people had to turn the other also. Yea, the Marquis of Montrose, who brought such military genius and dash to bear upon both sides of the controversy, gave hard knocks to the one cheek after the other. The very dogs of Aberdeen were made to feel the brunt of the unhappy times. Spalding, in his garrulous, gossiping style, tells us that when the first army (Covenanting) came here, "ilk captain and soldier had a blue ribbon about his craig—'true blue Presbytan'—in despite and derision whereof, when they removed from Aberdeen, some women of Aberdeen (as was alleged) knit blue ribbons about the messin's craigs,

---

* King's "Covenanters in the North" is a book that all should read who want to have particular information regarding the Covenanters in their relation to this part of the land.

whereat thir soldiers took offence, and killed all thir dogs for this very cause."

But who were the Covenanters? Just as there were reformers before the Reformation, such as Huss and Wickliffe, so the Scottish Covenanters, or rather those of them who were so by stress of religious conviction, and not from mere pressure of political circumstance, may be regarded as reformers after the Reformation. There were men who heralded the dawn, who anticipated and prepared for the crisis of the Reformation period; and there were men who afterwards, in a conspicuous way, contributed to give further prominence and fuller effect to the great principles involved in the historic struggle. Behind all subsidiary and incidental issues, the great cardinal principle contended for by the champions both of the Reformation and the Covenant was the supremacy of conscience in matters of faith. Was it right in anyone to submit to an imposition of belief or polity other than that which conscience, enlightened by God's word and guided by God's spirit, held to be true? Luther's contention ultimately resolved itself into this plain and simple issue—Was he accountable to the Pope in Rome or to God in heaven for the convictions which study and prayer had lodged in his mind?

That was substantially the position taken by the men who signed the Covenant in Greyfriars

Churchyard in 1638; with this difference—that the pivot of the controversy had been shifted from the Pope to King Charles the First.

No doubt it would be an easy thing to prove that many of the Covenanters were illogical and inconsistent, and were sometimes ready to deny to others what they were claiming for themselves; but the main drift and spirit of the movement was against interference with the rights of conscience, and, notwithstanding the mixed motives of some identified with it, was broadly favourable to religious life and progress.

The policy against which the Covenant addressed itself owed its existence partly to the spirit of the times, but mainly to the high notions of the Stuart dynasty as to royal prerogative in things religious as well as political. We cannot be unmindful of the fact that the Scottish Stuarts had a personal fascination of manner—an ease, a grace, and generosity which to some extent won the hearts of the people. They were patrons of literature and art, and had an eye and taste for the pleasures and elegancies of life; but their most undaunted apologists could not claim for them a plentiful possession of that intense spirituality of mind evinced in Malcolm Canmore's consort or in her son King David. It can be quite understood how the Stuarts and others of the same cast of mind should prefer a religion which did not make a direct appeal to the spiritual consciousness, but one that travelled to it by ancient and hallowed usage, and gave more scope for the graceful enshrinement of unseen things than Presbyterianism afforded. Is it doing an injustice to them to say that sentiment and imagination had a larger place in their religion than robust moral conviction and lofty spiritual aspiration? Nor were they very far behind the ideas of the time which those in power favoured when they desired that what they personally liked the people should adopt. But the blinding fanaticism of the Stuarts was shown in this that a hundred years' chequered experience failed to work the conviction in their minds that the high-spirited and earnest people from whom they sprung, and whom they ruled, while loyal, never could become subservient. With what fond tenacity did the Scottish people in direst trouble, and in the face of much exasperation from high places, cling to the principle of monarchy, and no race of kings would have been more honoured and loved than the Stuarts if only they had manifested more sympathy with that "soul" which Thomas Carlyle said was given to the nation at the time of the Reformation.

Against the attempt to enforce Episcopacy and the service-book upon the Scottish nation a bond of union or agreement embodying the Confession of Faith, subscribed by James VI., was, as we have already stated, drawn up and signed by persons of all ranks in 1638. That Covenant became a sort of symbol of religious liberty, and the visible embodiment of the protest of a nation against the unhallowed encroachment of an earthly potentate. It was hailed with great enthusiasm, and copies of it having been circulated over the country, it was signed by multitudes who could not be present on the eventful day when it was unfolded in Greyfriars Churchyard. Along with several noblemen, Andrew Cant, Alexander Henderson, minister of Leuchars, and David Dickson, of Irvine, visited the towns of the north as commissioners of the Covenant, their business being to obtain as many signatures to it as possible.

The General Assembly knew what it was about when it appointed Alexander Henderson as one of the commissioners to visit Aberdeen, and try to bring its recalcitrant inhabitants into line with the people of Scotland generally on the great subject that was almost monopolising the public attention. He was just the man to rein the impetuosity and temper the heat of Andrew Cant. Henderson's was the weightiest and most commanding personality of the period; his action and bearing ever manifestly had a broad basis of calm judgment and dignity, as well as immovable rectitude. He was staunch in his loyalty to conviction, and yet his moderation was known to all men. When once he passed over from the ranks of the Episcopalians to the Covenanters he was unfaltering in his allegiance to the Covenant, and yet, being delivered from the heat of extravagance and bigotry, he won and held the respect of his opponents as very few did at the time.

He had a rare tact and quiet humour, which frequently cut their way to the heart of the matter with the precision of a lance, wielded by a gentle but strong and steady hand. In one of his sermons he says—" When a kirk-man climb up as high as he can, till he win up to the kirk rigging (ridge), what good can he do there but ill ? While in the meantime it were meeter for him to stay down laigh in the body of the kirk and teach others rather than to climb up there, and both endanger himself and others."

At the never to be forgotten General Assembly of 1638, where he was moderator, he was put upon his mettle if ever man was in this world. When the crisis came and His Majesty's representative, after formally dissolving the gathering and protesting against the further continuance of business, withdrew, expecting that they would not dare in the face of the King's prohibition to sit longer where they were, Henderson, with a consummate address. as conspicuous as the firmness which it graced but did not conceal, pointed out to his brethren the duty of the hour. He said they could not but admire the concern which the Marquis of Hamilton had manifested for the honour of the King he so worthily represented, and his intense desire that due respect should be paid to royal authority. Situated as they were, they could not do better than imitate his excellent example, and be as unflinching in their loyalty to their King as Head of the Church as he was to his; and therefore he proposed as moderator that they should proceed to the next business to which, in the discharge of their duty, they had to give their attention.

We cannot recount all his public acts and services, such as his attendance at the Westminster Assembly of Divines, where his learning and geniality enabled him to take a leading part. Perhaps the best proof that he gave during his life, in which so many great occasions had a place, of his power to exemplify the "*fortiter in re*" with the "*suaviter in modo*" was in the correspondence he carried on with King Charles I. with respect to Church government. It says much indeed for Henderson that he should have been able to interchange views on such a subject with such a person, with the result that, while throughout he never swerved from his fidelity to the principles of Presbyterianism, he yet retained the deep respect of the King for his "learning, piety, and solidity."

David Dickson, another of the commissioners who visited Aberdeen, and who became minister of Irvine in 1618, was a man whose learning—which was very considerable, fitting him for eminent posts in the Universities in Glasgow and Edinburgh—was overshadowed by his deep spirituality and unction. He had much grace in every sense and meaning of the word. In proof of the intellectual activity of the time, as well as of the man, it may be mentioned that he proposed to have a more elaborate commentary on the Scriptures than had ever before been attempted in Scotland, the work being parcelled out to several competent men. But a rude interruption was given to his various labours by an order coming to him from headquarters to leave Irvine and go into exile in Turriff, Aberdeenshire, because of his nonconformity to the five articles of Perth, which enjoined practices that were deemed to savour of sacerdotalism.

Turriff, which had early been an ecclesiastical centre, like many places of the kind, when the form has supplanted the spirit, was one of the most backward parts of the county. Dickson complained that the devils of Turriff were far worse than the devils of Irvine; and work that he could have done in the latter place in a few hours took him as many days in the spiritually apathetic, cold north.

It was very characteristic that when the commissioners entered Aberdeen, and, according to the custom of the burgh, were offered a treat of wine for welcome, they rather unceremoniously declined the corporation banquet till they had some assurance that the magistrates would subscribe the Covenant. They evidently meant business, and were not to be put off with a Bon-Accord cup till it was ascertained that there was agreement of which the bond could bear witness. "Whereat," says Spalding, "the provost and baillies were somewhat offended, and suddenly took their leave; caused deal the wine in the beadhouse among the poor men, whilk they had so disdainfully refused, whereof the like was never done to Aberdeen in no man's memory." Poor baillies! it was rather hard treatment for men who wanted to be civil to all parties and commit themselves to none—or, at least, not to the Covenanters.

The commissioners were not allowed the use of any of the city churches on the following Sabbath, and were obliged to address the people during the interval of worship from the balcony of Earl Marischal's mansion, on the north side of the Castlegate. Dickson, Henderson, and Cant, the very flower of the Covenanting ministry, addressed them in succession, and appealed for sympathy and help in bringing the great religious struggle to a successful issue, Cant being chosen to be the last speaker, as no one was better fitted to drive in the nail which the preceding speakers had put in its place. But against the eloquence and fervid pleading of those masters in speech there was the extreme caution, not to say indifference, of the people, and only a very few signed the Covenant.

The celebrated "Doctors" of Aberdeen, who were the most formidable opponents the Covenanting commissioners met anywhere, were Dr. Alexander Scroggie, minister of Old Aberdeen; Dr. William Leslie, Principal of King's College; Dr. Robert Barron, Professor of Divinity in Marischal College; Dr. James Sibbald, and Dr. John Forbes of Corse, Professor of Divinity in King's College.* The last-named was the best man and the ablest scholar of them all. The son of Bishop Patrick Forbes, he had the advantage of the very best education that the country and the continent of Europe could give him. He improved what he had got in youth by a lifelong

---

* The following extracts from the diary of Dr. John Forbes, when the General Assembly was dealing with his case, throws more light upon his character than anything we can say:—

"Vpone the 30th day of Julie, 1640, in the morning early, revolving what hade passed yesterday I found that in my words before the Assembly there were some which I should rather not have spoken, and that I hade omitted some words which had been very convenient to be spoken; and fearing lest any offence have arisen thereby in the myncs of my brethren, and fearing desertion, I prayed and wept unto God for mercy, and that He would remeid and remoue all offences given by me to any, or taken by any at me, that day or at any tyme, and to be with my heart and with my mouth, and to grant me mercy and grace in His sight, and convenient mercy and favour in the eyes of all with whome I have to doe; and I was comforted in God: to Him be glorie for ever: Amen. Vpon

course of study. It was his misfortune, as a man not of affairs but of study, to have fallen upon unquiet times, by which his favourite pursuits suffered considerable interruption. The chief of his works is " Instructiones Historico-Theologicae," which was used up to this century as a college text-book in some parts of Europe.

the 31st day of Julie, 1640, I repeted the same petition to God and I was comforted.

"Vpon the first of August, 1640, I compeared before the committee of the General Assemblie, and, being questioned upon many things, I found God's mercifull presence so evidently with me as not withstanding of my scruples concerning the Covenant and of my writtings, yet they were pleased with me. . . . Now, all the dayes of the General Assemblie I prayed every day with groans and tears unto God to be with me and give me a comfortable outgett, and to forgive all my sins; and the Lord heard me: praised be the Lord.

"Vpon the 5 day of August, I was called and I compeared before the General Assemblie, and the moderator thereof, Mr. Andro Ramsay, said to me, in name and in presence of the whole Assemblie, that the General Assemblie had found me ingenuous and orthodoxe, and neither Papist nor Arminian, and as for my different judgment concerning the Covenant, they should intimate their will unto me the next morning."

He was eventually deposed, as he refused to "tacke the Covenant."—"Memorialls of the Trubles," p. 447.

CHAPTER XIII.

ANDREW CANT—1584-1663.

IT is unfortunate when a good man has a name with odious or ridiculous associations. Like a shabby coat or an ungainly manner, it is apt to create a prejudice against him. It is hard to say how much the famous Scottish Covenanter of whom we are to write, as the local representative of re-established Presbyterianism, has suffered from the fact that he bears a name which has anything but an excellent savour. The transition is so easy from Cant the man to cant the thing. An opening, and almost a challenge, are given to shafts of sarcastic wit from bows big and little.

The grievous injustice has actually been done to this worthy man of assuming that the word "cant" can be traced to his character and manner, just as macadamised roads owe their name to the genius of Macadam. Sir Richard Steele, in the "Spectator," says:—" 'Cant' is by some people derived from one Andrew Cant, who they say was a Presbyterian minister in some illiterate part of Scotland, who by exercise and use had obtained the faculty, *alias* gift, of talking in the pulpit in such a dialect that it is said he was understood by none but his own congregation, and not by all of them. Since Master Cant's time, it has been understood in a larger sense, and signifies all sudden exclamations, whinings, unreal tones, and, in fine, all praying and preaching like the unlearned of the Presbyterians." The etymological supposition is not very ingenious, and it is certainly far from accurate, as it can be easily proved that the word "cant" was in use long before the Aberdeen Presbyterian of whom we are writing was born. It is an explanation which probably owes its existence to some of Cant's virulent opponents, who had more exuberance of fancy than love for truth and fair play. The probable derivation of "cant," or sanctimonious affectation, which often gives effect to itself in sing-song and whining tones, is the Latin word *Canto*. It may be mentioned, by the way, that the great German philosopher Kant, who was undoubtedly of Scottish descent, is said to have been of the same family as the man who is the subject of this chapter.

Very little is known of the parentage and early life of Andrew Cant. He was born in Aberdeen in 1584; attended the Grammar School and King's College of that city, and graduated in 1612. There are little circumstances which point to the fact that he was of lowly birth, and, like many more of his fellow-countrymen, had a struggle to reach the goal of a place in the ministry. He was twenty-eight years of age before he was a member of the guild of accredited scholars; and, while he was not deficient in the needful equipment of scholarship for the position he held, there is evidence in his subsequent history to show that he owed more to natural gift than to academic acquirement in the success he achieved and the influence he wielded. He was a born speaker and a man who was constitutionally incapacitated for remaining in the background as a silent listener or spectator when stirring questions and decisive events held the field.

Through the kindly offices of Lord Forbes, after teaching for some time in Aberdeen, he became minister at Alford in 1617. The opposition that it was his fate to encounter to the very end of his days showed itself at the outset of his public life; for a considerable number of the parishioners would have preferred a man who gave their consciences less trouble, and was less furiously in earnest as a champion of the truth. They nicknamed him "Bobbing Andrew," probably on account of his animated movements in the pulpit.

His strong personality and ceaseless activity won fame for him beyond the limits of this northern district. He was so well known and so much appreciated in Edinburgh that in 1620 he was chosen by the people to exercise his ministry in that city. That, however, was an arrangement which Charles the First did not approve, as he saw that Cant would be a formidable antagonist to the policy that was to be pursued, so the needed royal sanction was withheld, and Cant met with the great disappointment of his life. Cant's antipathy to Episcopacy was something that almost amounted to a passion; and it is difficult to account for it unless on the supposition that the opposition of his uncongenial ecclesiastical environment in early days fanned the flame of conviction that was in his bosom.

In 1629 he took service as tutor in Lord Forbes's family, and in 1633 was made minister of Pitsligo. It was while he was minister of that remote and quiet parish that the principal part of his public work as an ecclesiastic or politician was done; for events were now hastening to a crisis, compelling men who had it in them to be leaders to take their stand. He was as ready to do that as the war horse is to enter the battlefield.

In the great and historic Assembly held at the close of 1638, when Episcopacy was displaced by Presbyterianism, we find Cant well to the front. Passages from a rousing and thorough-going sermon preached before the Commissioners at that gathering are still preserved, and they make good reading yet, there is so much virile force in them. He must have been, as Principal Baillie called him, "ane super-excellent preacher." It is incidentally mentioned in one of the Kirk records that an Act was publicly read in the Assembly by Mr. Andrew Cant, "he having a strong voice." He was, indeed, as is said on his tomb, a "Boanerges," and the times made such a man eminently seasonable. He could not be hid. His over-flowing energy, his hot and forcible eloquence, his power of moving the feelings of the common people, made him a marked man wherever honesty and courage and evangelical truth were appreciated. Andrew Cant was a later and abridged edition of John Knox. He had certainly much of the tempestuous vehemence, the glowing intensity, the absolute fearlessness, and occasional asperity of the great Reformer.

Andrew Cant was the very incarnation of the spirit of the Covenant, with which he was so intimately and honourably associated—resolute, whole-hearted, sturdy, and thoroughly surrendered to the cause with which he was identified. When men are rising to meet the weighty responsibilities of a providential crisis, a God-made epoch, and are laying the foundations of the future, they must be able to distinguish things that differ, so that sand shall not be mistaken for rock. It is needful to be sure of your ground when much depends upon your affirmations. He that offers to prescribe for the body will not be listened to if he is in doubt whether it is poison or medicine he is administering. Is it of less importance that a man should know what he is about in the higher region of life? Men who have a high sense of the value of truth, and valour of soul to stand by what they believe to be such, cannot help pressing in all legitimate ways what they deem to be for the world's good.

Let us give a few extracts from a sermon Andrew Cant delivered in Inverness as one of the Covenanting Commissioners, showing the power of the man—a man for the times, and not like Leighton, who, to a large extent, lived apart from the times:—

"Long ago our gracious God was pleased to visit this nation with the light of His glorious gospel, by planting a vineyard in, and making His glory to arise upon, Scotland. A wonder, that so great a God should shine on so base a soil! Nature has been a stepmother to us in comparison of those who live under a hotter climate, as in a land like Goshen or a garden like Eden. But the Lord looks not as man; His grace is most free, whereby it often pleaseth Him to compense what is wanting in nature: whence upon Scotland—a dark, obscure island, inferior to many—the Lord did arise, and discovered the tops of the mountains with such a clear light that, in God's gracious dispensation, it is inferior to none. How far other nations outstripped her in naturals, as far did she outgo them in spirituals. Her pomp less, her purity more: they had more of Antichrist than she, she more of Christ than they; in their Reformation something of the beast was reserved, in ours—not so much as a hoof. When the Lord's ark was set up among them, Dagon fell, and his neck brake, yet his stump was left; but with us, stump and all was cast into the brook Kidron. Hence King James his doxology in face of Parliament, thanking God who made him King in such a kirk that was far beyond England (they having but an ill-said mass in English), yea, beyond Geneva itself; for holy days (one of the Beast's marks) are in part there retained, which, said he, to-day are with us quite abolished. . . . But alas! Satan envied our happiness, brake our ranks, poisoned our fountains, muddled and defiled our streams; and while the watchmen slept, the wicked one sowed his tares: whence these divers years bygone, for ministerial authority, we had lordly supremacy and pomp; for beauty, fairding; for simplicity, whorish buskings; for sincerity, mixtures; for zeal, a Laodicean temper; for doctrines, men's precepts; for wholesome fruits, a medley of rites; for feeders, we had fleecers; for pastors, wolves and impostors; for builders of Jerusalem, re-builders of Jericho; for unity, rents; for progress, defection. Truth is fallen in the streets, our dignity is gone, our credit lost, our crown is fallen from our heads; our reputation is turned to imputation; before God and man we justly deserve the censure of the degenerate vine; a backsliding people, an apostate, perjured nation, by our

breaking a blessed covenant so solemnly sworn. . .
. . Though this north climate be cold, I hope your hearts are not—at least, they should not be cold. The earth is the Lord's and its fulness, the world and they that dwell therein; the uttermost parts of the earth are given to Christ for a possession; His dominion is from sea to sea, and from the river to the ends of the earth. Come, then, and kiss the Son; count it your greatest honour to honour Christ, and to lend His fallen truths a lift. Come and help to build the old wastes, that ye may be called the repairers of the breach; and then shall all generations call you blessed. Then shall God build up your houses as He did to the Egyptian midwives, for their fearing God, and for their friendship to His people Israel. Be not like the nobles of Tekoa, of whom Nehemiah complained that they would not put their necks to the work of the Lord. Be not like Meroz, whom the angel of the Lord cursed bitterly for not coming to the help of the Lord against the mighty. Neither be ye like those mockers and scorners at the renewing of the Lord's covenant in Hezekiah's days, but rather like those whose hearts the Lord humbled and moved. Be not like those invited to the king's supper, who refused to come, and had miserable excuses, and therefore should not taste of it. We hope better things of you; God hath reserved and advanced you for a better time and use; but if ye draw back, keep silence and hold your peace; God shall bring deliverance and enlargement to His Church another way; but God save you from the sequel! Nothing is craved of you but what is for God and the king; for Christ's honour and the kirk's

good, and the kingdom's peace: God give to your hearts courage, wisdom, and resolution for God and the king, and for Christ and His truths! Amen."

But that tongue, with the warm, honest heart behind it, which was his power, was sometimes also his snare. At one of the General Assemblies, when an important written declaration was being discussed, Mr. Cant was the first to rise and say—"It is so full of gross absurdities that I think the hanging of the author should prevent all other censures." Such an explosive speech met with the quiet rebuke of the moderator—"That punishment is not in the hands of kirkmen." His hot and unrestrained violence of utterance showed to the leaders of the Covenanting struggle that Cant was more useful in supplying needed motive power than in piloting the party through matters of intricate and delicate ecclesiastical statesmanship. They were anxious to have the benefit of his popular gifts and robust championship of their cause nearer the metropolis; so they got him translated to Newbattle, but his hasty and forceful manner made enemies for him there, and even estranged a few of his friends, so, after acting as chaplain to the Covenanting army for some time, he availed himself of the opportunity of returning to Aberdeen and filling a vacancy in St. Nicholas Church. "Bot the toune of Aberdeen at the cumming of this Cant,"—Spalding rather spitefully says—"wes not fully glaid—he was not veray welcome to all." That is perfectly true, Spalding. Andrew Cant would have been more acceptable to Aberdeen had he been more accommodating, just as Savonarola would have been more popular in Florence if his ideal for its inhabitants had not been quite so high.

For twenty years he laboured with unflagging zeal in his native town, concentrating his attention as life went on more upon pastoral duty and spiritual work. Those years were filled with incessant toil and battling for the truth. An evangelical ministry was almost a new thing to that generation in Aberdeen, and he had much to contend with and few to sympathise with him as he tried to shape things in the Church according to the mind of Christ. In purging away the old leaven, which had not been seriously touched for centuries, he needed all his noble audacity. He denounced and tried to clear away superstitious customs and Popish practices. He instituted lectures on Mondays, Wednesdays, Fridays, and Saturdays, and from the "night abouts," as they were called, "no honest persons durst be absent, but were rebuked and cried out against; nor durst any merchant's or craftsman's booth be opened, in order that the kirk might be better kept."

Not content with preaching to the people who came to the church to meet him, as we read in

Wodrow's "Analecta"—"He was singularly useful in Aberdeen, and multitudes ever soe great that he frequently preached at the great square at the Crosse of Aberdeen." On one occasion, we are told, when the people were crowded around him in the market-place, a dead corby (a raven or crow) was flung at him by some unknown hand. We are further informed that the preacher stopped, and, looking around him, said—"I know not who has done this open affront; but I am much mistaken if there are not as many gazing on him at his death as there are here this day." The historian relates that this was actually the case, for, as it turned out, the person who did it was executed for some crime at the Grassmarket, Edinburgh.

He was the same fearless man to all-comers. At the time Aberdeen was occupied by Cromwellian soldiers, some of them who happened to be in Mr. Cant's church heard him pray for "our banished king," and at another time they took umbrage at peppery statements the preacher made which were exceedingly distasteful to their party. They scowled and threatened, and at last, coming near to the pulpit with drawn swords, it looked as if a violent deed was about to be done. Wodrow tells us "Mr. Menzies, his colleague, was very timerouse, and crape in beneath the pulpite"; but Cant, baring his breast, said to the rough and incensed soldiers—"Here's a breast ready to receive the thrusts of any who will venture to give them for the truth"; and by his very boldness put them to shame.

But a contest into which he entered with his own congregation proved to be more formidable. He was grieved and burdened on account of the spiritual deadness and flagrant inconsistency of the lives of many under his pastoral charge, and so determined was he not to be a party to shameless formalism that he refused to administer the Communion. This denial of the privileges of the Church set all the "worldly professors," of whom there were many, against him. He was out of favour, too, with the Independents, as he was a strenuous upholder of the monarchy, though ready to rebuke the monarch, as he by implication did when preaching before Charles I., and insisting on the reservation of the rights of "King Jesus." But the worst opposition he met with came from those to whom the world, the flesh, and the devil were more than Christ and His cause.

It sounds strange to read of a man being deposed from the ministry in his old age and after long and faithful service, he having done more for the religious awakening and moral reformation of the north than any other man —but so it was: he was thrust out at the time of the Restoration. Three years later he died, saying on his deathbed—" My conscience bears me witness that I never gave a wrong touch to the ark of God in all my days." Thus passed away this truly Gideon-like hero, one of those whole-hearted, single-eyed men who in the hour of battle see nothing but the cause they have espoused, and which they have at heart more than lucre, or glory, or even the love of life.

In St. Nicholas Churchyard, at the west side, not far from the church, Andrew Cant's dust lies. All that marks the spot is a flat stone sunk into the ground, the lettering on which is much worn with exposure.

CHAPTER XIV.

THE QUAKERS IN ABERDEEN—1662.

IT may seem strange that Aberdeen of all places should have become the headquarters of Quakerism; but so it was, there being no place in Scotland, in the middle of the seventeenth century, where so many men of education and social position embraced the tenets of that sect. It would be a mistake, which no one who is acquainted with the religious condition of the time could fall into, to suppose that the comparative strength of Quakerism was owing to a deeper spirituality here than existed in the other large centres of the population in Scotland. The very opposite of this was the case, and the explanation, paradoxical as it may appear, is perhaps to be found in that fact.

There were Quaker settlements in Inverurie, Oldmeldrum, Aquhorthies, Kingswells, Kinmuck, and Aberdeen, and the two last named are all that now remain in our county. Ury, in Kincardineshire, attained to a world-wide fame in connection with the Quakers, through the influence of the Barclay family.

In order to understand aright the things done against and by the Quakers, we must remember that the times were unsettled and critical. The Presbyterian ministers of Aberdeen, filled with anxiety lest what had been gained might be lost through division, were naturally annoyed that pious men in the town should do anything to break the ranks of those who ought to stand with an unbroken front against the common foe. Andrew Cant, taking a comprehensive view of the situation, years before there was any formal espousal of the tenets of the Quakers, had little patience with his son-in-law, Alexander Jaffray, for allowing what he regarded as little things and extravagances, and errors to boot, to distract attention from what was of vital moment, if the liberties of the nation were not to be endangered.

The Jaffrays, the Barclays, and other Friends in the locality, sharing in the heated intensity of the times, felt that they were only carrying a little further the claims for liberty of conscience, and were as resolute in contending for what they deemed to be truth. The Presbyterian ministers, regarding this Quakerism as a foreign and noxious importation, denounced its local adherents as "demented, distracted, and devil-possessed," and, because they refused to take oaths and give "hat honour" to Magistrates, as "destructive of all good government."

Such gross misrepresentation, and the indignities and brutalities it led to, had their effect upon the Quakers, as oppression makes even wise men mad. We need to take account of the state of public feeling at the time before we can give due perspective to some of the extravagances laid to the charge of the Quakers. A Quaker writer, dealing with that period, says :—

"Subjected to these indignities, it does not cause surprise that two such gentlemanly and refined natures as Andrew Jaffray [son of Alexander] and Robert Barclay were each, at different times, led to make of themselves a spectacle to the persecuting citizens, by walking, stripped to the waist, through the streets, the one with sackcloth and ashes on his head, and the other holding of the filth that had thus been cast upon them in his hands, each uttering woes and judgments on the city if such course of insult and oppression were persisted in. These personal appearances by way of a sign, like the prophets of old, are not forgotten to be brought forward by those who reproach the early Friends with fanatical practices; but they never ought to be mentioned, as they mostly are by such, without due remembrance of the state of public feeling at the time, and the shocking indignities and brutalities an excited populace had inflicted on these peaceable citizens. The appearances of high-bred gentlemen in such a condition might be expected to have had more effect of shaming them into propriety than of offering any shock to those unacquainted with our modern ideas of social proprieties."

There are few local figures more impressive to the imagination than that of David Barclay, the laird of Ury, who, after being on many battlefields, retired to his estate, and gave himself up to the study of the New Testament, with the result that he espoused the cause of the despised Quakers. The grand old warrior presented a more noble aspect in his passive endurance as a persecuted Quaker than as a victorious general at the head of armies in Sweden under Gustavus Adolphus. As he said himself, he found more satisfaction as well as honour in his being thus insulted in his religious principles than when, some years before, it was usual for the magistrates, as he visited the city of Aberdeen, to go several miles to meet and conduct him to a public entertainment in their Town-House. One day, as he was being insulted while riding along the streets of Aberdeen, an old comrade, accompanied by soldiers under his command, offered to disperse and punish the mob, but Barclay would not allow him to interfere. It is to this incident that Whittier, the American Quaker poet, refers in one of his most spirited pieces. We subjoin two stanzas:—

> "Up the streets of Aberdeen,
> By the kirk and college green,
> Rode the Laird of Ury:
> Close behind him, close beside,
> Foul of mouth and evil-eyed,
> Pressed the mob in fury.

>"Yet with calm and stately mien,
> Up the streets of Aberdeen,
> Came he slowly riding;
> And to all he saw and heard
> Answering not a bitter word,
> Turning not for chiding." *

The following exquisite touch, from the pages of John Hill Burton's "Book Hunter," brings the old warrior Quaker, Barclay, more distinctly before our imagination:—

"After the religious change had come upon David Barclay, and he had retired to spend his latter days in his ancestral estate in Kincardineshire, a brother laird thought the old Quaker could be taken advantage of with impunity, and began to encroach upon his marches. Barclay, a strong man, and with the iron sinews of his race, and their fierce spirit still burning in his eyes, strode up to the encroacher, and with a grim smile spoke thus:—'Friend, thou knowest that I have become a man of peace, and have relinquished strife, and therefore thou art endeavouring to take what is not thine own but mine, because thou believest that, having abjured the arm of the flesh, I cannot hinder thee. And yet, as thy friend, I advise thee to desist, for shouldest thou succeed in rousing the old Adam within me, perchance he may prove too strong, not only for me, but for thee.'"

* "The Poetical Works of John Greenleaf Whittier," Vol. II., p. 31.

CHAPTER XV.

ALEXANDER JAFFRAY OF KINGSWELLS—1614-73.

OF all native Aberdonians who attained to historic eminence, there is perhaps none whose character is more beautiful and lovable than that of Alexander Jaffray, the Quaker. He came of a strong, thriving burghal stock, his father before him having won the confidence and respect of his fellow-citizens to such a degree as to have been called to the Provost's chair. While sitting in his official place one day, it is reported that some practical joker put a pie before him, to keep him humble, by reminding him of the fact that his grandfather had been a baker. But the faithful narrator adds—" He took no notice of it."

The prudent and dignified self-restraint then exhibited seems to have been a family trait, for, as we shall find, the subject of our sketch gave remarkable proof of his possession of that virtue in his stirring and eventful career. His transparency and quiet strength of character, along with his devotion to duty, drew discerning minds to him, and brought him into positions of trust and responsibility. He was twice elected Provost of Aberdeen. He was a favourite with Cromwell, who induced him to enter the "Barebones Parliament," and offered him a judgeship, which was declined. He was afterwards one of the Parliamentary Commissioners to negotiate with Charles II. for his ascension to the Scottish throne. Having received a good education, and being accustomed to mingle with men of all classes, he was often employed in public work requiring firmness and tact.

It was the lot of this quiet, contemplative man to spend his days in Aberdeen when feeling was high and hot as it never was before nor has been since. What with Covenanters, Cromwellians, and Royalists, society must have been very lively. As showing the difficult position which the inhabitants of Aberdeen had to maintain at that critical period, take the following extract from the diary of General Monk :—

"We had notice that our men were well entertained by the inhabitants of Aberdene, whoe made a banquett for them. They staid there 3 nights, and had very good quarters. They brought away 2 ships laden with armes and ammunition; fined the towne 1000 *l*. for assisting of Huntley." *

But while there was enough of interest in his outward life to ensure him an honourable mention in the annals of his native town, which he

* "Scotland and the Commonwealth—1651-53," p. 14.

did so much, by his blameless character and public spirit, to adorn, what gave him the very high place which he occupies in our reverent remembrance is the attitude he took in relation to spiritual religion, and the sacrifices he made to give effect to his convictions in the highest sphere of human thought. He seems to have been predisposed naturally by the elevated cast of his mind, his grave, earnest spirit and fearless love of truth, to give a hospitable welcome to the best ideas and influences of the times in which he lived. He was not the man to be the mere creature of convention and fashion, the echo of other minds, but brought an independent and inquiring spirit to bear upon the deep questions of life which were then agitating the thoughts of men. He had a strong realisation of the leading doctrine of Protestant Christianity, viz., God's direct immediate personal access to the soul; and following that truth with a noble carelessness as to consequences of a temporal kind, it led him first of all to the side of the Covenanters, latterly, by intercourse with Cromwell and John Owen, to the Independents, and farther still amongst the derided and persecuted Quakers.

The story of the discovery of Alexander Jaffray's long-lost diary is worthy of being told. In 1826 John Barclay, a descendant of the famous Quaker "Apologist," was visiting the home of his ancestors at Ury, near Stonehaven, with the view of ascertaining whether any documents could be found in the family archives that would shed light upon the days when Quakerism became a force in our part of the land. In a corner of the room that was the Apologist's study he discovered the earlier part of Jaffray's diary, along with other MSS. in a neglected condition. The paper was highly discoloured and the writing in some parts almost faded away, so that it was most difficult to decipher it. In the loft of a farmhouse not far from the old mansion detached fragments of another MS. were found among heaps of waste paper which was in the same handwriting, and proved to be the other part of the diary. After incredible pains, the whole was copied, and is given with wonderful perfection in the volume that was published in 1856.

Thomas Carlyle laments that our renowned fellow-townsman Jaffray should have devoted so much of his writing to an account of his introspective musings and devout contemplations instead of giving us information regarding men and things in the stirring times in which he lived. But it is possible to glean facts of historical interest relating to himself and others from among his spiritual meditations. In giving an account of his early days he says :—

"Being born at Aberdeen, in the month of July, 1614, I was bred at [the grammar] school there by my parents, and sometimes with my uncle [of] Pittodrie, and at Banchory under Gilbert Leslie, Mr. David Wederburne, Mr. Alexander Strachan, and Mr. Robert Dewine, as schoolmasters. . . .

"Having spent divers years very idly, from the time of my first entry at the grammar school, which was, as I suppose, about the ninth year of my age—sometimes with my uncle [of] Pittodrie in the Garioch, and in Buchan, where I had no occasion to learn any good thing, and for one year or two at the school in Banchory; by this unfixed and unsettled way of getting too much liberty I lost much, especially in attaining a knowledge of the Latin tongue. About the middle of the year 1631, being then about seventeen years of age, I came from the school in Banchory to the College, where, passing the first class, having made the manner to learn some Greek in Banchory, I entered to my logics under Mr. Hugh [or Howe] Gordon, regent, and Dr. Dune, then principal, who were both of them unfit for training up youths, so that I had no good example from them."

He then proceeds to tell us of his early marriage :—

"Having staid a short time in the College, and profited as little, I was, in the month of April, the last day thereof, in the year 1632, married to Jean Downe [or Dune], being then eighteen years of age. . . .

"In the month of June, 1633, the King being then to come to Edinburgh to be crowned, I went over and attended that ceremony.

"In July thereafter I came home, my wife being, before my coming, brought to bed of her first son, called Alexander. Shortly thereafter I went again to London in company with Robert Skene, Andrew Birnie, and George Jamieson, the famous artist. I staid some time longer, and . . . . on my return, went off the road and visited the University of Cambridge by the way. In September, 1634, I went to France; and there staid in Caen in Normandy, for the space of three months; in which time I learned so much of the French language that I was able to travel without a guide. From Caen I went to Rouen, and from thence to Paris, where I staid for the space of two or three months; from thence I returned to Rouen, and so to Dieppe, and in the month of June I landed in Leith. In September thereafter I went again to France, and staid five or six months, most part of the time in [Neufchatel] despatching some . . . , and had them with me and made some . . . , but to very little purpose."

Regarding the year 1647, he writes—

"The pestilence raged in Aberdeen for the space of five or six months. All this time my family was preserved, which was the more observable, as I was every day among the sick people, being a Magistrate—for the time I removed to Kingswells."

As one of the Commissioners appointed to arrange for the accession of Charles II., he gives an interesting account of his repentance for the part he took:—

"In the year 1649, I being then a member of Parliament for the town of Aberdeen, was sent unto Holland, with the Earl of Cassillas, Lord Brodie, and Lord Libertone, for to treat with and bring home our young king. I shall spare to mention many things for shortness; only, by the way, I must observe this, that having gone there in the simplicity of our hearts, minding what we conceived to be duty, it pleased the Lord to bring us safely off without any snare or entanglement. But, being again sent there by the Parliament, in the year 1650, for that same business, we did sinfully both entangle and engage the nation and ourselves, and that poor young prince to whom we were sent; making him sign and swear a covenant, which we know, from clear and demonstrable reasons, that he hated in his heart. Yet, finding that upon these terms only, he could be admitted to rule over us (all other means having failed him), he sinfully complied with what we most sinfully pressed upon him—where, I must confess, to my apprehension, our sin was more than his."

The battle of Dunbar and his narrow escape from death, and the effect it had upon his future are narrated with vividness:—

"The King being come home, we were not well landed, when England was on our border with an army, to succor themselves against our invading them. It is not my purpose here to speak to that business, or the unwarrantableness of it, or of our defence and the lawfulness of it; but the thing I aim at is—to remember (and O, that I could do it with a heart rightly thankful!) the just severity and yet merciful dispensation of my blessed Lord, who by a very sad blow at that battle of Dunbar, the 3rd day of September, 1650, brought me to the very gates of death—my horse being shot under me, and I having received two wounds in my head, one in my right hand, and another in my back. So good was the Lord unto me—that, albeit for my manifold guiltinesses, and particularly for my accession to and compliance in that matter of our acting about our King, he might have left me there—and for ever to His wrath in hell; yet—glory to his name! that guiltiness was blotted out, and all my sins pardoned through Jesus Christ."

He now writes of his intercourse with Cromwell and with the great Puritan theologian, John Owen, which was destined to tell so much upon his future:—

"During the time of my being a prisoner I had good opportunity of frequent conference with the Lord General [Cromwell], L. Gen. [Lieutenant General Fleetwood], and Doctor Owen; by occasion of whose company I had first made out unto me, not only some more clear evidences of the [Lord's] controversy with the family and person of our King, but more particularly the sinful mistake of the good men of this nation about the knowledge and mind of

God as to the exercise of the magistrate's power in the matters of religion—what the due bounds and limits of it are. The mistake and ignorance of the mind of God in this matter, what evils hath it occasioned! fearful scandals and blasphemies on the one hand, and cruel persecution and bitterness among brethren on the other!

"The thoughts of these things did for some months very much perplex me; and being over swayed sometimes with too many prudential considerations, I was brought very near to have fully waived and laid aside all thoughts of that kind, and to have suppressed them, because I saw reproach to come thereby, not only upon myself, but on the nation, and also so great appearance of suffering and hazard that way if the king's party, who were then in good hopes, should then or any time thereafter prevail. But, for all this, it could not be; the clear discovery of the thing being so made out to me, that I could not contain, but went to some few at Aberdeen, as Mr. Andrew Cant, Mr. John Menzies, Mr. John Rowe (Principal of the College), and Mr. William Moire. To all of them I not only spoke my thoughts freely, but gave them my notes before mentioned to read, which they did, except Mr. Andrew Cant, who refused to read them. Thereafter, having written to some good men in the south, and finding no satisfaction, I came south to them; and, by providence, found about fifty or sixty of them, ministers and professors together, about the very thing I was desirous of inquiring; and everyone speaking publicly what they thought might be the causes of the Lord's controversy with the land."

The circumstances connected with the setting-up of a separate congregation in Aberdeen are given in detail :—

"Some time after this some Christians in Aberdeen, men and women, having for a long time been convinced of these things (long before ever a thought of them was with me), found themselves obliged to endeavour to have the ordinances administered in a more pure way, than there was any hope ever to attain to have them in the national way. But before we would conclude to do any thing of this, it was thought necessary, first to impart our purpose to some Christian friends, and to be willing to hear what they could object against our resolution. Whereupon, by common consent, a letter was drawn up and subscribed, in the name of the rest, by Mr. John Rowe, Mr. John Menzies, Mr. William Moire, and me, and directed to the Lord Warristoun, Mr. David Dicke, Mr. John Levinstone [Livingstone], Mr. James Guthrie, and Mr. Samuel Rutherford, to be communicated to whom they pleased, which letter was of date, at Aberdeen the . . . day of . . . . jaj vj . . . and . . . ."

We learn that Jaffray was not without marks of appreciation and honours such as the world can give :—

"Thereafter I was called by the Judges at Edinburgh to be Director of the Chancellry, in the month of March, 1652, which I accepted of in the month of June.

"In the month of June, 1653, I was called, with other four out of Scotland, to sit as member of the Parliament of England. I came there the 5th of July, and stayed until the 6th of February, 1654. I had there good occasion to meet and be acquainted with many godly men, though I can say little of any good we did at that Parliament; yet it was on the hearts of some there to have done good for promoting the kingdom of Christ; but, the time not being come when these things were to be brought forth, we were dissolved the 12th January, 1654. I came for Scotland, the said 6th of February thereafter, having gotten at that time from the Lord Protector and his Council an order for paying to me by the Commissioners at Leith £1,500 sterling, for paying my part of that debt we contracted in Holland in the year 1650."

Does the following statement not reflect honour upon the Protector as well as upon Jaffray?—

"When that Parliament was broken up, I not being satisfied with the reasons thereof, was one of thirty or thirty-one that stayed in the house. Yet, the Protector was pleased to give me the aforesaid order, of which I got payment; and did offer me to be one of the Judges in Scotland; but this I refused, finding myself not capable for discharge of that duty."

Committed a prisoner on account of his religious views to the Tolbooth, Edinburgh, he tells us of his sufferings:—

"But here, it is to be observed, that in my case, not only fixedness and enlargement [seem suspended, or removed from me], but even words also many times so that I could not speak a word; and yet I could not tell wherefore or how it was thus with me, insomuch that upon the 6th of December I was necessitated to desire of Mr. James Simpson, my fellow-prisoner, to forbear to press me any more to perform that duty of praying publicly, as I was before accustomed to do in our little prison-family. I was above a month under this exercise before I did adventure thus to be forborne, fearing to be mistaken by him, and to give him offence. But having informed him a little of my case, and of the weakness and great infirmity of my body; and having a little reasoned with him about labouring to have our hearts more in a fittedness and disposition for prayer, before venturing so rashly on it as ordinarily we do—some discourse of this kind having past, at last he agreed for some time to forbear me."

After a life of incessant toil, much suffering, but, as his diary shows, not a little joy of a truly heavenly sort in his walk and converse with God, Alexander Jaffray died at Kingswells in 1673, and lies in the little graveyard in that estate, bearing evidence in the very situation of his grave how loyalty to truth sometimes involves separation.

The following is the minute of the monthly meeting of the Friends (one of the earliest minutes made by Friends in Aberdeen) respecting the end of Alexander Jaffray:—

"It pleased the Lord to remove out of the body our dear and precious friend, Alexander Jaffray, at his own house at Kingswell, the 7th of 5th month, 1673, at one in the morning; who was buried in his own burial ground there on the 8th. He was a sincere, upright-hearted man all his time, and one that had been a seeker of the Lord from his youth up, and had much of the life of Jesus and spirit of holiness attending his heart all along, as his conversation witnessed; and died with blessed and living testimonies to the honour of truth, before many professors and profane who came to see him."

CHAPTER XVI.

CHURCH LIFE IN THE SEVENTEENTH CENTURY.

LET us learn, in this chapter, of the worship and life of the people, their morals and manners, as indicated in the Presbyterial records of that period. On the Sabbath day the people were accustomed to meet in church half an hour before the minister appeared, when the reader or precentor read several chapters of the Bible as prescribed. When the minister came in, the reading was stopped and a psalm given out, which was sung till a sign came from the pulpit to cease. After that, prayer was offered, followed by the sermon, which at that period was usually delivered without the help of notes. After prayer and another psalm came the benediction. Almost the only difference in the service as conducted by Presbyterian and Episcopal clergymen was that the latter, in addition to the above, repeated the Lord's Prayer and Doxology at the end. In most places there was an afternoon service, which was shorter than the morning one.

The following entries, extracted from the records of Strathbogie Presbytery, give us glimpses of the disturbed times:—

"Att Botarie, 18 Februarii, 1645. No meeting

becaus of the enimie was for the tyme within the boundis of the presbyterie, so that the bretheren could not saiflie convein together ; but the Moderator by letter desyred the bretheren to meet that day fourteen days.

"Att Botarie, 5th March, 1645. No meeting for the reason forsaid, and besydes the sole bretheren wer forced to flie from their houses.

"Att Botarie, 19 March, 1645. Convened the Moderator and two of the bretheren next adjacent, all the rest being absent becaus of the broknes of the country."

The times were rough and wild in various ways, as the records of that same Presbytery abundantly show. The Church then was really the principal guardian of order, and was useful, not only for its spiritual ministrations, but also as a moral police. The reader of those entries is disgusted with the extraordinary number of persons charged·with uncleanness who came before the ministers of the district for discipline.

But probably it was the exceeding faithfulness of Zion's watchmen of that day which makes the immorality so apparent. Men were not let alone in their sin without words of warning and correction :—

"At Botarie, February 8, 1637. Mr. Robert Watsone regrated that Andrew Mackpharsone was very scandalous in his behaviour in that dweling in the conutrye and at the church style; he never came to the churche nor any of the familye. The said Robert was ordained to deal privatlye with the said Andrew, and if he found no guid fruit by his traveles, that he shall summond the said Andrew and his familye before the Presbyterie."

The "stool of repentance" was a great institution in those days. Female offenders were sometimes "put in the kirk wolt" or "doukit at the dam." The sentence occurs very frequently—"Ordained to satisfie in sackcloth three-quarters of ane year."

William Mitchell, of the parish of Keith, convicted of adultery: "was ordained to stand in the jogges and brankes with his head clipped and barefooted, in sackcloth, till the congregation was satisfied, or otherwyse to redeeme himself from the jogges and brankes by paying forty markes penaltye, and to stand only in sackcloth."

Some of the women, ashamed of their position as they sat before the gaze of the whole congregation, drew their shawl or plaid over their heads, so as to cover their faces, but they were ordered to desist from that attempt at concealment. The "stool" must often have had a hardening effect. We read of a man who is described as making a "moke of repentance by putting in of sneeshen in his eyes to make them tear and by laughing upone several persones in publicit." It must have been a character of that sort that made Alexander Phine say to his fellow-Presbyters that he "regrated the stoole of repentance was just above his deask quhilk he had erected, quher he was somquhat disturbit be ther motion in time of divyne service; neither was the said stoole so conspicuous to the congregation as it ought. The said Alexander promising to renew it upon his owne charges, was ordained to erect the said stoole of repentance to the for part of the common loft, so that it be without prejudice to the said loft."

Witchcraft, sorcery, and other relics of Paganism also received the zealous attention of the clergy in those days. "The General Assembly, in consideration of the growth of the sins of witchcraft, charming, and consulting, appointed a commission." Much complaint was made in Strathbogie of "the superstition of the Wallak Kirk." St. Wollok has left his mark on the parish of Glass, and great crowds, up to a comparatively recent period, resorted early in May to the pools on the Deveron which bore his name, the waters of which were supposed to have a healing efficacy. It was customary after using the water for the diseased person to leave his cap or some portion of his dress, which was supposed to represent the ailment that had been left behind, and was an act of homage to the saint. Pilgrimages were made to sacred wells and chapels, and a favourite one with the people of Aberdeen was to the saint's well in Bay of Nigg.

The most hideous example of perverted zeal shown on behalf of religion was in the suppression of witchcraft. The parish of Skene, it would appear, was specially affected with witches, as in 1602 a roll of them was ordered to be made up and transmitted to the Marquis of Huntly that "the land may be purgit of sic instrumentis of the devill." The purging was carried on with great energy, and the people of the city and the county seemed to have lost their heads in dealing with the poor unfortunate creatures, who from various signs were supposed to be in league with the Prince of Darkness. It was believed that certain persons were brought under the malign influence of the Evil One, that they made a compact with him, and were his agents in stopping mills, blasting crops, raising storms, causing cattle to die, and cows to cease to give milk. Terrible cruelties were perpetrated in the name of religion. In the course of ten years in the latter part of the sixteenth century no fewer than thirty persons, chiefly women, were put on their trial and burned alive beside the Heading Hill in Aberdeen. It did indeed look as if there were demoniacal possession in the accusers rather than the accused. Sometimes in their fury a tumultuous and howling crowd would drag suspected persons down the Shiprow and throw them into the harbour; if they sank there was an end of them, and if they floated they were guilty!

It must, in justice to the ministers, be said that those raids upon witches were due more to popular excitement than to the instigation of the Church. There was one form of superstition very prevalent that the Presbyteries set themselves against, and that was the "goodman's" lot. This was a survival of the old heathenism of the country, which had its place before the beneficent sway of Christianity began. To propitiate the devil he was called the "goodman," just as the fairies were addressed as "our good neighbours," and in recognition of him there was often a part of the farm left untilled. "In 1646 Scifwright and Stronach were accused of sorcery in allowing some land to the old goodman." At a visitation of the Kirk of Rhynie in August, 1651, Sir William Gordon of Lesmoir admitted that part of the Mains of Lesmoir was given away to the "goodman," and not to be laboured, "but that he had a mynd, be the assistance of God, to cause labour the same."

The times were trying to good men whose hearts were enlisted on behalf of the cause of order and righteousness. In the year 1651 Mr. Alexander Fraser, minister of Botriphnie, was deposed from the office of the ministry, and one cannot but sympathise with that parishioner who "entreated a preaching in that desolate congregation that they might have the occasione in like manner for taking order with the great enormities that were beginning to increase amongst them throughe the want of restraint and correction." Amidst the lawlessness which prevailed during the civil wars the dread of the reappearance of Popery often came into the hearts of Christian patriots, as they were ever on their guard against those who had converse with "excomunist persones or shall receipt seminarie priestis and Jesuits."

Great exertions were made to wean the people from Sabbath desecration. "The Laird of Avochy was found guilty of bringing home a millstone from Morayshire on a Sunday with a great company of horses and litters." At the Presbytery meeting in "Dunsfermand, September 29, 1636, it is ordained that the earth shall not be opened in the church till the buriall silver be payed. It is also ordained that drinkers in tyme of divyne service shall be punished as fornicators." In 1603 two of the baillies were "ordered to pass throw the townie everie Sabbath day and nott sic as they find absent fra the sermones ather of efoir or efter none." Persons absent from sermon were fined. The baillies were enjoined to go through the town on preaching days as well as on Sundays to "caus the people resort to the sermones." We learn that George Gordon of

Rhynie was brought under discipline for "gathering grosers in time of sermon." But the ministers of that date were as strict in dealing with each other as they could possibly be with the people under their charge. There were regular visitations of the churches within the bounds of the Presbytery, when searching questions were put as to the conduct and work of the minister. Here are some of the queries that were put—" Primo—" Iff there be preaching on each Lord's day, and how often: 2, Iff the minister preach to their edificatione and be careful in reproving of sinne; iff he keep at home, not steering abroad unnecesiarilie; iff he doth not without necessitie resort to tavernes; iff he be a good example in ordering of his own familie."

The elders were called in and asked to give evidence regarding the faithfulness of the minister, and they in turn were put through a similar ordeal. One minister tells us that he had on Sabbath "on lecture and on sermon on an ordinarie text," the lecture continuing one hour, the sermon two. Instead of having an afternoon service, which he could not get the parishioners to attend, he gave them full measure, heaped up and running over; but he was exhorted to be "more tymouslie on the Lord's day, preach shorter in the sermon and have ane afternoon sermon."

There are few things more striking in those

ecclesiastical chronicles of the seventeenth century than the discipline which the ministers imposed upon each other. Men who did not attend the Presbyterial gatherings were soon made to feel that indolence or occupation with less important matters brought its penalty. "At Botarie, Sep. 16, 1640, the said day it was ordained if any brother will be absent two dayes without ane sufficient reason shown to ther Presbyterie he should be suspended from the ministrie." A few years before we learn that "At Botarie, April 12, 1637, Mr. William Read and Mr. Robert Irving were excused for their absence the former daye by reason of their age and the boysterousness of the wind." But, as if they felt they had gone too far in brotherly leniency, we read that on "May 17, same year, Mr. Robert Irving excused his former absence by the tempest of (raine). His excuse was rejected by reason the raine was warm!"

But there were some tender touches of sentiment in those stern days, as what took place at a death bears witness. Notice was given to the "cryer," who, with a handbell, announced at convenient places — "Faithful brethren and sisters, I let you to wot that there is a faithful brother (or sister) departed as it hath pleased Almighty God. He or she was called (the name being given), and lived in ———."

CHAPTER XVII.

THE SECEDERS—1733.

BEFORE we can give an intelligible account of the genesis of the "Secession" movement, it will be necessary to take a general survey of the situation and state of the Scottish Church from the Restoration in 1660 to the period of which we have now to write. When, by the accession of Charles II. to the British throne, Episcopacy was established and the forms of worship and government to which the great body of the people tenaciously clung were proscribed, four hundred ministers, who were the heirs and representatives of the best traditions of the Reformation, and who preferred to serve God rather than man, left the parish churches and betook themselves to the conventicle and the field, where their congregations were to be found.

The persons who came to fill the pulpits of the ejected ministers when Episcopalianism was up and Presbyterianism down had as their distinctive appellation, in which there was a touch of scorn, the "curates." Many of them were from the north, and from all accounts they were no credit to the country from which they came. Bishop Burnet's loyalty to the Stuart dynasty and to Episcopacy cannot be impeached in the face of the following extract from the preface to his " History of the Reformation ":— The Church "was again restored to its former beauty and order by Your Majesty's [Charles II.] return!"* Even he describes those "curates" as a "sorry lot." "They were generally," he says, " very mean and despicable in all respects. They were the worst preachers I ever heard. Many of them were openly vicious. They were a disgrace to their orders and sacred functions, and were indeed the very dregs and refuse of the northern parts."

Now, when it is remembered that hundreds of such persons thus described by a friend of their order were admitted into the reconstructed Presbyterian Church after the Revolution settlement of 1688, it cannot be doubted that those who ate the bread and performed the sacred functions of the Church were bound to be for years to come a very mixed multitude.

The spirit of compromise was abroad in the councils of State and Church in, and for some considerable time after 1688. King William was essentially an Erastian; he was a Presbyterian by training, but did not attach much importance to ecclesiastical or even

* Burnet's " History of the Reformation "—dedication to the King.

theological differences, and by his Dutch blood and phlegmatic temperament was far removed from the consuming earnestness of a religious enthusiast. The policy he favoured was comprehension, a basis so broad and a banner so colourless that men of all shades of belief might live together under the same roof, if not on the ground of affinity, at least on that of toleration. It may be said, indeed, that from his position as a civil ruler he could not well have done otherwise; and any truth there is in such an observation militates, some think, against the alliance of two things which in the interests of both ought to be kept apart—Church and State. Thus while the "glorious Revolution" of 1688 could not but have its bright side as a release from captivity—the fit sequel to what took place a hundred years before, the dispersion of the Spanish Armada in 1588—yet it had its less happy side in the cold, calculating, temporising policy which prevailed under the reputable name of moderation.

It has also to be borne in mind that the Restoration did not leave Scotland as it had found it. The strong and trusted leaders of the Church, the story of whose brilliant achievements is an inspiration, had died, and a generation had grown up under influences such as might be expected in an age of subserviency to a Court of which Charles II. was the head and ornament. No one who has any claims to be heard as a historical authority ever pretends to deny that there was a general deterioration of morals from the time that Charles II. ascended the throne. The kingdom that was coming during his reign was the very antipodes of that which is righteousness, peace, and joy in the Holy Ghost. What else could be expected when the best elements of the nation were driven into hiding-places, and the lower tendencies of human nature came to the front, and basked in the sunshine of royal favour and example?

On the flag of the frigate which bore the Prince of Orange to our shores he caused the words to be inscribed, "I will maintain the liberties of England and the Protestant religion," and in justice to his memory it must be owned he kept his word. But while 1688 is indeed a red-letter year in our history, as it was the close of a long, weary struggle with the forces of ruthless despotism and cruel persecution, yet, looking forward from that time, there was not much to rouse religious enthusiasm.

The Church, under leaders lacking in the spiritual elevation of those of the Reformation and Covenanting periods, began to move on a lower plane. High spiritual ideals, conviction that burned and glowed in the soul, heroic enterprise, consuming devotion to the great practical aims of Christianity, and prayers that were mighty in wrestling with God belonged to the past; the prevailing temper now was one of placid accommodation to things as they were—the reign of Moderatism was about to begin.

But God was not without His witness in that degenerate Church. There was a godly remnant that had too much of the ancient spirit of Knox and Rutherford to acquiesce in a downward course. There were some who had sufficient spiritual vitality and warmth to overcome the benumbing effects of the many icebergs which were around them; and when Patronage was forced upon the Church in 1712 by the anti-evangelical party, which commanded a majority in the Church Courts, there were many strong, if ineffectual, protests uttered against such an interference with the rights of the people.

What helped to keep experimental religion alive during the ascendancy of Prelacy, and when the people were debarred from the ministrations they loved, was the private praying society which existed in almost every parish. In some parishes there were two or three such meetings, for prayer, reading of the Scriptures, and mutual edification, which gave a popular backing to evangelical leaders in the General Assembly, and paved the way, as we shall see, for the Secession movement. It is questionable whether even students of Scottish Church history have yet realised how much the religious life of the people was indebted for its maintenance at a trying period to those scattered and obscure "praying societies."

The part that was taken by the majority of the General Assembly in 1720 in connection with what was called the "Marrow controversy," revealed their negative spirit and growing bias against evangelical doctrine. A book called "The Marrow of Modern Divinity," published by a graduate of Oxford, in 1645, had been brought to Scotland by a soldier from the wars of the Commonwealth. A copy of it was discovered in a cottage in the parish of Simprin, by Thomas Boston, who turned the attention of his fellow-countrymen to its contents. The main object of the book, which consists of extracts from the writings of Luther, Calvin, and other eminent divines, is to set forth God's free offer of salvation to sinful men. Cunningham, in his "Church History of Scotland," acknowledges that if "that celebrated treatise diverges from the standards of orthodoxy, it is only by a hair-breadth." Grub, in his "Ecclesiastical History of Scotland," says—"The doctrines of the book were nearly the same with those held by leading divines of the Protestant Church in the seventeenth century, and were eagerly supported by all who retained the old Covenanting opinions." Yet that book was formally condemned by the General Assembly, and twelve of the best members of the Church suffered severe rebuke as its upholders. Such a straw shows how the current was going. It was a sign of deep degeneracy, and a precursor of the procession of secessions which took place, weakening the State Church, but conferring untold benefit upon the country.

One of the most prominent men of the minority was Ebenezer Erskine, whose fine figure and impressive manner gave such dignity to his utterance that a Scottish divine of last century was accustomed to say, "He that has not heard Ebenezer Erskine preach the gospel has not heard it preached in its *maagesty*." Erskine's spirit was greatly stirred by the defections of the times, and having the courage of his convictions, he took the opportunity, when he had to preach a sermon as moderator of the Synod of Perth and Stirling, of delivering his soul. That sermon was the first shot in the battle which issued in the Secession Church. The Synod, after long discussion, decided that his utterances were censurable. The case passed on to the General Assembly, which rebuked and admonished Erskine. He lodged a protest for himself, and for three ministers—William Wilson, of Perth; Alexander Moncrieff, of Abernethy; and James Fisher, of Kinclaven, who appealed against the sentence of the Synod, and adhered to the protest of Erskine. The Assembly and Commission took very high ground, and treated the "four brethren" with great severity. Because, as earnest and honest men, they lamented the deadness of the times, and in the exercise of the right of free speech, reproached the Church for not bestirring itself more to champion the liberties of the people, and meet the spiritual wants of the country, he and his associates, on 18th November, 1733, were released from their charges, and their churches were declared vacant. Alarmed at the resolute attitude those Secessionists took, and seeing that they were evoking a great deal of popular sympathy, the leaders of the Church changed their front, and in 1734 so eager were they that the brethren should return to their place in the Establishment, that they actually rescinded some of the obnoxious legislation, because it was found to be "hurtful to the Church," and recommended the Synod of Perth and Stirling to restore the "four brethren." The Synod did so, and even went beyond orders in appointing Mr. Erskine moderator of Stirling Presbytery.

But with the experience they had had of the want of spiritual sympathy in the Church, and the views they now had for the future, for Erskine and his associates to have gone back would have been to sacrifice spiritual ends for the sake of an ecclesiastical connection. So they formed themselves into a Presbytery, and, as indicating the spirit in which those men entered upon their new responsibilities, it may be mentioned that before any formal arrangement was made the greater part of two days was spent in prayer.

Another secession took place in 1752 by the deposition of Gillespie, who, as a member of the Presbytery of Dunfermline, refused, along with other ministers, to take part in the ordination of a man to the parish of Inverkeithing, because he was obnoxious to the parishioners. The highhanded men who led the Church in those days, utterly out of touch with the people's feelings and needs, decided that Gillespie should be the scapegoat of the Presbytery, and they without any compunction cast him out. He and those who afterwards joined him, not prepared to enter the groove of the Erskine movement, became what was called the Relief Church, as indicating the relief they had got from the yoke of patronage.

Those Seceders were grave, solid men, with a decidedly old-world strain in their theology and phraseology. In their independence, staunch adherence to conviction, and readiness to testify against what they deemed to be evil or error, they gave a pronounced embodiment to some of the sturdiest characteristics of the Scottish nation. Narrowness and hard-and-fast dogmatism were amongst their most obvious shortcomings. "An entangled scrupulosity," Bishop Burnet said, is one of the characteristics of the Scottish mind, and it certainly comes out in the history of the

controversies in the Secession Church. They
needed to have repeated to them the words of
Oliver Cromwell to an assembly of Scottish
divines—" I entreat you, my brethren, I entreat
you, by the mercies of God, to remember that it
is possible that sometimes you may be mistaken."
The first Secession Church gave evidence of this
tendency to allow too much scope to an argumentative and opinionative state of mind by
dividing itself into two bodies—the Burghers
and Anti-Burghers, as they were called, the
former thinking it quite legitimate to take the
Burgher oath, the other considering it improper, and refusing to make this difference the
ground of mutual forbearance.

This is part of the oath that was taken at
the time :—

"Here I protest before God and your lordships
that I profess and allow with my heart the true
religion presently professed within this realm, and
authorised by the laws thereof. I shall abide there-
at, and defend the same to my life's end, renouncing
the Roman religion called Papistry."

Some members of the Synod judged that the
clause in the oath, " the true religion presently
professed within this realm," was equivalent to
an approbation of all the errors and defections of
the Established Church, against which the
Seceders had testified. Others maintained that
the clause simply bound the person taking the

oath to approve of the true religion itself, and that the Seceders might lawfully swear the oath: hence the disunion. The same scrupulousness was manifested in the discipline they maintained amongst the Church members, especially of the Anti-Burgher body. A member of the Secession Church at Clola was severely rebuked and admonished for having attempted to pass the tollbar at Peterhead without paying toll. A bleacher in Stuartfield was taken to task for allowing his yarn to remain on the green over the Sabbath, and the case was accounted so difficult that it was referred to the Presbytery for settlement!

But with all their defects, which many laugh at who have not a tithe of their sturdy conviction and moral worth, the Seceders were for many years the salt of this part of the earth. Much of their power lay in prayer. They had societies all over the country which were centres of spiritual life, and rallying points for the godly of the district. Much of the most solid piety and devoutness of the eighteenth century were to be found among the Seceders. What is the witness of Thomas Carlyle on this point? He says that in his early days "a man who awoke to the belief that he actually had a soul to be saved or lost was apt to be found among the Dissenting people, and to have given up attendance on the Kirk."

So mightily grew the word and prevailed, and so much were the Seceders in the current of the sympathy of the best part of the nation, that in the year 1765 the statement was made in the General Assembly that "there are now one hundred and twenty meeting houses erected, to which more than a hundred thousand persons resort, who were formerly of our communion, but have separated themselves from the Church of Scotland ; and this progress of Dissent is most evident in the greatest and most populous towns."

It is noteworthy that such a large proportion of men trained in the Secession Church have taken a prominent place in the civic life and general business of large centres of population. Some of the leading business firms in Glasgow were made by Seceders, who, by reading the Bible, pondering its contents, and grappling with its truths, acquired an independence and force which became of account in the ordinary affairs of the world.

Wherever there were praying societies of men there were demands for Secession preachers too numerous to be readily met. A drover from a southern market met a farmer in one of the secluded vales of Aberdeenshire, and as they sat on a stone together they talked about the revival of religion through the instrumentality of the Erskines and their associates, and that led to the formation of a Secession Church not far from where they met. A few fishermen from Rosehearty, landing one day at Leith, witnessed the observance of the Lord's Supper in a Secession Church, which so impressed them that, through their efforts, a church of that order was formed in their village. The origin of the Secession Church at Lynturk, near Alford, can be traced to the offence caused to the parishioners by the minister ordering the precentor to discontinue the reading of each line of the psalm before singing it! That was in 1760, when the practice which had prevailed since the Reformation was being abandoned.* One of the four brethren who were the founders of the Secession Church, Mr. Moncrieff, visiting Peterhead for the benefit of his health, spent some time in the house of his friend, Mr. Ferguson of Kinmundy, and preached to the people of the neighbourhood. That, along with other kinds of preparation which had been going on for years among the evangelically disposed people of the district, led to the formation of the Craigdam Church, of which Mr. William Brown was ordained minister in 1752.

The Secession movement made great progress in Buchan, notwithstanding the strong opposition it met with, such as is shown in the following postscript to the advertisement of some farms that were to let—"*Cairds* and Seceders need not apply." Dr. Ferguson of Kinmundy delivers the

* Mackelvie's "Annals and Statistics of the United Presbyterian Church," p. 80.

P

following valuable testimony as to the interest awakened in the north-eastern part of Scotland by the Secession preachers:—

"From ten, fifteen, twenty, and even twenty-five miles did some of them go and return to obtain their spiritual food. As this statement may appear almost incredible to some, I may state the following fact, which rests on the authority of an acquaintance of my own, and may be safely relied on. She, being an elderly woman, was well acquainted with at least one of the Rosehearty fishermen who walked from that village to Craigdam. On asking him how it was possible for them to overtake such a journey, he informed her that they prepared for the Sabbath by retiring early to bed on Saturday evening; and, rising early, they were ready to leave home about three next morning, so that they reached Craigdam in time for some rest and refreshment before service began; on their return they were accustomed to rest for some time at a place where the roads diverged, by which the companies from different districts departed to their respective homes; having there engaged in prayer, which gave to the spot the name of "The Praying Knowe," they went on their way, and by the time they reached Rosehearty it was generally time, if the weather permitted, to go to sea, and preparations having previously been made, they, without going to bed, proceeded to follow their usual occupations."

Mr. John Bisset—born in 1692, died in 1756—was the precursor of the Secession body in the city of Aberdeen. After labouring for eleven years in Newmachar, he was called to St. Nicholas Church, and for nearly thirty years was a thorn in the side of the Moderate clergy, who, from their numbers and social influence, tried to carry things with a high hand. Having preached a sermon before the Synod of Aberdeen, in a strain similar to that of Ebenezer Erskine, in which he testified with no uncertain sound against the defections of the times, some of his co-Presbyters were anxious to institute proceedings against him, with the view of compelling him to withdraw some of the statements he made. But Provost Cruickshank rose up and warned the members of the Court that Mr. Bisset was not the man to retract anything he had said, and that unless they wished to see a thousand Seceders in Aberdeen on the morrow, they had better forbear. It is quite consistent with the above to find it inscribed on his tombstone in our town's churchyard that "through the whole course of his ministry, particularly in the latter part of it, he encountered many difficulties and the most violent opposition."

Before Mr. Bisset died he recommended members of his congregation who consulted him on the subject to connect themselves with the Burgher Synod, as there was little expectation of a successor being appointed in the East Church whose ministrations would be such as they desired and needed. They took his advice, and the first Secession church was formed in 1758 in the Weigh-house, Mr. Alexander Dick being chosen as minister.

In the inscription on his tomb in the town's churchyard there is the following sentence:—" Whose religion was strict but not morose, warm but not enthusiastical, and regular but not formal."

The Burghers and Anti-Burghers were re-united in 1820, and the Relief Church joining in 1847, what we know as the United Presbyterian Church came into existence.

CHAPTER XVIII.

THE MODERATES.

THE term "Moderates" came into use about the middle of the eighteenth century to denote a party in the Church of Scotland whose tendency was to oppose popular claims and discountenance "enthusiasm" in religion. As the century advanced, the term became more fully developed in its application and significance, and, while ever somewhat vague and indefinite, yet it came to have a recognised value as opposed to pronounced Evangelicalism.

The great aim of the Church generally, under the leadership of Robertson, the historian; Dr. Carlyle of Inveresk, and Blair, the preacher of smooth platitudes, was to improve the social manners and literary style of the clergy, to tone down fervour, to substitute for enthusiasm and uncompromising Evangelicalism a calm, finished, man-of-the-world style of religion, by which the upper classes would be conciliated. Moderatism, it is said by Dean Stanley and Principal Tulloch, was a reaction from the narrowness, not to say the fanaticism, of the Covenanting period. There is a measure of truth in that presentation of the case. It is so difficult to combine intensity of feeling with breadth of view and toleration.

When soldiers are concentrating their energies upon some point in the citadel, it is not easy at the same time to give due attention to all the outlying places. Wallace and Bruce, struggling as true patriots for the vital interests of their country, were to be excused if they at the same time did not do much for its literary culture and social amenity. So the Covenanters were not to be condemned because, in contending for the fundamental truths of our faith and those liberties which are the first condition of civilisation, they were not as alert as they might have been on behalf of toleration, charity, and other Christian graces. There are times when some things can be gained, it would appear, only by the sacrifice or the abeyance of others. When a man's house is on fire he is not to be greatly blamed if his movements do not show all the ease and elegance we like to see. Are, then, the Covenanters to be reproached because, in those times of strife and distraction, they lacked some things in life which are the fruit of calm and leisure? It must be owned that the Covenanters went a great deal too far in depreciating grace of form in worship and preaching, and some of them were prone to identify godliness with rudeness, spirituality with baldness in its vesture and setting.

But admitting that the Church in Scotland, having fought and won its battles with Popery,

Episcopacy, and civil despotism, was now free to cultivate those amenities of form which join sweetness to strength, there was surely nothing to justify that abandonment or concealment of the great mysteries of our faith, which was the characteristic note of a great deal of the Moderatism of the eighteenth century. If a lecturer on physiology were to confine his attention to the heart, lungs, and stomach, and say nothing of the action of the skin, that would not justify the person who supplanted him, in making the function of the skin his chief subject of study and discourse. The best of the Moderates wanted to give a wider view of life and duty, which was perfectly justifiable; but many of them swung round to the fatal extreme of making form and manner more than substance in religion. They betook themselves to the functions of the skin, and gave the vital parts too little attention. They made a great effort to win educated but unspiritual men to their side. But to bid too high for the support of the world sometimes defeats its own end, as Carlyle of Inveresk found on meeting David Hume after the famous sceptical writer heard him preach. Being on a visit to Gilmerton, Sir David Kinloch constrained Hume to go on Sunday to Athelstaneford Church, where Carlyle was to preach for John Home. "What did you mean," he said, "by treating John's congregation to-day with one of Cicero's

Academics? I did not think such heathen morality would have passed in East Lothian." Contrast with that the remark which Hume made after hearing John Brown, of Haddington, preach—"That's the man for me; he means what he says; he speaks as if Jesus Christ were at his elbow." Consistency is a virtue in the pulpit or out of it, and honest men like it.

The leading intellects during the reign of Moderatism made the great mistake of putting themselves out of touch with the most genuine and fervid piety among the people, with the result that the ranks of Dissent were largely recruited, and the Church was robbed of needed elements of the highest power. The Church was certainly not bound to perpetuate the lowly manners and unschooled narrowness of the godly peasantry of Scotland; but it should have kept itself in sympathy with their faith, their devotedness, their fidelity to gospel truth. As showing the spirit of Moderatism which held the majority of the General Assembly under its grasp for more than a century, there is scarcely a beneficent enterprise or helpful agency which has won a place for itself in the Church that was not opposed by it. Modern religious life and progress are what they are in spite of Moderatism. Missions to the heathen, Sabbath schools, the abolition of patronage, would not have been if the Evangelical minority, which became a majority, had not fought and beaten Moderatism.

But there were able and faithful ministers classed with the Moderates who owed that questionable distinction not so much to the want of faith and zeal as to family connection, to a peculiarity of temperament, to habit of mind, or to the fashion of the time. It must be remembered, also, that in those days Evangelicalism was deemed by some to be associated with gushing emotionalism, and if a man had a strong intellectual bent, he not unnaturally gravitated to Moderatism. That partly explains why Aberdeenshire should have been stigmatised as the "dead sea of Moderatism." There is an untempered intellectual robustness in the north which shows a predilection for those parts of the Christian religion which the logical understanding can grasp, but there is not a corresponding fineness of perception for the spiritual contents of our faith. We of the north are of the school of Aristotle rather than that of Plato. We are followers of the practical, matter-of-fact, ethical James; and the Apostle John, as he soars, would need to lend us his wings before we could rise to his level.

It is true we have a Beattie whose "Essay on Truth," and still more his "Minstrel," prove that the finest sentiment and poetical genius can root themselves in any soil and thrive in any clime. But Reid, who became the parish minister of Newmachar in 1737, afterwards Professor of Moral Philosophy in King's College and in Glasgow University, presents to us the typical northern intellect under the most favourable conditions. He, had such a humble estimate of his powers that he occasionally read to the Newmachar parishioners a sermon written by Tillotson rather than one of his own, and yet in his "Enquiry into the Human Mind on the Principles of Common Sense" he has given to the world a contribution to the discussion of psychology which led to a new and distinct school of philosophy, and reveals to us where the strength and the weakness, or rather limitation of the northern Scottish mind lies. Alexander Gerard, too, by his "Essay on Truth" and his "Essay on Genius," shows us the bent of the stronger minds in the ministry in these parts in those days, and shows us also how naturally we take to metaphysics rather than to the visions and raptures of saints of a southern latitude. Yet while Moderatism is not an unnatural excrescence of northern Scottish human nature, it is no essential and permanent part of it. The *perfervidum ingenium* which is lying latent soon comes to the surface when the soul-kindling inspirations of experimental Christianity have had a fair opportunity of showing what they can do.

It must in fairness be owned that philosophy, literature, and intellectual culture generally, were greatly furthered by the best of the men who were ranked amongst the Moderates. Many of the "Paraphrases" appended to the metrical psalms came from their pen. They did a great deal to maintain, or, rather, introduce, elegance of manners and classic refinement of taste. But an icicle, however clear and shapely, is out of place in the pulpit. Much as chasteness of style and beauty of form are to be admired, the Kingdom of Heaven in its aims and ends cannot be reduced to the narrow limits of such a ministration. What might be fitting enough in the academy or in the professor's chair was intolerable in the pulpit, which is not much if it is not the symbol of a doctrine as high as heaven, as deep as eternity, and as intense as life itself. "Religion is the banquet of the spirit, not the feast of the mind, and therefore danger is ever present when men begin to listen to the sermon as a manifestation of intellectual force, and not for its spiritual power." It is true that religion should have a right relation to every part of human nature, and intellectual feebleness or dulness is a hindrance and not a help to the ministries of heaven; but the function of the understanding is not to retain God's truth for its own delectation; it is to hand it on to the heart, conscience, and life.

Moderatism represents a certain attitude of the mind in relation to the verities of religion which is never entirely absent from the Church, and may be seen in the present day under modern conditions. Just as Erasmus was a disciple of the Renaissance and Luther a herald of the Reformation, so men, according to the proclivities of the mind and the experiences of the soul, go out to culture or rise to faith. The ministers of God who have rendered most valuable service are those who combined both in due proportion. Humanism, with all its light and sweetness, is certainly a poor substitute for divinity.

CHAPTER XIX.

PRINCIPAL CAMPBELL—1719-96.

THE famous Dr. George Campbell, like many of Scotland's eminent sons, was a child of the manse, his father, the Rev. Colin Campbell, having been one of the ministers of this city. Born in 1719 the youngest son of a considerable family, made fatherless when he was only nine years of age, and left in not very affluent circumstances, he was from his earliest years disciplined into habits of self-reliance. The Grammar School and Marischal College did for him all that they could, though, like many who afterwards win distinction, he was not a recluse or a bookworm in his early years. After graduating, having made marked progress, especially in the study of Greek, he went to Edinburgh and served a regular apprenticeship to the law, which may partly account for the method and precision of expression observable in his writings. Not relishing the profession to which he appeared to be destined, he returned to Aberdeen, entered the Divinity Hall, and threw himself with ardour into studies that were more congenial and afforded greater scope for the powers with which he was endowed.

As illustrating his intellectual zeal and his acute perception of the possibilities of any situation, practical or literary, it may be mentioned that while he was a divinity student he took a leading part in the formation of a theological club for the free discussion of subjects of special interest to embryo ministers. The original members of that society must have been astute persons, for no one could apply for admission into it, and only those were taken in who were deemed to be of such parts and habits as would make them a real acquisition.

After his course of study was finished and he was licensed as a preacher, much against the wishes of many in the parish he was ordained minister of Banchory-Ternan in 1748. It need scarcely be said that he soon gained the confidence and affection of his parishioners by his sterling character and assiduous devotion to duty. His plain, practical expositions of Scripture—"lecturing," opening up the word—were greatly appreciated, and they put him on a line of study which afterwards developed into his published "Translations of the Gospels." The quiet country parish, by the side of the Dee, did for him what such a place has done for many ministers who rose to conspicuous place and wide public usefulness. The foundation of his greatness as a thinker, lecturer, and author was laid during the nine years of comparative obscurity in that rural region. He had leisure to read, to ponder, to master many things, especially himself. A man who formed the habit of beginning his work at five or six o'clock in the morning was sure to experience the truthfulness of the proverb that the hand of the diligent maketh rich. That, too, was done with a physical frame which was by no means robust. In view of his prowess as an antagonist in argument, we are apt to think of him as a big, muscular man. On the contrary, he was under the average stature, and was subject to fits of dyspepsia, for which his most effectual cure was abstinence from food till the digestive organs were restored to healthy action.

In 1757 he was translated to the city of Aberdeen, in room of Rev. John Bisset. Here also his entry was opposed by many of the parishioners, and the event was signalised by the separation of a considerable number, who, as we have seen, formed the nucleus of the first Secession Church in Aberdeen. The transition from Bisset to Campbell must indeed have been felt to be abrupt, and Patronage in that, as well as in many other instances, did not appear to follow the line of evolution. Bisset was an evangelical of the evangelicals, and while a man who rendered splendid service to the cause of vital godliness in Aberdeen, being to some extent a later Andrew Cant, yet, like some excellent men of his school of theology, he was deemed to be narrow, imperious, and intolerant. For example, he was almost as much opposed to the appearance of Whitefield, the great preacher, in his pulpit, when on a visit to Aberdeen in 1741, as he was to the advent of Charles Stuart, the Pretender, regarding whose movements he made such copious notes in his diary.

A few months after Dr. Campbell's settlement in Aberdeen, a new society, Phœnix-like, rose from the ashes of the former one we have referred to, which included in its membership such men as Gerard, Beattie, and Reid, of whom the world has heard. It was on a wider basis, and was more literary and philosophical than theological. Reid's "Inquiry into the Human Understanding" and some of Campbell's best-known works first saw the light as seedlings in that select circle of intellects, as keen as ever met at any time or at any place in Aberdeen. At no time indeed, in the history of Aberdeen, did so many men live and write within its borders who have won world-wide fame. It was a period more brilliant by far than that of the "Doctors," for in addition to scholarship, there was original research and vigorous thought displayed by that galaxy of talent at the close of the eighteenth century.

In 1759 Dr. Campbell was made Principal of Marischal College, and by the publication of his "Essay on Miracles" not long after, he proved himself worthy of the dignity to which he had been promoted. Hume's "Essay on Miracles" was the great sensation of the eighteenth century in the learned world, and many Davids did it call forth to meet this infidel Goliath. For style, sentiment, and fervour, Beattie's "Essay on Truth" was by far the most popular effusion on the subject that emanated from this part of the land. It was easily read, and George the Third could compliment the author by saying it was the only book he ever stole! But by discerning minds, capable of weighing the merits of an argumentative treatise, the palm was awarded to Principal Campbell. Like most controversial works, it had its day, and the "fashion" of it passed away, as a defence of supernatural intervention. At the time it was admitted to be a masterpiece, and was speedily translated into French, Dutch, and German.

It is this "Essay on Miracles" more than any other book he wrote which entitles Campbell to be called "the Paley of Scotland." The heightened, luminous "common sense" which was the distinguishing note of the school of thought to which he belonged, and which prevailed in Scotland at the time, is most conspicuous in this writing. Hume had taken the position that our experience of uniformity in nature is such that no human testimony can make a miracle credible. Here is a specimen of Campbell's illustrative rejoinder:—

"I have lived for some years near a ferry. It consists with my knowledge that the passage boat has a thousand times crossed the river, and as many times returned safe. An unknown man whom I have just now met tells me in a serious manner that it is lost; and affirms that he himself, standing on the bank, was a spectator of the scene, that he saw the passengers carried down the stream and the boat overwhelmed. No person who is influenced in his judgment of things, not by philosophical subtleties, but by common sense—a much surer guide—will hesitate to declare that in such a testimony I have probable evidence of the fact asserted."

It should be mentioned as one of the "curiosities of literature," and as illustrating the extraordinary candour and courtesy of Dr. Campbell, that, before publishing the "Essay," he sent the manuscript to David Hume, and begged him to correct any misstatement, and expunge any expression which gave just offence. We give the first sentence in Hume's letter, in which he handsomely acknowledges the author's magnanimity:—"It has so seldom happened that controversies in philosophy, much less in theology, have been carried on without producing a personal quarrel between the parties, that I must regard my present situation as somewhat extraordinary, and have reason to give you thanks for the civil and obliging manner in which you have conducted the dispute against me on so interesting a subject as that of miracles."

In 1771 Dr. Campbell was elected by the

Town Council of Aberdeen, Professor of Divinity in Marischal College as successor to Dr. Gerard, who was removed to the same chair in King's College. The spirit in which he conducted the work in the class-room is well indicated in the following sentences which he addressed to the students at the outset of his career:—

"Gentlemen, the nature of my office has been much misunderstood. It is supposed that I am to teach you everything connected with the study of divinity. I tell you honestly that I am to teach you nothing. Ye are not schoolboys. Ye are young men who have finished your courses of philosophy, and ye are no longer to be treated as if ye were at school. Therefore, I repeat it, I am to teach you nothing; but by the grace of God I will assist you to teach yourselves everything."

As a teacher he was in many respects a man before his time; he was so open and independent, so untrammelled by artificial systems and standards, so fearless and thorough-going in his love of truth. In urging his students to go to the Bible with an unbiased mind, and seek what God's Spirit leads them to find, we hear the utterance of the spirit of the later years of the nineteenth century rather than that of a hundred years ago.

Among the students under the Divinity Professor in his later years was James Kidd ("Dr. Kidd of Aberdeen"), and doubtless the prince of polished Moderates had his own opinion of the energetic and unconventional Irishman, who, like a stranded boulder belonging to far away formations, had found his way to this northern land. The peculiarity of Mr. Kidd's position in relation to Dr. Campbell was that, while a student, he was also a colleague as Professor of Hebrew in Marischal College. The young Irishman had to deliver a trial discourse before Dr. Campbell, and, being a busy man, and not very particular at any time about form and appearance, Mr. Kidd had not been at pains to elaborate his sermon upon sheets of paper in the ordinary way, but brought a sheaf of loose MSS., the outcome of which, as might be expected, was rather disjointed and crude; at least it was so in the eyes of Dr. Campbell, who had a classic finish and neatness in all he said and did. "Now, Mr. Kidd," said the doctor mildly, " it would ill become me to criticise severely the production of a gentleman holding the position of a colleague. I would just advise you, when you next come up with a discourse, to have it arranged a little more methodically."

His " Philosophy of Rhetoric," published in 1776, was one of the many contributions of that period to the study of literary composition, and it has received many glowing encomiums from masters of that subject, such as Archbishop Whately. Rhetoric was one of the favourite topics of the clergymen of the Moderate party. Educated Scotland was then trying to reach that purity and elegance of English diction which was exhibited by such writers as Addison; and Blair, Gerard, Beattie, and many others, along with Campbell, in Scotland helped the movement both by example and precept. That the style is the man comes out strikingly in the writings of Campbell; it is simple, perspicuous, nervous—the fit vesture of his mind.

Of all his works, none gave rise to so much controversy as one that was issued a few years after his death—his "Lectures on Ecclesiastical History." In that volume he gives expression to views regarding the origin and structure of the primitive Church, which some deemed to be dangerously democratic, with a leaning, indeed, towards Congregationalism. He is very hard, too, upon those who make apostolical succession the basis of church order and authority. He refers to persons who regard

". . . as the sole authentic evidence of our being Christians the examination of certain endless genealogies, as if Christ had intended that all His disciples should be antiquaries; because otherwise they could not have the satisfaction to know whether they were His disciples or not. Unfortunately for those people, all such spiritual pedigrees are so miserably lame that if their rule were to be admitted we should be involved in darkness on this subject from which no antiquary could extricate us, and there would not remain the slightest evidence that there was a single Christian on the earth." *

Such trenchant and rather provocative writing could not but give offence, but Dr. Campbell was like the blacksmith who hammered the iron while it was hot and never minded where the sparks went.

What a splendid directness there is in the letter to the Presbytery of Aberdeen, in which, owing to the frailties of old age, he resigned his professorship :—

"It is my firm opinion that when a man is conscious that he is no longer able to perform properly the duties of an office, and is providentially in a situation of living independently of its emoluments, it is an indispensable duty to resign, that a fit person may be timely found to supply the place, for the sake of the community at large, that the public may not suffer, compared with which the accommodation of the incumbent is, and ought always to be, regarded as but a secondary consideration at the most."

He was succeeded both in the Principalship and in the Divinity Chair of Marischal College by the accomplished Dr. William Lawrence Brown.

On the 6th April, 1796, in the seventy-

* "Lectures on Ecclesiastical History," by George Campbell, Aberdeen, 1815. An account of the life and writings of the Principal is given by the Rev. George Skene, Keith, to which we are indebted for many of the facts here stated.

seventh year of his age, there passed away Dr. George Campbell, who for masculine vigour of mind may be said to be a typical Aberdonian, and the highest development of the race. If he was a Moderate, he was certainly one of the best of them. Party classifications and labels are often a grievous injustice, as there are some men, and those often the best, who, from constitutional proclivity or early training, present a certain example of religious life that defies all partisan assortment. Within his own range, Dr. Campbell was a master in Israel. His mind was that of the cultured Scot, argumentative rather than imaginative, logical and not at all intuitional or mystical. He was not content to leave a subject till he had seen through it to the other side, though perhaps he was not always able to penetrate to its deepest parts or reach its hidden roots; but, alike in the quality of his mind and its limitation, there is no finer specimen of the prevailing type in these northern parts.

The house in which Dr. Campbell lived for the greater part of his public life was that now known as 49 Schoolhill.

CHAPTER XX.

JOHN SKINNER OF LINSHART—1721-1807.

IN depicting the many-sided religion of the north as it has been evolved from a remote past, we come now to the Scots Episcopalians as they appeared after the Revolution, and no better representative of them could be found than John Skinner of Linshart. The study of such a man is interesting, were it only to show how plain living and high thinking can go together—how character, genius, and highest pursuits are not dependent upon earthly environment and the prizes which time sometimes bestows. It has been said that Wordsworth rendered greater service to the peasantry of Cumberland by the noble simplicity of his life than he did by the most magnificent of his poems. The spectacle before their eyes every day of a man communing with the highest and yet showing in his household life how by frugality a little money can go a great way, and how personal dignity is not to be identified with the length of the purse in one's pocket or the upholstery that is in his house — such an object-lesson was a positive means of grace. In some such position John

Skinner stood in relation to his contemporaries and neighbours in Buchan for upwards of sixty years.

John Skinner was born in the parish of Birse in 1721, his father being the schoolmaster of the place, and one of exceptional learning and ability. Apt and diligent as a scholar, John, under the competent and stimulating tuition of his father, soon attained to such proficiency in his studies, especially in Latin composition, that he took a considerable bursary at Marischal College when he was only fourteen years of age, which went far in securing his maintenance during his four years' curriculum.

At the close of his University course it was his happy fortune, after teaching in Kemnay School for a few months, to obtain a situation as assistant to the schoolmaster of Monymusk, the natural scenery of which almost equals in interest its ancient ecclesiastical associations. Here his muse, which had made its presence felt at a very early period, now took higher wing than it ever did before, and a " Poem on a Visit to Paradise" (the one in Monymusk) having come under the notice of Lady Grant, she encouraged him to visit Monymusk House, and gave him free access to its library. He came while there under the influence of an Episcopal clergyman in the locality, which led eventually to his passing from Presbyterianism to Episcopacy.

There can be little doubt that conviction and nothing else accounted for this change. There was scarcely any room at that time for the play of inferior motive. Episcopacy was not then on the sunny side of the road; fat livings and the smiles and favours of men in high place in Church and State were then reserved for Presbyterians. But to a resolute, high-spirited man like John Skinner there would be the charm of romance in the very adventure and probable worldly loss involved in such a step.

Passing to Shetland in 1740 to enter upon a tutorship, he met an additional argument to confirm him in his adhesion to Episcopacy in the daughter of an Episcopal clergyman, with whom he fell in love and soon married. In 1740 he was called to Longside, near Peterhead, where he remained for nearly sixty-five years. It may be safely affirmed that among the attractions that rooted him to that spot for such a lengthened period richness of landscape and geniality of climate cannot be named. John Hill Burton has described Buchan as "a spreading of peat moss on a cake of granite." No "Buchan body," none of "the folk in the corner," as they have sometimes been called, however intense his loyal patriotism, could make the north-eastern part of Scotland a figure of that ideal country of which it is the duty of a minister to speak. Yet there are sweet spots in it, as at Old Deer, to relieve the general flatness and bareness, and in the bleakest parts there, are always wide views to be had and plenty of sky overhead!

Our townsman Dr. Walter C. Smith thus sings of it :—

> "Where Ugie winds through Buchan braes—
> A treeless land, where beeves are good,
> And men have quaint, old-fashioned ways,
> And every town has ballad lore,
> And every hamlet has its song,
> And on its surf-beat rocky shore,
> The eerie legend lingers long."*

In that monotonous land he lived a full and happy life, and one charged with varied interest. It would be difficult to find in the north a better example of the typical country parson, such as poets sing about—homely, kindly, the man of his people, ever ready to succour and counsel, living among them and for them, and yet ever having an inner life in his study which he nourished with much reading.

While it would appear there was still enough of the old Presbyterian leaven in him to make him thoroughly loyal to the Government, yet he suffered in common with his Episcopalian brethren after the tragic events of 1745. Many of the people of that persuasion, believing in the divine right of the Stuart dynasty, manifested a

---

* "Selections from the Poems of Walter C. Smith," p. 72.

chivalrous devotion to the "Pretender," which makes one of the most romantic episodes in Scottish history. For the sake of an idea, and no doubt also from the feeling that the return of the exiled family would bring their Church once more into the sunshine, they risked their all. Culloden not only dashed their hopes to the ground, but also brought the avenging law on their track, and occasionally the innocent suffered with the guilty, and John Skinner was one of that class. He was no political conspirator; there is no evidence that his people showed any Jacobite leanings in church, such as a traveller reports of a certain Episcopal congregation in the city of Aberdeen after the collapse of the rebellion. The clergyman of the place had taken the oath of allegiance to King George, and when in the act of praying for the reigning monarch, the people assembled, we are told, who had been joining with the utmost devoutness to the prescribed prayers up to this point, immediately began to betray their want of assent and consent to the testing but unpopular petitions by taking out their snuff-boxes, and, with much noise and demonstration, using their contents till once they got past King George!

But John Skinner was apprehended on the ground that he had violated the law which was passed with the view of stamping out disloyal Episcopacy, that no clergyman was to minister to more than four persons at a time. It is believed that he owed those attentions which the Government paid him, to the officious zeal of a lady "of some rank" in the district, who so pestered the powers that be that they were compelled to enforce what was not intended to be too rigidly carried out. He was sentenced to six months' imprisonment in Old Aberdeen, and he afterwards averred that he never, in his long life, had such an unbroken period of study! Happily constituted man; contented, spirited, resourceful, he had the knack of yoking all experiences into his service, and exacting helpful contribution from the most untoward events. He needed all his staying power in those disturbed times. One night, on coming home, he found some of Cumberland's soldiers standing at his door with fixed bayonets, and others plundering indoors. He was stripped of all his valuables, and his chapel was burned to the ground by a lawless soldiery. But his cheerful heart and nimble wit soon enabled him to rise above such disasters.

When without a building in which to conduct worship, and obliged to gather the people into and around his humble thatched cottage, little better than a "but and a ben," an incident occurred that had great effect upon his future pulpit ministrations, and which also shed much light upon the man and the times. One Sabbath when Mr. Skinner was about to begin reading his sermon, which in detached leaves was placed upon a temporary desk, a hen which had found its way into one of the apartments began to cackle, and when an attempt was made to chase it outside it became flurried and flew over the papers, scattering them among the people so as to render their recovery to be of use at the moment impossible. As the people were hastening to gather the bits of paper, their minister said, "Never mind them; a fowl [Scottice, *fool*] shall never shut my mouth again;" and ever afterwards he preached extemporaneously, and often for forty minutes. He once said to a friend who expressed surprise at the ease and fluency of his address in the pulpit—"Does a man require study and preparation to talk to his own family? Of the numerous congregation which you saw assembled in chapel to-day I have baptised more than three-fourths. I therefore consider them as my children, and surely he feels not as a parent who does not address his children without awe or restraint."

Dr. Walker, in his interesting life of Mr. Skinner, has put in print many of his sayings, which were for generations current in the district. Unable to dissuade a conceited tailor from abandoning his trade and entering the ministry, the Linshart pastor "chaffed" him by asking if he could measure that angel for a suit of clothes who stood with one foot on the land and one foot on the sea. The tailor was nonplussed, and was told to go home and learn his own business before thinking of another! A good, honest farmer who was spending an hour with his minister, could not be convinced that the earth moved at all. "The earth," he maintained, "never gaes oot o' the pairt, and it maun be that the sun gaes roon, for we ken that it rises in the east, and sets i' the west," and then as a decisive argument he added—"If the sun didna gae roon, foo is it said in the Scripture that the Lord commanded the sun to stand still?" "Ay," responded Mr. Skinner, dryly, "it's very true that the sun was commanded to stand still, and there he stands still, for he never was commanded to take the road again!"*

With an income that was even less than that of Goldsmith's parson, who is said to have been "passing rich on forty pounds a year," he thought he could meet the increasing demands of a growing family by becoming farmer as well as minister. He leased a farm, but soon found that the proverb is indeed true that the cobbler should stick to his last. There are ministers who make good farmers, but, as a general rule, it is by the minister losing himself in the farmer. The Linshart minister was too devoted to his own

* "The Life and Times of the Rev. John Skinner, M.A., of Linshart, Longside," by the Rev. William Walker, M.A.

proper work and to the pursuits of literature to be a successful farmer, and, at the end of seven years, he was glad to be liberated from bondage which in every way was having a crippling effect upon him. He resolved, as he said in a poetical effusion on the subject, to

> "Sell corn and cattle off; pay every man:
> Get free of debt and duns as fast's I can;
> Give up the farm with all its wants, and then—
> Why, take me to the book and pen."

In his "closet, five feet square," during the rest of his life he had better company than creditors and dealers, as he wrote with the air of a man who was so happy after his release from sore captivity—

> "With a few of the Fathers, the oldest and best,
> And some modern extracts picked out from the rest,
> With a Bible in Latin and Hebrew and Greek
> To afford him instruction each day of the week."

He had the habits of a student, and his life shows how a scholar, living on the pittance that is given to a peasant, can yet succeed in nourishing his mind, and by his utterances in the press direct and entertain his generation. Far from public libraries, and unable to buy many books, he tells us how he kept up his reading:—" When visiting any neighbour possessed of such a library as country gentlemen might be supposed to have, I took down in writing what I thought worthy of notice in any book that came in my way, and, collecting the most material of these extracts into a common-place book, I could have recourse to it as often as I found occasion for such a reference. . . . My common-place books through fifty-seven years and the blessing of a most tenacious memory have been my storehouse, and from their contents I have done what once on a day I could never have expected to do."

Ramsay, in the Ochtertyre papers, gives some interesting reminiscences of the pastor of Linshart. In 1795 he writes:—

"Next Sunday I went out to Linshart and attended divine service, which was almost as great a treat to me as the English cathedral worship is to a raw Scotsman. I saw what I knew would shortly be seen no more, viz.—an old-fashioned Episcopal clergyman who did not affect to tread in the steps of his English brethren, between whom and the parochial ministers of Scotland before the Revolution there was little similitude. The first thing that struck me was the strongly marked faces of the people, which betokened not only sense and sharpness, but also a serious frame of mind. In point of mode and plainness their dress reminded me of that of our country people more than forty years ago, bonnets and party-coloured plaids being frequent. To my great surprise the service began with a psalm taken from the Assembly's version, which he said was more intelligible to a country congregation than Tate and Brady's. This, with the precentor's tone and style of singing, made me fancy myself in a Presbyterian church, till the reading of the liturgy dispelled the illusion. . . . The service being finished, the venerable old man gave us a sermon—that was pious, rational, and impressive, calculated to edify peasants and philosophers. It owed nothing to the graces of his delivery, which looked liker familiar conversation than a studied discourse delivered in public; and its length and the want of papers were equally extraordinary in an Episcopal chapel."

His principal works by which he challenged the attention of the world were a "Preservative against Presbytery," written when the fortunes of Episcopacy were at a low ebb; a "Dissertation on Jacob's Prophecy"; an exposition of the Song of Solomon; and a popular ecclesiastical history of Scotland, dedicated in elegant Latin to his son and bishop. The latter was a contribution to the elucidation of a subject that has since been a favourite one with members of his Church. Tytler, Hill Burton, Skene, Robertson, Cosmo Innes, Grub, and other sons of the Scottish Episcopal Church have placed the country under deep obligation for their painstaking and scholarly researches into the remote and shadowy past of our people and institutions.

But what won fame for him above all things were two poetical effusions, the casual offspring of his genius, upon which he never dreamt of staking his reputation as an author—"Tullochgorum" and the "Ewie wi' the Crookit Horn." The former was written at the request of a lady for the famous reel, and the other piece was the filling up of what Beattie had sketched out in two or three lines. "Tullochgorum" was said by Burns to be "the best Scotch song Scotland ever saw," and a most interesting correspondence passed between the two poets in consequence of an interview that the Ayrshire bard happened to have while passing through Aberdeen with the son of the Linshart parson, which does credit to them both.

Skinner was a thorough Scotchman, steeped from his earliest days in Scottish poetry and sentiment (he committed "Christ's Kirk o' the Green" to memory when he was twelve years of age, and turned it into Latin in his old age), with an eye and heart for the lighter as well as the graver sides of life. He was very human; perhaps some might say that he not only carried the man with him wherever he went, but occasionally ran the risk of losing the divine in the man when the convivial spirit was upon him. His broad, kindly sympathy, ready wit, and cheerful heart made him a favourite far and wide among all creeds and classes in the district. It cannot be said that he did anything to abate the Moderatism of the eighteenth century; but his memory is cherished as that of a strong, gifted man, who served his generation with fidelity, and ever showed himself, above all things, to be one who could link himself to any part of a broad, common humanity.

After being for nearly sixty-five years in Linshart, he, in his extreme old age and frailty, removed to his son's house in Aberdeen, where he lived for only a few days.

CHAPTER XXI.

THE METHODISTS—1747.

THERE is no Protestant denomination throughout the English-speaking world that has won so many adherents as Methodism, in its various branches; but, like the Friends and some of the other smaller religious bodies, its promoters are obliged to own that Scotland has not been a congenial soil for the transplanted system. A Wesleyan writer says—" Wesleyan Methodism as an instrument for the conversion of sinners and for the establishment thereby of a Church of Christ has made less progress in Scotland than in any other part of the world in which it has had the opportunity to make known its principles and exercise its power." This is all the more remarkable when it is remembered that Wesleyanism came, not to proselytise, but to convert, not to propagate a particular form of ecclesiasticism, but to take its share in that great pioneering work that should be regarded as common to all the churches, and for the furtherance of which it is not possible for us to have too many labourers. "Therefore," said John Wesley at the outset to the agents of this new movement, "spend and be spent in this work; and go always not only to those who want you but to those who want you most. Observe, it is not your business to preach so many times, and to take care of this or that society, but to save as many souls as you can; to bring as many sinners as you can to repentance, and with all your power to build them up in that holiness without which they cannot see the Lord."

The fact that Scotland was sternly Calvinistic in its theology, that its people are severely reticent and constitutionally averse to the free expression of emotion, more especially in connection with the sacred subject of religion, and above all, that Presbyterianism is rooted in the patriotic associations and affections of successive generations—all that is enough to account for Methodism being treated very much as an exotic. The sense of nationality, strengthened by the prolonged and embittered struggles which they had long ago to make for its maintenance, tended to lead the Scottish people to look askance at anything which had the brand of the other side of the Border, and was different from their own chosen and beloved Presbyterianism.

But as a contributing force to the religious life of the north in the dreary days of Moderatism, and as being successful in rearing individuals who have rendered conspicuous service to the community, Methodism is entitled to a place in this history.

It is recorded that Dr. Memyss, who came

from England to reside in Aberdeen, formed a small society in our city about 1747, and requested assistance from Mr. Wesley. Although Edinburgh and Aberdeen are mentioned in the minutes of 1749 as distinct circuits then formed, it was not until about a year and a half afterwards that John Wesley or any of his preachers visited Scotland. It does not appear that any agent from headquarters visited the small society in Aberdeen till Mr. Christopher Hopper came in 1759. During his stay in Aberdeen, which was for nearly two years, he preached on the Castlehill every morning at five o'clock! The statement may sound incredible, but it can be verified by a reference to an authoritative record of the times. Like many other prophets who brought new light to Aberdeen, he at first got a reception other than cordial. He was stoned, and dead cats were flung at him, as he called upon men to flee from the wrath to come; but, like all men who prove themselves to be the unselfish promoters of the world's good, he eventually established himself in the respect and confidence of the community.

In 1761 Mr. Wesley paid his first visit to Aberdeen, and while here he added forty to the membership of the society, and it then numbered ninety persons. Thereafter Mr. Thomas Olivers was appointed to labour in Edinburgh, Dundee, and Aberdeen, and Mr. Wesley himself visited

Aberdeen almost every alternate year until 1790, the year before his death.

There are circumstances connected with Mr. Wesley's first visit to Aberdeen which are of general interest, and on various accounts are worthy of being recorded. That great man, besides being conspicuous for his firm resolution and high purpose, had a fine tact and urbanity, which gained for him the goodwill of those who might otherwise have been hostile. Besides, his world-wide fame made people of all classes anxious to see and hear him. He preached on Sabbath to great crowds in the "College Close," and on taking a walk to King's College on the Monday following, he found a large number of ladies assembled in the hall, with several gentlemen, one of whom said, after some hesitation—"We came last night to the College Close, but could not hear, and should be extremely obliged if you would give us a short discourse here." Thereupon Mr. Wesley preached on the words—"God was in Christ reconciling the world unto Himself." The professors and ministers showed him marked attention, and he appears to have been as favourably impressed as they were, for he afterwards said—"I have scarce seen such a set of ministers in any town of Great Britain or Ireland."

On the following day he rode over to Monymusk, where he was the guest of Sir Archibald

Grant. At six o'clock he went to the Parish Church, "which was nearly filled with such persons as he did not look for so near the Highlands. But if he was surprised at their appearance, he was much more so at their singing. Thirty or forty sang an anthem after sermon with such voices as well as judgment that he doubted whether they would have been excelled at any cathedral in England." That was in 1761! The explanation is that the laird and his lady had taken a close personal interest in the psalmody of their church.

In May, 1763, Mr. Wesley paid his second visit to Aberdeen, regarding which he thus expressed himself — "Surely never was there a more open door. The four ministers of Aberdeen, the minister of the adjoining town, and the three ministers of Old Aberdeen, hitherto seem to have no dislike, but rather to wish us 'good luck in the name of the Lord.' Most of the townspeople, as yet, seem to wish us well, so that there is no opposition of any kind. O, what spirit a preacher ought to be of, that he may be able to bear all this sunshine!" In all the entries in his journal Mr. Wesley speaks well of Aberdeen and the treatment he received from it. Doubtless his standing as a clergyman of the Church of England and his gentlemanly bearing had something to do with the marked attention that was paid to him in our academic city. That he should again and again have preached to large multitudes on a week evening, in the "College Close," on simple Gospel themes, with heart-searching application, is proof of the respect in which he was held. It must have been from what he had heard rather than what he had seen that he, after one of his visits to Bon-Accord, said of its people that they were "swift to hear, slow to speak, but not slow to wrath." Mr. Wesley paid, in all, seventeen visits to the town of Aberdeen, and an interesting relic of one of the later occasions is an old carved chair on the platform of Crown Terrace Wesleyan Church, which he brought with him from Banff, but found to be rather cumbrous in his carriage, and he parted with it when he came to this place.

The little struggling societies dotted over the north, the members of which sought to edify one another with their class meetings and other agencies, and did not forget their duty to the ungodly around them, were blessed with the visits of less celebrated but faithful preachers who were prepared to endure hardness for the Lord's sake. One of them—Thomas Rutherford—writes of his work thus—"Having spent some time in Aberdeen and regulated matters as well as I could, on January 10, 1775, I set out on the northern circuit, which was above a hundred and fifty miles round, through a waste and desolate country and bad roads. My first place was Inverurie. Being obliged to go several miles round on account of the ice on the river, I did not get there till after dark. On the Sabbath afternoon I went to Old Meldrum, where there was a loving and lively society. Tuesday I rode through a dreary country and deep roads to Huntly." In 1784 another preacher says—" I returned to labour in the country between Elgin and Aberdeen, where I found everything disagreeable to flesh and blood except the kindness of the people."

It is evident that the preachers, who were mostly from England, did not regard the circuits in Scotland as prizes; they were only opportunities for hard discipline and heroic endurance. One writes in 1772—" When I took leave of my friends in those parts (in the north of England) my inexperienced heart was pained, and I felt a degree of reluctance in going to Scotland which made me ashamed of myself. I was grieved to find an unwillingness to go to any place, suppose it had been to the ends of the earth, to preach Jesus Christ, and endeavour to bring lost sinners to Him." That same preacher, in trouble over some obstreperous people in Arbroath, wrote to headquarters, and received the following very shrewd reply:—" Do you remember what a certain author (Dr. Cotton Mather) advises ? He says—' You will meet with *unaccountables* and *incurables*. Do not too much trouble yourself with them, but lay them up in two different heaps, and let them lie!'" He then added—"I have often observed when there is a commotion among our people that time will cure what reason cannot."

There can be no doubt that the rise of the Secession movement, which took such a hold of the country a few years before Methodism had a footing in Scotland, gave less of an opportunity to the latter system, and many of the societies started at first had to be abandoned. In the early part of this century there were societies in Aberdeen, Inverurie, Old Meldrum, Peterhead, Hatton of Fintray, Newburgh, Stonehaven, Fordy, Cothal Mills, and Cove. Of these, the Aberdeen, Peterhead, and Inverurie societies alone remain. But the others did not exist in vain. They were temporary evangelistic stations, the fruit of which remains unto this day. They contributed an element of fervour to the pulpit of the north. A Presbyterian baillie in Inverurie was accustomed to say—"I like to hear the Methodists; they harrow me up, man—they harrow me up."

Mere numbers are no criterion of the worth and work of a religious body. There must have been some element of power in the Methodists of Aberdeen before Thomas Rutherford could write of them as he did in 1775—" I took leave of the society there, with difficulty tearing myself away from the affectionate people, who with their love and tears, were ready to break my heart." The Methodists of the north can show a fair proportion of picked men, whom they have trained and to a large extent made what they are. The little society in Inverurie has given two Provosts to the town, and others noted for their public spirit and usefulness. One of the baillies carried the phraseology of the Methodist chapel with him to the bench, and was accustomed to put his question to the accused—" Well, how say you to that, brother? Are you guilty or not guilty ?"

The Aberdeen Society held its first meeting in Barnett's Close (leading from the Guestrow to Flour Mill Brae); then in a house on the north side of Queen Street, and thereafter in Lodge Walk. In 1764 the Society acquired a piece of ground near the north-east end of Queen Street, and upon it erected an octagonal chapel, the form of building preferred by Mr. Wesley. In 1818 Longacre Chapel, which was then the bishop's, and known as St. Andrew's Episcopal Chapel, was purchased, the deed providing that the building was not to be called St. Andrew's, which name was retained by the Episcopalians for their new place of worship in King Street. In 1873 the present chapel in Crown Terrace was erected.

It may almost appear from the different religious sects which in the course of years came into existence as if the Church of modern times in this land were only so many detached fragments. The reproach is brought against the Protestant Church that it is a thing of sections, that it lacks the unity which existed in the Church previous to the Reformation. But it would not be difficult to prove that much of the boasted unity is shallow and mechanical, and that all the principal divisions which we now see in the Protestant Church existed in the Roman Church in germinal if not in matured and definite form. Were Jansenist and Jesuit not as different from each other as Calvinist and Arminian? Could fervid High Churchman and semi-rationalistic Broad Churchman be further apart than were Bernard and Abelard? If we have our Quakers, were there not inside as well as outside the Church in ancient days the Quietists and Mystics? Did not also the preaching friars answer to our brethren the Methodists? Moreover, there may be deeper spiritual unity, though perhaps we are only now beginning to recognise it, pervading all those Protestant religious bodies with their different administrations and distinctive tenets than what existed in the huge iron-bound hierarchical system which was so shaken three centuries ago.

CHAPTER XXII.

GEORGE COWIE OF HUNTLY—1749-1806.

ROWLAND HILL, when travelling in the north of Scotland, wrote thus in his journal:—" Wednesday, July 3rd, 1799.—Travelled through a dreary country till we came to Greystone (in Culsalmond). Here I met with one whose character I had before known by report. As soon as I conversed with him he stole into my heart. Shall I tell his name? Shall I mention his denomination? George Cowie, the Anti-Burgher minister of Huntly." In another part of the journal he says:—" Cowie and his elders are men to be wondered at." There is no exaggeration in such praise. No name stands higher in the Strathbogie district than that of George Cowie. There is much in the memories of the people besides what is recorded on his tombstone in the churchyard of Dumbennan to preserve his remarkable career from oblivion. He was an Aberdeenshire Great-Heart, well called the "Whitefield of the North."

Such a man was needed in Strathbogie, for it proved itself for generations to be one of the most stubborn districts of the north, and ill-affected to Gospel truth. In 1650 the verdict of the Synod of Moray respecting Kinnoir and Dumbennan was that—" The Gospel had never been in power in these congregations. They are nurseries of gross idolatry, heresy, and superstition." In 1745 the official record of the Presbytery of Strathbogie is—" Kinnoir and Dumbennan are distinguished above all others for malignancy and fomenters of our troubles."

George Cowie was born in the parish of Ordiquhill, near Banff, in 1749. Sent to the Grammar School at the age of seven, he was a successful competitor for a bursary at Marischal College when not more than twelve. Appointed schoolmaster of Rothiemay when he was sixteen, brought that same year under deep conviction of sin and guided to Gospel light and peace by the ministry of the Anti-Burghers, with whom he became united, and in consequence was ejected from his school in the Establishment when he was seventeen—such is an epitome of the early life of George Cowie. He was persuaded to become a student of divinity in the theological seminary of the Church to which he had attached himself. In the year 1769, when he was only twenty years of age, he was sent from it to labour in Huntly, where a few praying people were banded together and had made request for a preacher.

Preachers were scarce in those days, and the little "praying societies" throughout the north were eager to have the services of men, whose preaching somewhat resembled in simplicity and warmth of earnestness, what they were accustomed to find in the Acts of the Apostles and the Epistles of the New Testament, which were their daily study; so he had to labour in Grange, Keith, and Cabrach, with Huntly as a centre. A small company had been gathered at the Cabrach eight years before, which was greatly augmented by his ministrations. The congregations at Keith and Grange appear to have been due almost entirely to his labours. At a somewhat later period a cause was established by him in Culsalmond. He had thus the superintendence of five congregations for several years. It does not surprise us that he died before he had reached the close of his sixth decade! When he preached in Huntly, many came to the central church from each of those places, and returned to their homes before the Sabbath day was done. It was his practice in the early days of his ministry, as he himself described it, to take his staff in hand, bread and cheese in his pocket, and when he was weary to sit down and eat his frugal fare, drink of the bubbling spring or " of the brook that runneth by the way," and thus refreshed resume his journey. Often did he arrive at his destination much fatigued, but greatly cheered and revived by finding large numbers eager to hear the Word. So abundant were his labours, and so blessed of God, that each of those congregations became strong enough to support a minister of its own.

But it was in the town of Huntly that the deepest imprint was made by Mr. Cowie's undaunted faithfulness and consuming earnestness. He, as a spiritual husbandman, found the district to be virgin soil, and largely overgrown with weeds and thorns. When he came it was the practice of the lads of the town to play at shinty in the Castle grounds on Sabbath when the "kirk scaled." Grieved and burdened, he went amongst them, and, as the result of persistent pleading and praying, he at last succeeded in inducing them to abandon such desecration of the Lord's day.

But he had a stiff and, at first, almost singlehanded battle to fight. Unaccustomed to such an outspoken and fervid preacher of righteousness, some of the inhabitants of Huntly were disposed to resent his presence amongst them as an intrusion. The baser sort lay in wait at the street corners on the dark evenings and pelted him with rotten eggs as he passed by. It is related that on one occasion when he was preaching, the service was interrupted, and the congregation thrown into excitement, in the following manner. Before a place of worship was built for him, he preached in a house in the "Old Road," then called the "High Street;" it was open from end to end, and with the rafters visible. Certain garden vegetables belonging to the owner were tied two and two together, thrown over the cross beams, and left there till needed. Some young men of loose character, instigated, it is said, by older persons, got up one night on the rafters and commenced pelting both minister and people with the onions. The confusion and uproar in the crowded house caused by such extraordinary behaviour can well be imagined. But Mr. Cowie was determined not to be put down by such sons of Belial. The tide of popular feeling in the town was at the turning, and his righteous boldness converted what might have been an ebb into a flow. He faced the fellows, to whom, though preacher, he had to look up, and told them he would preach though they might be devils in human shape. They were overawed and silenced, and for the rest of the evening sat still in their uncomfortable position, glad, doubtless, for various reasons, when the service was brought to a close.

It was Mr. Cowie's hard fate not only to have to fight with practical heathenism in the world, but also with bigotry in the Church. He was a man before his time, and had far larger ideas than most of his brethren. The spiritual intensity and Puritanical strictness of the Anti-Burghers drew him to them; but their narrowness and intolerance repelled him. He did not hesitate freely to express his approbation of the preaching of Whitefield and of the revival at Cambuslang; his disapprobation, also, of the separation of the Burghers and Anti-Burghers, which independence and frankness led to his ordination being delayed. When the feeling was abroad in the land among God's people that the obligation was laid upon them to do something in execution of the Master's commission to go and preach the Gospel to every creature, Mr. Cowie and his people proceeded to take practical action, and on 10th March, 1796, a local missionary society was formed. Within a year of that date, Mr. Cowie succeeded in collecting in the Huntly and neighbouring congregations no less a sum than one hundred pounds, which was sent to the London Missionary Society, and many more precious gifts came in due course—men who offered themselves to the service and distinguished themselves in it. Shortly after that, one of the earliest, if not the first, Sabbath school in the north was established in connection with Mr. Cowie's church; and far and wide such schools were planted, which did their work so well that in many of the places where the good seed was sown for years there are now thriving Christian congregations, mostly belonging to the Free Church.

Mr. Cowie was bursting one after another of the swaddling bands of his sectarian connection.

When James Haldane, along with Messrs. Aikman and Rate, visited Huntly in October, 1797, Mr. Cowie and his elders gave him the use of their chapel. Unable to go against what he believed to be a work of God, and yet not willing to give unnecessary offence to the Anti-Burghers, who forbade their ministers from identifying themselves with such "irregular" services, he in the morning sat at the open window of the manse, which was close by the place of meeting, and heard all that was said. He was so delighted with the preaching of James Haldane, and so abundantly satisfied now that the work of the "Missionars" was of God, that in the evening he could not restrain himself from throwing prudential scruples to the winds and going boldly into the chapel when the hour for the evening meeting came round. That act sealed his ecclesiastical fate.

Mr. Cowie and his session were summoned before the Presbytery for their alleged irregularities, and eventually their case came before the Synod in Edinburgh, which "agreed unanimously in declaring that, as lay preaching has no warrant in the Word of God, and as the Synod has always considered it a duty to testify against promiscuous communion, no person under the inspection of the Synod can consistently with their principles attend upon or give countenance to public preaching by any who are not of our communion; and if any do so, they ought to be dealt with by the judicatories of the Church, to bring them to a sense of their offensive conduct." He and his session were thereafter deposed, and public intimation was made of the same by the minister of Clola on 18th May, 1800.

On that same day Mr. Cowie preached on the words—"If God be for us, who can be against us?" Valiant, heaven-enthralled, clear-sighted, because large-hearted, Cowie! he is worthy to take his place among the Confessors of old, who are confined to no age or clime, but have this as their distinction—that the Creator is more to them than the creature. His refusal to submit to men who objected to Sabbath schools and missions and lay preaching gave an immense impetus to his usefulness. All his people clave to him with the exception of four or five, and many came to him from other parts who disapproved of the high-handed proceedings of the Synod.

Mr. Cowie's congregation gradually, but slowly, came to be recognised as one of the newly-formed Independent Churches, though in every other respect except its independency it remained exactly the same during his lifetime as it was before. He was one of those men who make things denominational a mere platform on which to stand while doing God's work.

If the platform should give way, or become too narrow for the larger ideas which had entered his heart, he was ready to leave it for another, as he could never bear to sacrifice the end for the sake of the means. The Church must be true to its essential principles and dominant objects, whatever comes of the iron bands of a cramped ecclesiasticism.

He died in 1806. He passed away when he was only fifty-seven years of age, as his herculean labours were enough to break down prematurely the strongest constitution. But the cause he built up remained.

Mr. Cowie trained his people not only to hear, but to serve; not only to receive, but to give. His was a congregation of workers. Not content with getting their own portion in the house of God, they went from it singly or in little bands to the various schools and stations to break the bread of life. A person still alive writes of Cowie's men:—"Since I came to Huntly an old man died who for thirty-five years travelled, summer and winter, seven miles every Sabbath day to the braes of Gartly to teach a Sabbath school." He adds:—"The sight of that old cobbler plodding along, wet day and dry day, year after year, to his Master's work was a glorious object lesson."

CHAPTER XXIII.

THE INDEPENDENTS—1797.

SCOTTISH Independency is not the extension of an ecclesiastical system that had its origin in England, into the land which since the Reformation has been almost exclusively occupied by Presbyterianism. It was not imported; it sprang from forces operating within our own borders. While that particular form of Church polity is substantially the same as, if not identical with, the Independency of Owen, Cromwell and Milton, yet it cannot claim to be a direct offshoot from that body, which took such a prominent part in a brilliant period of English history, and has, by its renowned names and splendid achievements, shed unfading lustre upon Independency wherever it is known.

Scottish Independency, like most things that take root among the sturdy people who inhabit this part of the isle, is indigenous, or, rather, one of the incidents of a general religious movement at the close of the eighteenth century, which can be so described. It is scarcely conceivable that it could have been otherwise. The Scots have ever respected and jealously guarded the idea of nationality, and in former days, more than now, were disposed to look askance at any ecclesiastical importation that came from England, which was always willing to cast its shadow upon its smaller neighbour. The desperate conflicts which Scotland had to wage for centuries with England had so driven and burned the passionate longing into the hearts of the people for the maintenance of nationality, which expressed itself in the whole environment of life, that no polity or Church which had a foreign aspect had a chance of gaining a footing a hundred years ago. There was a keen, almost morbid and ludicrous sensitiveness with regard to intrusion or meddlesomeness of any kind, especially from the South. Every institution had to be as distinctive and as much their own in Caledonia as the thistle and the heather. The imprint of the genius, or at least the seal of the approval of Scotland, was necessary as a passport to favour. Presbyterianism was that which was taken three centuries ago as a substitute for the Popery that was rejected, and the people who, in the days of Queen Mary, took, and ever since have more or less kept, their affairs in their own hands with characteristic tenacity and fervour, clung to the Church system of John Knox, which was the child and companion of their emancipation from priestly thraldom. Other Churches might be good enough for other countries, but they as a nation had made their choice, and they resented the invasion of competing sects. What hindered the progress of Episcopacy in our land as much, perhaps, as anything else, was the fact that it was established in England, and now and again ruthlessly but impotently thrust upon Scotland, and within the memory of many, if not up to the present day in rural parts, every church of that persuasion was called the "English chapel."

By what vital and assimilative process, then, did Independency become one of the factors in the religious life of this part of Great Britain? As an incidental, almost accidental, product of a period of quickened religious life. No restless sectary said "Go to, let us rear a new denomination"; no student of ecclesiastical history, struck with the supposed superiority of this mode of Church life as expounded in books or exemplified with such intellectual and moral grandeur by the Puritans of England, brought it here as a zealous propagandist. It came unlooked for when the minds of those who became identified with it were bent upon the possession of what was of far greater importance.

There were, indeed, straggling Independents —"Brownists"—from the time of the Commonwealth, before what is now known as Scottish Independency began its course. One Ferrendale came to Aberdeen in 1642 who was accused of "Brownism." Local records tell us that he was "trapped" holding a "nocturnal meeting," *i.e.*, an evening meeting for Christian fellowship and prayer, and put in jail. Spalding says that in the Provincial Assembly at Aberdeen in 1642 there was "great business about Brownism, lately crept into Aberdeen and other parts." Farther on, John Glass, minister of the parish of Tealing, near Dundee, was, in 1730, deposed by the General Assembly of the Church of Scotland in consequence of views which he had adopted and published concerning the nature of the Kingdom and Church of Christ, his personal worth being acknowledged by his most strenuous opponents. He and his followers, including Robert Sandeman, who has by his name almost eclipsed his master, were known as Independents but they soon became a vanishing quantity.

What, however, is known as Scottish Independency, which has been about a hundred years in the country, is the outcome of a revival of religion associated notably with the names of Robert and James Haldane, regarding whom Dr. Charteris, Professor of Biblical Criticism in the University of Edinburgh, thus writes:—" Men of zeal, fortitude, and faith, they did more to bring Scotland into living sympathy with missions in heathendom, and with the reviving faith in the Churches of the Reformation, than any Court of any Church in the beginning of this century."

Robert and James Haldane, born respectively in 1764 and 1768, were members of an old

Scottish family which belonged to Perthshire. In education, tastes, and surroundings, they were in their early days about as far removed from what they afterwards became as it was possible for them to be. They had high birth, a wide, aristocratic connection, ample means, and all that the world can bestow upon those who are considered to be the darlings of fortune. Nothing could have more surprised them when they were men of the world and spirited officers of His Majesty's navy than to be told that they would yet find their vocation and glory in street preaching and tract distribution and as founders of Congregational and Baptist Churches.

Brought under the power of New Testament truth, they consecrated themselves and their substance to their Divine Master. There are few things in the history of our land nobler than the story of Robert Haldane selling the romantically-situated estate of Airthrey, near Stirling, that the £70,000 thus liberated might be used for the support of evangelists, the erection of chapels, and the distribution of religious books. There is much that is picturesque in the scenery of Airthrey, but there is not anything so lovely in its rocky cliffs and grassy lawns and charming stretch of water as the spirit of the man who was constrained to turn his back upon it all for the sake of Christ and his fellow-countrymen. Few spots upon earth have associations that, to the thoughtful mind, bring heaven nearer. In the neighbouring castle of Stirling, where the Stuart sovereigns lived, we have the splendour of royalty in the memories which cluster around its weather-worn walls; in the field of Bannockburn, not many miles away, we have suggested to the mind the splendour of patriotism; but in Airthrey the man who has an eye for the finer things of life cannot think of what was renounced a hundred years ago without being impressed with the exceeding splendour of experimental Christianity.

"Christianity," said Robert Haldane, "is everything or nothing. If it be true it warrants and commands every sacrifice to promote its influence." Hindered by the East India Company from carrying out his first intention after conversion, which was to go with a large company as a Christian herald to India, he turned his attention to the spiritual needs of his native land, and made it the scene of his life-long labours.

The plan of operations adopted was to secure the co-operation of persons like-minded with themselves, Robert Haldane backing up with pecuniary assistance all pioneering efforts for the spiritual awakening of the people. James Haldane, who was the better speaker of the two, would set out in a carriage or on horseback, having John Campbell or some other friend of kindred spirit with him, and always in addition an abundant supply of tracts. When they reached a town the drummer or bellman was sent round announcing a religious meeting. One or both of them would speak at the Market Cross, the churchyard, or some other place of concourse; tracts were distributed, and an exhortation given to the persons assembled to cleave unto God. James Haldane was young and handsome, of commanding presence and powerful voice, and the fact that he had the bearing of a gentleman dressed according to the fashion of the time, with his powdered hair tied behind, and had been a captain in His Majesty's Navy, gave a piquancy to his street preaching. He was opposed, scoffed at, persecuted, especially by those of his own station, but this sailor-missionary had acquired the power of weathering storms of various kinds. Here is the account that Mr. J. Haldane gives of his first appearance in Aberdeen in the summer of 1797:—

"Intending to preach out-of-doors on the Lord's Day evening, I was told that the College Close would be an excellent place. So the town drummer was sent round to give notice. On Sunday morning, before breakfast, I received a message from one of the Magistrates, who was also a professor, that he wished to see me. On presenting myself, he inquired how I came to intimate preaching in a place which was not public. I replied that I had been informed that there would be no objection in any quarter. 'Who told you so?' I replied that I was told it or believed it, but would not say by whom [rumour said it was Dr. Kidd]. He pressed the matter very much, but saw I was firm. I had been so told by one highly respectable, who spoke in good faith, but whom I would not implicate. But I said, 'Since it appears that I was misinformed, I have no wish to persist, and I would preach elsewhere.' 'No,' said the Baillie, 'that will be worse; it will occasion a riot, and our windows will be broken.' 'Then,' said I, 'as you wish it, I will preach,' and accordingly I did so, to a very great congregation."

The Haldanes and their coadjutors had no thought of setting up a new denomination in Scotland. Their one absorbing desire was the dissemination of Scriptural truth that their fellow-countrymen might become alive unto God. They were no more ecclesiastics than John Wesley and his brother Charles when they began their Gospel work in England sixty years before. Their desire at first was to remain in the Established Church if the needful conditions for carrying on their converting work were not withheld. They felt they were called to a mission of awakening—and nothing on earth was to be allowed to stand in the way of its execution—by the use of open-air preaching, tract distribution, Sabbath schools, and other agencies which were deemed to be suitable points of contact between the truth of God and the need of man. And all the reliable records of the period bear witness to the fact that the need was great.

The Church of Scotland, however, did not appreciate the help they were receiving from the Haldanes, accompanied by Rowland Hill and others, as the following testifies :—

"On the 28th May, 1799, an overture was presented from the Synod of Aberdeen and that of Angus and Mearns respecting vagrant teachers and Sunday schools, irreligion, and anarchy. The Assembly unanimously agreed to the overtures, and prohibited all persons from preaching in any place under their jurisdiction who were not licensed as above; and also those who are from England or any other place, and who have not been educated and licensed in Scotland—and resolved that a pastoral admonition be addressed by the Assembly to all the people under their charge."

As is always the case, ecclesiastical repression of that sort only fanned the flame instead of extinguishing it. The Word of God was sounded abroad, and had much effect in spite of the ban which the Moderates of the day had put upon its "vagrant" agents.

Congregationalism, with its simplicity and freedom, seemed to the Haldanes and those associated with them to consort with their practical aims and with the example of the primitive Church which they accepted as a model; but in planting Churches of that order throughout Scotland the Haldanes, Ewing, Aikman, and others who were banded with them, did not consider so much where the conditions of a thriving ecclesiastical interest would be found as where the spiritual need was most pressing. That accounts for Aberdeenshire having a larger number of Congregational Churches than any other rural district in Scotland. But, as illustrating the sturdy individuality of the folk of our county, from the very beginning they differed from the Independents of other parts of the land (having come to some extent under the influence of English Congregationalism) in some of their usages, as, for example, their preference for monthly Communion, instead of weekly which the Haldanes favoured.

The parent church of the north was George Street ("the Loch Kirk") now known as Belmont Street, whose ministers—Dr. Philip, Alexander Thomson, and David Arthur—are remembered with respect in Aberdeen.

The new development of religious life in our city identified with Congregationalism was directly due to local instrumentality. A few good men, having George Moir, a hosier, and Alexander Innes, a dyer, as leaders, met together privately for prayer and spiritual edification. Eventually, under the direction of Dr. Bogue, of Gosport, on 15th September, 1797, they formed themselves into a church. Nine persons were thus banded together, and they drew out a most excellent statement of the principles they adhered to, each one affixing his signature to the same. Their first place of worship was opened by Dr. Bennet, of London, on the 2nd September, 1798. The members were full of missionary fervour, and had preaching stations in and around Aberdeen, the little church at Blackhills, now called Westhills, being part of the fruit of that period of abounding evangelistic zeal. Shortly after, churches sprung up in Inverurie and other parts of the county, in connection with which faithful men laboured not only as pastors, but as itinerating evangelists. They preached often during the week as well as on Sabbath, taught schools and classes, and instituted libraries and centres for the distribution of religious tracts. Among the Independents in this part of the country who, in addition to those already named, have attained to eminence, mention must be made of Joseph Morrison, of Millseat, and John Murker, of Banff. There are now, including the two Evangelical Union congregations, seven churches of the Independent polity in Aberdeen.

The Baptists, who are Independents, but have as their distinctive denominational basis a difference of belief as to the proper subjects and mode of baptism, came to have a footing in this part early in the present century. In 1803, five persons who held Baptist principles met together privately for fellowship: in 1809 the celebrated Andrew Fuller and Dr. Stuart, of Edinburgh, visited Aberdeen and advised the brethren to constitute themselves into a Church, which they did in the following year—that being the beginning of what was afterwards called "Silver Street Church."

In 1821 John Gilmore, who had just finished his studies, came to Aberdeen, and after preaching in St. George's Lodge with great fervour and practical effect, gathered together a number of worthy persons who formed themselves into another Baptist congregation, now known as Crown Terrace Church. There are now four Baptist congregations in Aberdeen.

Some of the most eminent citizens of Aberdeen have been connected with this body, such as M'Allan, M'Combie (of the *Free Press*), Macdonald, Stewart of Banchory, and the revered Dr. Anderson, of the Gymnasium.

CHAPTER XXIV.

DR. KIDD—1793-1834.*

DR. MASSON, a native of Aberdeen, in one of a series of articles which he wrote in the early numbers of *Macmillan's Magazine*, of which he was then editor, on "Dead Men Whom I Have Known," delivers a remarkable testimony regarding the effect of Dr. Kidd's presence and labours in furthering the cause of Evangelicalism in our city. He says—"Ere long the taste for his style of preaching spread beyond his own congregation, till the whole city became in the main Evangelical in its notions of doctrine, and the other pulpits in it were filled with men supplying similar doctrine after their various native fashion, and only in the country round did Moderatism still prevail, though even there largely modified. All this was not owing to Kidd, for the *Zeit-geist* was at work, but much of it was owing to him. He was a flame at which many lit their candles."

There can be no doubt that in the early part of this century Dr. Kidd was one of the great

* These dates indicate the duration of Dr. Kidd's ministry in Aberdeen.

popular and shaping religious forces of this city. It does not lie within the scope of our present purpose to attempt even an outline of the life of this remarkable man, and that is rendered all the more unnecessary as his character and romantic career are depicted with minuteness in the volume that was published in Aberdeen two or three years ago, and to which we are indebted for all that is here given.*

An Irishman, a "self-made man," educated in Ireland, the United States, Edinburgh, and Aberdeen, Professor of Hebrew in Marischal College, and minister of Gilcomston Chapel of Ease, by the sheer force of personality and unflinching fidelity to God's truth, Dr. Kidd did more than all other men in the city combined, to prepare for the spiritual and ecclesiastical developments which took place after his death. This gallery of portraits would be incomplete without a chapter on him. Let us therefore keep company with him for a single Sabbath morning in Gilcomston Chapel that we may discover if possible the secret of his power.

Gilcomston Chapel, which was then in what was a suburb of Aberdeen, was a large, square-built, plain building, with galleries on both sides, the pulpit at one end, and a gallery at the other, with a "cock loft" above it to accommodate the increasing congregation attracted by Dr. Kidd's

* "Dr. Kidd of Aberdeen," 1892.

powerful preaching. The exterior was more than severely simple; it was bald and barn-like. The interior made no pretension to elegance of any kind; the only thing visible which hard, matter-of-fact utility did not demand, was the model of a ship hung in front of the end gallery, a symbol of the consequence of the seafaring calling to the population of that period, that was to be seen also in some of the other places of worship in the city.

There being no vestry attached to the chapel, the Doctor, as was his wont, made a virtue of a necessity, and, walking from his house attired for his ministerial duty half an hour or so before worship began, made the pulpit his waiting place. There he sat primed and ready like a man who was longing for the opportunity in which he gloried as a preacher of Christ's everlasting gospel. He had been engaged in work already in the early part of the Sabbath, which only whetted his appetite for more. Besides meditating and praying from an early hour in his study, he had opened a class and addressed one or two of his Sabbath schools, and so it had been proved beyond doubt that the pump was not "off the fang."

As the Doctor sat there on his lofty pedestal surveying the assembling multitude, he, with his observant eye and wonderful faculty of recognising individuals, was able to keep up acquaintance with his members and their families. The faces of most of those before him indicated the grave purpose and alertness of persons who had come to do business and to get something. They had not the dull, sleepy air, not unknown in parish churches of the time, of churchgoers who were merely conforming to decent custom, and meritoriously assisting at a formal celebration. No doubt they were a mixed multitude, with not a few black sheep amongst them; but, taking them as a whole, they were a douce, earnest-minded, hard-headed people, the progenitors of a great deal of the robust Evangelicalism of the town.

On his yearly Communion Sabbath in July the immense congregation must have presented an imposing spectacle. People came then from other congregations in town and country in large numbers, and the place was packed with human beings, many of whose faces revealed that their spirits were touched with the exaltation and solemnity of the occasion. No wonder the Doctor, when standing up in the pulpit to begin the service, and looking out upon this vast sea of faces, should have been constrained to remark, as he once did—"This is a day for a death-bed!"

The scene was not without its touches of picturesqueness and human interest, even to the ordinary observer who laid no claim to intense spiritual sympathy. The Communion Sabbath was the great day of the year for putting on one's finest and newest clothes. It is a true instinct which prompts one to put on "his best" when appearing before God in His public sanctuary. So on that day the young women had on light dresses and the men "drill" trousers. With a profusion of white "mutches" and a sprinkling of red-coloured cloaks among the elderly dames, there must have been something to please the eye even of those who were not "on the mount," and saw nothing that lay beyond the outward and earthly aspect of the scene.

As the people were taking their places in the pews under the Doctor's eye, occasionally little incidents occurred which told their own tale of human vanity and selfishness, and revealed the fact that Gilcomston Chapel had not yet fulfilled its task in seeking to bring Aberdeen men and women to perfection. One day, as will happen sometimes even yet in the House of God, strangers who wanted to go into a certain pew where there was abundance of room, met with a passive resistance on the part of those sitting at the end of it, and as passing people in the narrow space between seat and bookboard was next to impossible, they could only stand and look and wonder at the inhospitality of the professed worshippers of God. Roused to anger by the incivility shown to visitors, the Doctor, who took in the whole situation at a glance, thundered out—" Sit up, proud flesh, and let the people have a seat as long as there is one to give them." So great was the demand for sittings that there were folding seats in the passages, which were usually filled. Old men and women might be seen sitting on the pulpit stairs, and on stools on any empty space not too far from the minister.

Having a keen appreciation of the value of time, punctuality was a virtue which Dr. Kidd practised with conspicuous constancy. But his was an Irish kind of punctuality, for, as Dr. Bain tells us, he regularly rose to begin the service five minutes before the hour. The first exercise was a brief exposition of the psalm that was to be sung. In that way he helped the people to give reality and significance to the praise, and, when the time came for it, they were better able to sing "with the understanding." An old woman of those days, but belonging to another parish, once said, "I thocht the psalms were jist to gie the minister a breath." They knew better than that in Gilcomston. He took up the psalms in consecutive order, giving so many stanzas each Sabbath.

In like manner, when he announced the passage of Scripture to be read, the Doctor proceeded to give a brief analysis of its contents, and a summary of the lessons taught. His great aim was to make every part of the service real and vital to all who were before him. He was at pains to enlist their intelligence and sympathy, and to shut dull apathy and dreary formalism outside the gates of Gilcomston. Having stated the general scope of the chapter, he proceeded to read it with that true and powerful elocution which does not draw attention to itself, but to the matter in hand. His sonorous voice was well modulated, and the rich Irish accent, instead of detracting from the effect, must, to Aberdeen ears, have lent the charm of piquancy to his delivery. Professor Masson says—" His slow and impressive reading of the psalms was, I remember, a never-failing source of admiration and delight to the Aberdonians. He was a real Chrysostom."

Then came the prayer, in which the man, in the depth and tenderness of his nature, stood revealed. Prayer was to him the very soul and breath of religion. He knew the value of it for himself, and he pressed its importance upon his people, sometimes in the pulpit taking up a psalm, and, there and then, like a father dealing with his children, showing them by actual experiment how it could be turned into prayer. Dr. Bain and others, who attended Gilcomston in their youth, testify to the unique power, the freshness and seraphic fervour of the man in prayer. Dr. Bain says—" The first occasion when I resumed attending the church I was taken all of a heap with listening to his first prayer; the easy flow of language, the choiceness of his topics, and the brevity of the whole, came upon me like a new revelation." Dr. Bain also tells us that it was a common habit with the Doctor, in his prayer, to "address the three persons in the Godhead in consecutive order, adapting the petitions to the specific personality of each," and he adds, "I never heard this done by any other preacher." One secret of Dr. Kidd's extraordinary power in prayer was that he did not trust entirely to the mood of the moment for the subject matter of his petitions. Besides constantly breathing the atmosphere of prayer, he secured coherency, freshness, and variety in those all-important exercises of the Church by prolonged premeditation and careful selection of topics.

The sermon was also the outcome of well-digested knowledge and intense thought, though delivered extemporaneously. His method was exposition, having from beginning to end a practical edge. "He was mighty in the Scriptures." Generally, though not invariably, he took for exposition the historical books of the Old Testament in the forenoon, the Gospels in the afternoon, and the Epistles in the evening. In the course of his Gilcomston pastorate he, in his expository discourses, went over the whole

Bible twice, and had begun the third series when he died. An old man, whose character in youth was formed under the preaching of Dr. Kidd, in recounting the scenes of Gilcomston, used to wind up his remarks by saying—alluding to the fervour of the ministrations, as well as to the crowded congregations—" Eh, sir, it was a het hoose."

The Sabbath spent in Gilcomston was an educational as well as a religious force to the great body of the people of that generation in Aberdeen. Many young men, some of whom have won distinction in their chosen spheres of activity, had their mental powers awakened by grappling with the doctrine of the Gilcomston pulpit, and reproducing for the benefit of others the arguments and illustrations with which it was supported. For the Doctor, though he was ever impelled by a consuming earnestness, allowed himself considerable latitude in the topics he chose and the manner in which he treated them. The millennium, the evils of Popery, and the glories of prophecy might be sprung upon his people at any time. Things civil, political, and local, the resources of literature, and the examples of history, as well as the general information which could be gathered from all parts of the world, were woven into the texture of his Sabbath discourses. It would be a stretch of fancy for even the most enthusiastic Kiddite to lay it all to the credit of the

Gilcomston pastor, but it is certainly, to say the least of it, a most remarkable coincidence that so many youths belonging to the district, and who were brought more or less under the influence of its chief luminary, though not all belonging to his congregation, should have risen to place and fame. Phillip, the painter; Dr. Bain, the logician and metaphysician; Dr. John Hill Burton, the historian; Dr. Masson, professor of English literature; and Dr. Walter Smith, the minister-poet, occur among many names that might be mentioned in this connection. We know that his pastoral oversight did win the gratitude of "Rabbi" Duncan, whose genius, though erratic, and prodigious learning have brought honour to the city of his birth.

Many others, too, whose distinction is known only to the records of heaven, were inwardly nourished by the weekly "feast of fat things" provided for them, and had their lives redeemed from sordid tedium by the inspiring motives and splendid visions exhibited to their view. How could they do other than throng Gilcomston Chapel? If it had no loveliness in itself, yet within its walls the beauty of holiness was revealed to their souls, and aspiration was kindled within them as they were made to feel that the higher life by which they became sharers of the divine was a possible possession to craftsman and peasant, to the poor and illiterate, and even to the vicious and abandoned. To many who, during the week, were tied from early morn till late at night to the loom and the lapstone, and to whose minds the Gilcomston sermons introduced an ideal element, by providing material for thought and discussion, which lifted them above their monotonous and toilsome drudgery, but did not unfit them for their duty —to many such the lines of Herbert were indeed true—

"The week were dark but for thy light;
Thy torch doth show the way."

Gilcomston Chapel was a kind of university for the multitude, the place where ideas were propagated, where life was placed in its proper perspective, where truth and righteousness were shown to be more than bread, and where eternal and immutable principle was held up against the the most specious and prosperous expediency. Above all, sitting in that chapel, men were made to feel that it was indeed the house of God; for if they went to it in a right spirit what was best in them rose to the surface, what was mean and earthly was rebuked; and, heaven becoming an experimental reality, they, on leaving the place for their homes, felt constrained to try again, with the help of Him of whom they had heard, to live according to the "pattern shown to them on the mount."

CHAPTER XXV.

PATRICK ROBERTSON OF CRAIGDAM—1777-1867.

THE spot in Aberdeenshire called Craigdam is in the parish of Tarves and district of Buchan, about eighteen miles north-east of the city of Aberdeen. It derives its distinction from the fact that the first Secession Church of the north was planted there; and for more than a century and a half it has preserved the continuity of its character as a rallying-point for spiritually-minded men and women, and the centre of a widely-diffused evangelical influence.

It is a striking tribute to the power of Christian Voluntaryism that church and manse should have stood there all those years, "a city set upon a hill," among the green fields, miles away from any town or village. No Act of Parliament or legal statute of any kind has given security of tenure to this institution; it is to be traced to nothing but the in-working of faith in those who used it. Also, the succession of richly-endowed and faithful ministers that have stood in its pulpit has contributed greatly to the continuance of its vitality.

The first pastor of Craigdam—Rev. William Brown, ordained in 1752—was enough to give character to any church. The father of Provost

Brown, the bookseller, the grandfather of the venerable Principal Brown, of the Free Church College, Aberdeen, and the ministerial founder of the Secession Church in the north, he has many claims to a place in our local annals. His worldly prospects were not bright when he accepted the call to Craigdam, as at the outset of his ministry the people did not undertake to give him more than fifteen pounds of an annual income! He was called the "rinnin' minister," as he was fleet of foot, and seemed ever in haste, as having something important on hand; and, considering the demands that were made upon his time and energy at the beginning of the Secession movement in the needy north, he could not well afford to walk at a leisurely pace. He did not spare himself in breaking up the fallow ground, putting heart and soul as well as earnest study into his work; so that his name is still fragrant in many parts far beyond Craigdam. It was a common saying among the sermon-loving peasantry of the north that Mr. Cowie of Huntly upon "black natur'" and Mr. Brown of Craigdam on the love of Christ—"an' they canna be dung," *i.e.*, excelled.

His grandson, Principal Brown, remembers an old man describing a service conducted by the first minister of Craigdam at Knock, near Portsoy. One thing in the sermon which came to him and was indelibly imprinted upon his memory was the vivid and fervid way in which the preacher used the historical incident of Simeon holding the child Jesus in his arms:—"There did not appear to be much in the old man's arms, and yet the salvation of the world was dependent upon what was there—all was wrapt up in that Jesus held by Simeon." Then, holding out his own arms as if embracing that which Simeon esteemed to be so precious, Mr. Brown, with tearful urgency of voice cried to the people assembled —"Have you, my freens, taken a grip o' Jesus?" He died in 1801, in the seventy-third year of his age and the forty-ninth of his ministry, and was buried in the family vault of the Kinmundy family (he was married to a daughter of that house) in the church of Old Deer.

Mr. Brown was succeeded by Patrick Robertson, who was born in Perth, July 16th, 1777. His family was closely connected with the Secession Church, his father having been an elder in one of the congregations in that city. Patrick distinguished himself as a scholar in the Perth Grammar School, and, having studied in Edinburgh University under Dugald Stewart, Playfair, and other men whose names were an inspiration to youth, he, at the age of twenty-one, had to decide what his future profession was to be. He was offered a situation as tutor in a family of great influence on condition that he ceased to be a Dissenter, and the prospect of a presentation to a parish was held out as an inducement. Attachment to principle overcame the temptation to seek worldly advantage, and in 1798 he entered the Anti-Burgher Divinity Hall in Whitburn, where he had as fellow-students, James Templeton, Aberdeen, and Thomas Stark, of Forres, the latter of whom became the most influential minister of the body in the north.

On leaving the Hall, to be called to Craigdam not long after, Professor Bruce addressed him thus:—" Now, Patrick, you have talents which very few possess to the same degree; you are gifted with a powerful imagination; this may be of great service to you as a minister, but watch it, and do not let it run wild." That professor must have been able to read character as well as books, for both in the prophecy and the warning he suited the word to the man.

On entering upon his duties in Craigdam, Mr. Robertson found that a scholarly, polished style kept him at a distance from the peasant farmers who constituted the bulk of his congregation, and he resolved to acquire the broad Buchan dialect, so as to speak to the people in their own mother tongue. No missionary who goes to heathen parts could be more assiduous in the study of the language of the people, among whom he is to labour, than was this Perth scholar to become all things to the inmates of the scattered cots and crofts around Craigdam, for whose everlasting welfare he had so far become responsible. Deliberately, and from the highest motive, he laid aside, as a useless garment, the correct English into which he had been drilled, and learned to speak as one of the natives.

One can understand how at that time Mr. Robertson might reap considerable advantage in his public work by the effort. To a Scottish ear there is something "couthy" in the dialect of our country and district. What constitutes a barrier to the appreciation of the genius of Burns by readers of his poetry outside of Scotland, is exactly what deepens the regard that is felt for him by those of his own kith and kin. There is music to the heart as well as to the ear in the speech of the people that is so rich in associations that are dear, so laden with the memories of early days. To give direct expression to feeling is against the canons of Scottish temperament and taste, but how often we can obliquely insinuate a considerable measure of tenderness by one of those diminutives which abound in the north! "Pretty child" is not so euphonious in this latitude as "bonnie bairnie." Mr. Robertson was not far wrong in his philosophy—at least at the time and in the place—when, in referring to the pronunciation of a young preacher who had been officiating for him, he said—"Fin ye are preachin' ye say 'devil'; noo, I widna say it that wye: I say 'deevil'; it's mair kindly like!"

As to Mr. Robertson's numerous exercises in the vernacular, some of them quaint and pithy, and not a few of them ludicrous, we must refer the reader to that racy book—"Craigdam and its Ministers," by George Walker, to which we are indebted for much that is in this chapter. In reading such a book, however, we are apt to make the mistake of regarding the choice tit-bits as the staple of Mr. Robertson's preaching, and to conclude that he was more of a joker than a Christian herald. A greater mistake could not be made. We have to remember that for every sentence of pleasantry and eccentricity which retains its place in the memory, there are thousands of sober sense and Christian instruction which did their work at the time, though they are not reproduced in conversation or in writing.

There was much practical wisdom and point as well as pawky humour in some of his descriptions. When preaching on the temptations that assail Christians, and on the doubts and fears which arise in consequence, he said—" But, ma freens, aifter a's deen, these doubts an' fears will sometimes be permitted to come, as we a' ken to oor cost an' skaith; an' sae ye maun jist dee wi' them as ye dee at your wark i' the fields. The black craws 'll come, an' afttimes in vera croods; ye canna help though they flee ower your heids, but surely [Luther uses the same figure] ye can prevent them settlin' an' biggin' their nests there." On another occasion, when lecturing on Jacob's ladder and the angels of God ascending and descending it so easily, he contrasted this with the "awkward sprawlings of the self-righteous sinner on the rungs of the ladder." "Ma freens, he may get up sae far, but jist the farrer he thinks he is abeen his fellowmen, an' the nearer he thinks he is to the yetts o' heaven, jist the sairer will be the clyte he will get whan he does fa', for fa' he will."

The minister of Craigdam was very outspoken, and could be sarcastic, but always with an undercurrent of kindly, fatherly feeling. Referring to the Mosaic law of sacrifice, which required that the animal should be perfect and without blemish, he said—"It wis a very necessary law, for mony a ane, then as noo, wad look oot the scabbiest stirkie o' a' the lot an' think it was gweed eneuch for the Lord." His rebuke was sometimes severe, but only when it was needed. Some of the people had an incurable tendency to rise and make for the door before the benediction was finished. One day on holding up his hands as usual, he noticed some beginning to move, and broke out as follows:—"Ye jist mind me o' Frosterhill's nowte fan they're a' stannin' in their sta's: nae sooner dis the herd pit his han's t' their collars than ilka heid is turned t' the door." A member of the congregation, after his week's toil in the open air and his long walk to church, often succumbed to the close atmosphere of the building in which they worshipped, and one day in his slumberous noddings he lost his balance and fell into the passage. The minister stopped, and looking at the unhappy man recovering his seat, addressed him thus—" Ah, Tammas, Tammas, ma man, the Deevil's been rockin' ye for mony a day, but he's coupit ye at last!"

An old man, who was a member of the Whitehills U.P. Church, remembers Mr. Robertson being present there at a Communion service in 1825. He lectured on the ten virgins, and when he came to that part of the parable where the foolish virgins said, " Give us of your oil, for our lamps are gone out," he wheeled round in the pulpit and said—" Leein' jades; their lamps were never lichtit!"

Patrick Robertson had a plentiful supply of that kind of brilliancy of imagination which easily flashes into wit and humour; and you could not well have him without them, in the pulpit or anywhere else. It might have tended to increase the weight of his influence with some if he had disciplined his natural genius more, but perhaps the broad popular effect would have been less marked. We must ever distinguish between the man whose aim is to divert and entertain and the single-eyed servant of Christ who happens to have a vivid imagination and a picturesque style, which, if he is to be natural, are bound to sparkle now and again.

But what he will be chiefly remembered for is unquestionably his quaint, forcible descriptions in the vernacular. Could anything be better than his word-picture of the sisters Mary and Martha—" Mary wis a fine, quate, decent, crettur, but Martha wis a bickering, bumptious, rampagin' bodie, an', like a lot o' ither women, she had a gey lang tongue o' her ain whan she could fa' foul o' the vera Saviour Himsel'."

What is quite as good is his comparison of Saul and David. Mr. Robertson had occasion to lecture on the Scriptural incidents connecting the lives of Saul and David; and in the course of his remarks he said—" Ma freens, I dinna ken what your mind is aboot the personal appearance o' Saul an' Dawvit, but I'll gie ye my mind. Saul wis a great muckle chield, jist like the miller ower there [pointing to the individual in his audience who formed the point of his similitude]; an' then for Dawvit, he wasna a muckle giant like Saul, but a ticht, delver strappin' fellow jist like Jeems Smith, the tailor, sittin' doun there afore me."

It would be foreign to our purpose to follow Mr. Robertson in his experiences after he left Craigdam, for it was in that place where his best and most distinctive work was done.

CHAPTER XXVI.

THE DISRUPTION OF 1843.

IT is generally admitted that the first half of the nineteenth century was in many respects one of the most brilliant periods in the history of Britain. Men awoke from the long slumber of the previous century, and turned their wakefulness to some account. They began to think and to search as they had not done for many generations, to contemplate ideals and possibilities in all spheres open to human intelligence.

There came an unprecedented outburst of energy in the domain of physics. Invention—the utilisation of the resources of nature for the convenience of man—set in like a spring tide. The railway, the steamship, the power-loom, the telegraph, and a thousand useful appliances of the energy in steam and electricity came upon the scene.

It was also a period of quickened and heightened intellectual life, as was evidenced by the noble succession of poets—real, genuine poets—with which this country was favoured. Not since the time of Queen Elizabeth has this nation had such men of the highest creative genius as Coleridge and Wordsworth. And other writers, notably Tennyson, Browning, and Ruskin, proved that the middle and latter part of this century had not lost sight of the rich vein of highest intellectual power which had been disclosed.

Men also became politically awake and alert. Anomalies—inequalities in the social system—were detected and exposed. The demand of the people for the rights of free men culminated in the Reform Bill of 1832.

Now, religion flourishes most when men are intellectually awake, and when they arise from the rut of spiritless acquiescence. No doubt an excess of activity on purely secular lines tends to an impoverishment of the higher life by denuding it of its rightful share of energy. Still, it cannot be gainsayed that mental life and activity are helpful to the interests of true religion. Ignorance may be the mother of superstition, but not of enlightened devotion.

In England, the Pusey or Oxford movement was one of the most noticeable manifestations of awakened life. The old formalism, so respectable and self-complacent, was shaken if not shattered, and men who had given themselves to the ministry began to enquire whether a quiet, comfortable living in the Church and compliance with time-honoured forms were to take the place of aspiration after a higher life. The zeal of the movement, as many think, was largely misguided; still, it was the warmth of revived life.

In the United Presbyterian and Congregational Churches in Scotland there was also a considerable stirring of life, which issued in a stiff controversy about those metaphysical questions which lie behind the doctrines of grace. The Morisonian or "New View" crusade had a beneficial effect, along with other contributing causes, in liberalising the theology of Scotland; the Evangelical Union Churches in St. Paul Street and John Street being the local outcome and embodiment of that movement which took definite shape in 1843.

But years before the "New View" movement there was the Voluntary controversy—the question whether the Church should be supported by the State or by the freewill offerings of its members. That discussion excited strong feeling, and champions on both sides lectured throughout the land on the subject. It was at that time that the Church of Scotland took decided action on behalf of missions, Dr. Duff going out to India in 1830.

Amidst all this life-stirring, it was not to be expected that the people could continue to submit tamely to the bondage of Patronage, which had always been a hateful yoke to the pious and high-spirited in the land. Patronage might evoke no protest when religion did not mix itself with the sympathies and vital interests of the members of the Church. But as soon as religion became of consequence to the people they naturally desired a pastor who could minister to their deepest needs, and one whom they chose with that view—not the mere nominee of patrons, who were frequently influenced by other considerations than the spiritual fitness of the person presented. The popular pressure became so strong, as reflected in the speeches and votes of the General Assembly, that in 1834— the Evangelical party now having a majority —what was called the Veto Act was passed, which gave power to the majority of the heads of families in a parish, to interpose their veto against the entrance of any presentee who was obnoxious to them.

But in spite of the Veto Act which the majority of the General Assembly had passed, patrons of the Moderate school, who sometimes did not belong to the National Church, persisted in the exercise of their legal rights, and thus there came to be a collision between the civil and ecclesiastical courts of the land. An incident of the "conflict" in our own county helped to precipitate the crisis. A majority of the Presbytery of Strathbogie in ordaining Mr. Edwards as minister of the parish of Marnoch against the emphatically expressed wishes of the people, and therefore against the law of the

Church as it then was, so shocked the moral sense and stirred the feeling of the whole country as to make decisive action of some kind or other inevitable. The scandal, too, of the enforced settlement at Culsalmond in the same year drove the conviction further home that something must be done, and done soon, in the name of order and religion to make such scenes impossible.

The question came to be—Would the civil law be altered to agree with what had become the law of the Church? A great national crisis had been reached. The Evangelical section of the Church had come to a parting of the ways. They had either to succumb to the law on the civil statute-book, which was against the law of the Church, and be traitors to their consciences, denying the headship of Christ, or they had to make a sacrifice of position, stipend, and manse, and cast themselves adrift upon the world.

There was, indeed, a third course possible— viz., that, in deference to the strong remonstrances of the Evangelical clergy, headed by Dr. Chalmers, the Government of the day would move for such an alteration of the law as should bring it into agreement with the wishes of the people and the law of the Church. But by a strange infatuation, a judicial blindness, the statesmen then in power failed to realise the significance of the crisis. They thought they had only to be firm and those fiery and restless ecclesiastics, "high-fliers," would be brought to their senses and kept within the bounds which had been imposed. They never dreamt that so many men, the very strength and flower and glory of the Church, would leave their secured position, their emoluments, and manses for the sake of a principle.

They were misinformed and ill-advised. They had too open an ear for the representations of the active opponents of the popular party, and to the last they never supposed that more than a mere fraction of the Church would take what they deemed such a desperate step. The cynical view of human nature is sometimes proved to be a mistake. Worldliness may miscalculate. The Devil is sometimes outwitted when he is too sure of the answer to the sneeringly-put question—"Will a man serve God for nought?" You do not know how far men may go when they are carried along by a moral principle, which is to them as the declared will of God.

The leaders of the Non-Intrusion movement —Candlish, Cunningham, Gordon, Guthrie—were remarkable men, made for and by the times, but the popular party owed more, in the providence of God, for their cohesion and courage, their Christian gallantry, and the magnificence of the moral demonstration of the Disruption, to the inspiring presence of Dr. Chalmers than to any other cause in this world. Dr. Chalmers was one of those men with whom the world is favoured now and again, and who need a great historic epoch to exhibit the full proportions of their noble manhood. After his conversion in Kilmany and his pronounced adhesion to Evangelical doctrine, he was the greatest force in Scotland since the days of Knox. It was not only his intellectual prowess and his irresistible oratory, but his simple-hearted devotion to the higher ideas of life, which won for him the position he has in the reverent regard of Scotchmen of all creeds and classes.

The "Ten Years' Conflict" was practically the revival of the old question, which has so often come to the front during the last three hundred years, whether the Church was to be a thing of earthly potentates and statesmen—a creature of the State—or to be undivided in its allegiance to Christ, its only legitimate Head. It had to be decided whether the Church was to be Erastian or Evangelical. It was the same controversy which the Covenanters had to face, under modern conditions. The justice of the contention made fifty-three years ago, and which was resisted by the Moderates and the Court of Session, has been practically vindicated. Patronage is now abolished, and the right has been tardily conceded to the people of choosing their own ministers; but it needed the Disruption to drive the lesson home. After the members of the Assembly had met in St. Andrew's Church on 18th May, 1843, and the Moderator had taken his place, he said :—

"Fathers and brethren, according to the usual form of procedure, this is the time for making up the roll. But, in consequence of certain proceedings affecting our rights and privileges, proceedings which have been sanctioned by Her Majesty's Government and by the Legislature of the country, and more especially in respect that there has been an infringement on the liberties of our Constitution, so that we could not now constitute this Court without a violation of the terms of the union between Church and State in this land, as now authoritatively declared, I must protest against our proceeding further."

Thereupon Dr. Chalmers, Dr. Welsh, and other eminent members of the Assembly marched out to the street and headed a procession from St. Andrew's Church to Canonmills, where the Free Church was formally constituted. Four hundred and seventy-four ministers, with a large body of elders and members, made what is called the Disruption in the Scottish Church. In connection with this historic event, Aberdeen has the distinction of being the only large town in Scotland where all the ministers "came out."

We subjoin a list of ministers who left their

charges in the Presbytery of Aberdeen, May, 1843:—

Dr. Alexander Black,	Professor of Theology.	
Rev. William Primrose,	Melville	Church.
" James Foote,	East	"
" John Murray,	North	"
" Hugh M'Kenzie,	Gaelic	"
" David Simpson,	Trinity	"
" Gavin Parker,	Bon-Accord	"
" James Bryce,	Gilcomston	"
" Abercromby L. Gordon,	Greyfriars	"
" Alexander D. Davidson,	West	"
" John Allan,	Union	"
" Robert Forbes,	Woodside	"
" Alexander Spence,	St. Clements	"
" James Stewart,	South	"
" William L. Mitchell,	Holburn	"
" John Stephen,	John Knox's	"
" John Longmuir,	Mariners'	"

In country charges within the bounds of Aberdeen Presbytery:—

Rev. Robert Thomson, Peterculter.
Rev. George Moir, Newmachar.

It is not reasonable to expect that those who took the opposite side in the controversy should be able even yet to view the Disruption as do their brethren of the Free Church, or even as neutral spectators or non-Presbyterians. But time, with its healing and soothing touch, brings calmness and clearness of judgment. As the British, after the lapse of a hundred years, can gracefully acknowledge the heroism of Washington and his compatriots in their attitude of determined resistance which culminated in the Declaration of Independence, so Scotchmen of all Churches will yet echo the language that Lord Jeffrey used on the day of the Disruption—" I am proud of my country."

Every such tribute offered to conviction, every sacrifice that a nation or considerable section of a nation makes for conscience and principle, is a distinct augmentation of that moral force which is the salt of the earth. Some think the position which the Free Church took at first was illogical; and yet they feel that the ecclesiastical creed, as held at that time, cannot eclipse the imperishable renown of those who forsook church and manse and emoluments, when, as they believed, they could no longer have them without the surrender of the crown rights of the Redeemer.

Who can calculate the measure and the quality of the service rendered to the cause of unfeigned religion when the testimony was borne home to those in high places, as it was to the members of the British Cabinet of the day, that it is unsafe to assume that, when a choice of motives is open to Christian men, the worldly, sordid ones are sure to prevail? It was an astonishment to astute men of the world when it was demonstrated beyond all contradiction that there was such a large number of the ministers of religion in Scotland who were faithful to their interpretation of New Testament teaching and apostolic tradition, to the extent of submitting to the spoiling of their goods, rather than abandon their convictions. It is this which enables many in Scotland, who, while not accepting the Free Church theory of 1843, that is now in some of its distinctive parts, through half a century's marvellous experience of the power of voluntaryism, being quietly relegated to the archives of the past, to put the Disruption among events in the same rank as Iona and St. Andrews among places, and to hold that Chalmers is a name worthy of being placed alongside Columba and Wishart, as noble examples of what Christianity can do for men in provoking and sustaining sublime devotion to the higher claims of life and duty.

Is the ground not being rapidly cleared for a conflict that shall be wholly spiritual, ecclesiastical differences being lost in the consuming desire that is possessing all Christians for union against the common foes of unbelief and debasing worldliness? There is a growing impatience under the terrible waste of time and energy in the maintenance of mere sectarian rights and interests. Cannot each body of Christians be loyal to its own tenets, and yet be a part of a great spiritual federation that shall make the Holy Catholic Church a reality as well as a name, such as it has never yet been in our land?

Spenser, the poet, said that the chivalry of feudalism that was crumbling to pieces in his day should be superseded by the finer chivalry of an elevated and magnanimous Christian morality, knightly valour turning its attention from fantastic points of honour and frivolous contests to the real and formidable foes of lust, oppression, and ignorance. Is not ecclesiasticism very much in our day what feudalism was in Spenser's? It is an expiring force. It is more than time that the purely spiritual work for which the Church exists engrossed the energies of all true-hearted followers of Jesus Christ. What need there is for a combination, a brotherly alliance, among all evangelical denominations, in order that the earth, which is the Lord's by creation, may become His in a deeper and holier sense!

CHAPTER XXVII.

THE REVIVAL IN ABERDEEN OF 1858-60.

THE city and several parts of the county of Aberdeen between the dates at the heading of this chapter were favoured with a remarkable season of grace, the fruits of which were precious and abiding, and some of them remain with us unto this day. About the close of the sixth decade of this century there was a mysterious spiritual susceptibility abroad in different parts of the world; and notably in America, Ireland, and Scotland, men in large numbers were brought under the powers of the world to come to a degree that astonished and rebuked the formalism of Christendom. Aberdeen was in a measure prepared for a revival work, which in its effect is simply a deepening interest in the central verities of our faith, and a more complete obedience to what it involves; not a few within our borders were praying and expecting that the spiritual world would make its presence felt by a striking demonstration of its power upon the consciences and hearts of the people. A daily prayer meeting had been begun in the city in July, 1858, and to the feeling indicated by the existence of such a meeting a great deal that followed could be traced.

By invitation of Professor Martin, of the Moral Philosophy Chair in Marischal College, Mr. Reginald Radcliffe came to Aberdeen on an evangelistic mission on 27th November, 1858. Mr. Radcliffe had already proved himself to be a man specially gifted for work of that kind. A gentleman by birth and education, trained for the law, he found what was evidently his divinely-appointed vocation in philanthropic and spiritual work. In looking at him and listening to him it was at first difficult to account for his power; it was so quiet and unobtrusive. There was no oratorical display, not even what could be called eloquence; he had not the intellectual robustness of some of his coadjutors, such as Brownlow North; yet no man in such a short time ever so drew and stirred Aberdeen, and was the instrument of leading so many to cry out—"What must we do that we may be saved?" The man's power lay to a large extent in his entire self-effacement; and in the circumstance that he happened to come to Aberdeen at a time when the people were prepared to receive and profit by simple statements of gospel truth.

Considerable prejudice had to be broken down in Aberdeen, before the methods and agents God was to use for the special work that was to be done were duly acknowledged. Some of the churches did not view with favour the new earthen vessels into which the treasure was to be put, forgetting that the Master had ordained that there should be evangelists as well as pastors and teachers, and that a layman's testimony from experience, given in a plain, pointed style, may prove to be a most valuable auxiliary to the ordinary preaching of the Word. Mr. Radcliffe's operations at first did not extend beyond Albion Street Congregational Church.

The extraordinary feature of this movement was that it began amongst the young. The children came, and they by-and-bye brought their parents. All the blossoms did not come to fruition, but not a few converts have stood the test of time, and are now most useful church members and the most distinguished of our self-denying Christian workers.

Principal Brown was forward among our leading men in discovering and expressing his belief in the genuineness of this work among the young, and in giving it his hearty and continued co-operation. When present in the General Assembly of the Free Church about thirteen years after Mr. Radcliffe's visit, he had the gratification to hear a minister who had been commissioned to inquire into the state of religion in Aberdeen remark that the religious work among the young in 1858-60 must have been very profound and widespread, as he had met so many decided Christians in the city who had been converted at that time. Thereupon the Principal rose up and said he had been "in the thick" of that work, and could testify to its thoroughness and blessedness, and he added that a member of the present Assembly, who had taken an active part in its business, began his Christian career under the influences of that period. For twelve years did our venerable Principal continue to preside at the prayer meeting, which was held every Sabbath morning in Marywell Street School from the time of Mr. Radcliffe's visit to our city.

Some knotty points in ecclesiastical order were incidentally discussed and dealt with at that time. The churches gradually opened their eyes to the fact that a work of God was going on amongst them, and some of the ministers invited the evangelists, not into the pulpit at first, but into the precentor's desk. It was held to be unfitting that a layman should occupy a pulpit and that what he said should be called a sermon. So the evangelists, becoming all things to all men, and content with the lower seat of the synagogue till they were bidden come up higher, took the precentor's box and called what they uttered an "address."

Besides some of the churches of other denominations, the Greyfriars Parish Church was opened for this work, and its minister, the Rev.

James Smith, had to answer to his co-presbyters for daring to allow this new expanding life in Aberdeen to burst asunder the swaddling-bands of ecclesiastical rule and precedent. On consulting Dr. Norman Macleod as to what course he should follow, he got for reply that "he had no sympathy with Puseyism in Scotland any more than in England, and that he would admit a layman to the pulpit at once."

The case, however, went against Mr. Smith in the Aberdeen Presbytery and also in the Synod. His appeal to the General Assembly met with a different reception. Some of the men who had the ear of that august body were far removed from the ways of the ecclesiastical martinet, and having largeness of soul enough to take in the significance of such a great spiritual movement, were prepared to adapt the channel to the stream that was flowing. This was how Dr. Norman Macleod spoke in the General Assembly:—

"A few Christian men came to Aberdeen, and were brought within the sacred walls of one of the churches there. He did not know whether they preached a sermon or not; he did not know whether they stood in a pulpit fifteen feet high, or on a platform seven feet high, but he knew that they addressed people upon the unsearchable riches of Christ, and that as Christian men they spoke from their hearts to thousands. The only fault found with these men seemed to be that they addressed immortal souls on the truth of Christianity within the walls of a church; but he had been brought up in the belief that the Church of Scotland attached no peculiar sacredness to stone and lime. It had been pleaded at the bar that these men might go to the street. But there were many laws that were tolerable only because they had liberty occasionally to break them, and surely all church laws must subserve the one grand end for which all churches exist. They might have decency, regularly appointed licentiates, and regularly ordained men, and death all the while. This was not a time—when there was so much necessity for increased spiritual life—for the General Assembly to occupy a whole night in finding fault because a minister permits a layman to preach the gospel from a pulpit."*

Mr. Radcliffe continued to be the leader in this mission, and he did not spare himself. The meetings were crowded, and often after the people were dismissed they came back to hear the same old story. Thousands in the Castlegate or Links would hang upon the lips of an evangelist who could not have sustained the interest of an audience for ten minutes on any other theme than that of the gospel. Having few hymns which they could use at such meetings in those days, they were never tired of singing over and over again the 126th Psalm and the 41st Paraphrase. These were sung

* "Memoir of Norman Macleod," Vol. II., p. 89.

thousands of times during the course of the mission, with a freshness of interest which came from the soul.

In the towns and villages on the shores of the Moray Firth a great work was going on about the same time. Mr. Turner, of Peterhead, went from place to place like a flaming seraph, and by his addresses, and still more by his prayers, became a channel of power to multitudes.

Aberdeen was moved: men were to be seen in the streets and in the railway trains reading their Bibles; some young men had all-night meetings in Rubislaw Quarries; a great many shop assistants were brought to religious decision, and it may indicate the kind of feeling that was abroad to learn that it was not uncommon for them, after sales were effected, to have a talk with customers about eternal things. All over the town, at leisure moments and when opportunity occurred, there were hundreds doing what Christ and the Apostles did eighteen centuries before—seeking to bring men to God; the feeling in enthusiastic minds was that the millennium was at hand.

Do not say that this was mere emotional excitement, that passed away like the blaze and crackling of thorns, without leaving anything behind but black ashes. Much of the Christian philanthropy that has been in our city for the last thirty years owes a great deal to the impulse received at that time. Institutions that flourish amongst us to-day, having for their object the uplifting of our fellows, have their roots in that movement.

Amongst the men not belonging to the city who actively co-operated with Mr. Radcliffe were the forcible and incisive Brownlow North, and Hay Macdowall Grant of Arndilly, the latter remembered with gratitude for his gracious work in the ladies' boarding schools of our city. It is remarkable that the north country should have been favoured at that time with the presence of so many persons of high social position who were conspicuous for their devotion to the interests of experimental religion. Besides the persons we have already mentioned, there were the Duchess of Gordon, the Earl of Kintore, John Gordon of Parkhill, and others, who were neighbours, and whose names, not to speak of their labours, helped to give importance to a movement, especially in the eyes of those who are ever prone to ask the old question—" Have any of the rulers believed in him ? "

The above-mentioned persons are all gone from us, but a landed proprietor whose name has ever been identified with God's work in this part of the land is with us still—Alexander G. Burnett of Kemnay.

By the labours of the American evangelist,

Mr. Moody in 1874, Aberdeen was greatly quickened, but not nearly to the extent that it was sixteen years before. Although the movement was less profound and widespread, much good came out of it, one of the standing witnesses of that being the Young Men's Christian Association buildings in Union Street, which, through the stimulus received by Mr. Moody's visit, were purchased and put to their present use, and the large hall added behind. The Church should expect and be prepared for these intermittent revivals. "The course of the Christian heavenward," someone has said, "is a series of impulses. Between the impulses, however, there is the measured and normal movement of habit. The fresh impulse of extraordinary effort, and the well-regulated step of habitual or ordinary exertion, alike harmonise with and result from the laws which limit and govern all human activity."

A revival of religion just means that religion by a special effort inspired from above is trying to raise itself to the level of something that is adequately alive and efficient, something that is trying to be what it professes to be, and is fitted to serve the ends for which it was brought into existence. There is no cause that continues upon the earth and is of service to humanity that has not its revivals. Especially is that so with regard to everything of a spiritual nature, man being so unspiritual in his proclivities, and so prone to mistake traditional form and mechanical routine for something better than they are.

Doubtless in all revivals the baser elements have too prominent a place, and one of the cheapest ways of obtaining a reputation for sagacity is in pointing out the shortcomings of such good movements. When a number of men are really and intelligently moved by sacred conviction, many around them will be touched with the contagious excitement generated in the community; and, of course, if that does not deepen into something more worthy, it will be as sparks shot from the anvil rather than as iron that is heated at the core and then beaten into the right shape.

The history of religious revivals is a history of divine power and of human weakness. We have many living witnesses of the power, just as we have, alas! too many strong proofs of the weakness. But we do not cut down the fruit tree because some of its blossoms come to nothing. We do not believe that Pentecost was a figment, a fond imagination of the spiritual visionary, but a fact in the history of the Church. Such a fountain-head leads us to look for corresponding streams.

CHAPTER XXVIII.

THE CHRISTIANITY OF THE PRESENT DAY—1896.

IN bringing this succession of pictures of local religious life and ecclesiastical history to a close, it may not be an unprofitable task to inquire what the Christianity of the present day has to say for itself after all the travail and discipline of the centuries through which it has passed. We have seen that there has been much shaking: does anything remain which this age should cleave to? One earthen vessel after another has been broken before our eyes; is the divine treasure left, and is it really such to us of the present day?

No stranger can visit our city and cast his eye abroad upon its principal streets without meeting abundant evidence of the fact that Christianity still exists, and can erect for its worship and work edifices which are the ornament and pride of the place. The crowded appearance of Union Street, also, on a fine Sabbath morning, a few minutes before worship is begun, demonstrates that the Christian Church still has a hold of the population.

But is not the hold slackening? "Yes" and "No" can be answered to that question. Mere external authority and conventional restraint are unquestionably less potent than they were a generation or two ago, in securing church attendance. In these days, when freedom is not unfrequently interpreted to mean self-will, the yoke of established custom is disdainfully dropped by some who deem it possible now to maintain "respectability" outside the Church. Formalism is to be seen flinging aside its irksome mask and revealing itself as unabashed indifference or even avowed hostility.

But most persons who feel that man shall not live by bread alone, who are conscious that they have a moral and religious nature which it is their duty to nourish and discipline, acknowledge that they are as much dependent on the verities of which the Church is the witness and vehicle, as were their ancestors a thousand years ago. Advancing civilisation has no more made the Christian religion unnecessary than gas and electricity have lessened the importance of the sun.

It must be admitted that a great deal which the people of this country held most tenaciously, and for which they sometimes resolutely contended, is now regarded with a languid interest. Questions of metaphysical theology and theoretical Church polity do not engage the popular mind as they once did. In so far as that arises from a better perspective of truth and a more practical use of religion, there is cause for thankfulness. Breadth and catholicity of feeling are on the increase. Men are beginning to realise as perhaps they never did before, that where Christ is, there is the Church, and consequently they are ready to recognise as brethren all who "hold the Head," even though they may differ in their views of Church government and on minor points of doctrine. There is now a more thorough discrimination between things essential and things non-essential, and even where there is no immediate prospect of ecclesiastical incorporation, there is to a large extent a real sense of spiritual brotherhood among all truly evangelical Christians.

But we should ever be on our guard lest we mistake the chilling effect of a lowered temperature of Christian feeling for the wisdom which is joined to love, and which enables us fittingly and usefully to distribute our intensity. Changes we must have, as the generations succeed each other, but the best theological change is often little more than a shifting of emphasis. An easy-going laxity is to be avoided, as it is a bastard kind of liberality. A Gallio's unconcern is a miserable substitute for true catholicity. While it is a decided advantage that we should be able to distinguish clearly between sheath and kernel, there will be no great gain unless we at the same time hold what is central and vital in our common Christianity with an added firmness. And while we have learned that it is wisdom such as humility begets, to keep a tight rein upon merely curious and speculative propensities, restraining ourselves from the attempt to reach definite conclusions about what is not clearly revealed, and which therefore lies beyond the immediate interests of life and duty, yet we ought to have an intelligent apprehension of the things most surely believed amongst us. Much of the blatant talk that is meant to discredit theology, only goes to show that the talkers depreciate earnest purpose and exact thought, with regard to the most momentous theme which can engage the mind of man. Theology is no more than religion as it shows itself to the thought of man. Loose or inaccurate thinking cannot fail to be bad in its effects, into whatever department of human interest it is allowed to creep. Who ever sneers at sound thinking in social economics? Is it not as important that we should get at the truth in the economics for eternity? No doubt hard, dry, sapless dogmatism has much to do with the suspicion under which theology has fallen in these days. But it is the lifelessness, not the accuracy, that is at fault. Theology is the teaching of Scripture as it reflects itself in human intelligence. It cannot be regarded as a small matter by any sane mind to try to hold up a flawless mirror to the Word of God, as mere human opinion which is not the

x

reflection of truth is but the bubble that bursts in the air, but the fleck of foam that melts on the shore.

The spirit of the age is putting the Church of the present day to the proof in many ways. The very intellectual progress of which we are the heirs and gainers, and which, also, enlightened religion has done so much to promote, has sometimes seemed to array itself against us. Nothing escapes the searching, critical inquiry of this scientific age, and the Scriptures, which are the depositories and symbols of that which is dearest to us, have been scrutinised within the last two or three decades as they never were before. Scholarly experts are leading us to views regarding the literary origin and structure of some parts of the Bible different from those which tradition upheld. The time of transition involved in this readjustment is trying, not so much to those who have faith, as to others who are only as yet halting inquirers; but the crisis has been made needlessly acute by the rashness of a few men who have more learning than judgment, and seem to have a predilection for the most extreme view which the facts, with the utmost stretching, will allow, however shocking to simple faith. But more sober, not to say more reverent, minds, with a full equipment of scholarship, yet weighted with a grave sense of responsibility to those who come not within the precincts of the academy, are gradually bringing the Church to conclusions regarding its sacred writings, which, though different in some respects from those which were previously held, are yet consistent with an undiminished and even added appreciation for the worth, and more thorough submission to the authority of the Word of God. Every part of man's nature must be brought into living relation to the revelation of God, the intellect as well as the heart and conscience; and "criticism" has its mission, as Pressensé says, in "disengaging the everlasting Gospel from the superstition of orthodox scholasticism in order to reconcile it with the conscience, while taking away nothing of the divine 'foolishness' of the Cross."

The danger besetting a period when sifting intelligence is specially at work is to emphasise what is doubted or denied rather than what is held. We have to remember that when the mind is more enthusiastic about the negative than the positive part of its religious creed, the face is set in the direction of death; for it is by affirmations that we live. Criticism, to the mind in a healthy state, is but clearing the way for better access to the truth, for which pearl of great price we are willing to sell all that we have. As the Germans put it, in emptying the bath we must be careful, lest we throw away the baby as well.

Another trial which the Church, as representing things spiritual and eternal, has to bear in the present day is the extraordinary and embarrassing influx of interest in material things, which is a striking feature of this age of physical discovery and enlargement. Things tangible and visible are opening up to us all round, yielding outlets, conveniences, and gratifications in such abundance that there is the risk of intoxication if a persistent effort is not made to live "in the spirit." The world of sense is able to do a great deal more for us than it did for former generations, and we are bound to believe that all this material progress is the gift of Heaven, which will lead to a real expansion of life after the excitement connected with our new possessions has subsided, and we, without going against the due order and proportion of things, are able to accommodate ourselves wisely to our providentially-appointed environment.

In former days in Scotland the contents of the Bible and the sermons the people heard were not only nutriment to the soul, but also were largely helpful in maintaining an intellectual interest in life. Now, a world of varied interest comes daily into the home of every artisan through the afternoon newspaper; and the Scriptures and the Church must take their place along with other things in stimulating mental activity. The task before the Church of the present day is to encourage the people to think on whatsoever things are true, and pure, and of good report, and yet to remind them that to have the mind secularised is to have its noblest parts deadened.

Should not the Church of the present day maintain that the Kingdom of God ought to come here and now in larger measure in all the many-sidedness of its advent, temporal and spiritual; that physical science and social economy ought to make the earth a more attractive dwelling-place for all its inhabitants; and, at the same time, should it not fearlessly declare that man cannot be "groomed and foddered into blessedness;" that you can no more put right what is wrong in human nature by a mere improvement of circumstances than, as Jeremy Taylor says, you can cure a man of the colic by brushing his clothes; that no one can live the life of the mere worldling without shutting up and shutting out what is man's best part; and that life which does not link itself with heaven is like earth without a sky, or the sky without its sun?

But in order that the Church may be able to hold its ground as a witness for spirituality, it must itself be free from the taint of sensationalism in its worship and methods. The temptation besets us all, when, owing to prevailing spiritual indifference, we do not get the "success" we desire on Scriptural lines, to come down to lower ideals and content ourselves with social and other results—but the temptation is to be resisted. The prime question is not what will draw a crowd and please it. Statistics, enlarged communion rolls, which are sometimes a sad study, and popular support are no infallible criterion of real prosperity. Multiplied activities, accompanied with a diminished interest in prayer, may only mean that we are trying to spend more spiritual energy than we are really succeeding in generating. Organisation is good if there be the life to organise, but the Kingdom of Heaven never has come by activity of any kind, in which prayer has not been what the soul is to the body.

The best gift the age can have is praying men and women in the pews and brave men in the pulpit, who, overshadowed by eternity and determined at all cost to deliver the divine message with which they have been entrusted, will speak with a view, not so much to the taste and liking of men as to their profit. The truth of heaven never was palatable to proud, unspiritual men; nevertheless, any progress that the world has made is due to its fearless utterance. Was not Thorold, the Bishop of Rochester, right when he said—"But this I am sure of, that if we had a little more of that despised Puritanism—without its flaws and defects—there might be more substance in our sermons, more backbone in our manhood, more honesty in our markets, and more purity in our homes?"

A gain that the Church of the present day can count as belonging to it, and yet one that is accompanied by a measure of danger, is the large attention that is being paid to the ethical or practical side of the Christian religion. The pulpit of Scotland to-day is exhibiting and applying as it never did before the moral teaching of the New Testament. We have swung from Paul to James, and we speak less of the doctrinal basis of Christianity and more of the superstructure of life and conduct than our forefathers did. This plain and palpable reaction shows itself in various ways. The human and outward life of our Lord is most minutely and vividly pourtrayed; the Gospels are favoured more than the Epistles, and those mystical phases of the divine life which John makes it his special business to set forth are not the favourite studies of the present day. The complaint is heard that the modern pulpit says little about sin, the Atonement, and the necessity for conversion, and leaves other parts of the foundation work of the ministry somewhat in the background.

If it be so, it will soon be found out that ethics are of little avail without those energies which come through the exercise of faith in a living and saving Christ. It is by the Fatherhood of God, of which the Incarnation and the Cross are the witness, that we have learned of the brotherhood of men. In so far as the Socialism of the day is sound and practical, it assumes and takes to its credit the moral capital which Christianity has accumulated. It is only, therefore, as we continue to give height to our religious feeling that it can find its proper breadth. A New Testament theology which develops love for God is the root from which spring the stalk and branches of love to our fellows. Charity to the poor, mercifulness to the conquered, hatred of war, care for the sick and aged may all be the developed and inherited results of a Christian experience which is not possessed by the very persons who favour such graces, and therefore may be embraced in a worldliness that has no eternity in it, no sense of sin, and no vital union with Christ; and not only so, but history does not bring before us the case of any nation being enabled to retain a permanent hold of such virtues and graces without continued faith and worship as the soul of such a beautiful ethical body.

We have to be on our guard, too, against the tendency to substitute the discussion of religious subjects before men for the application of religious truth to men. Columba and the long line of illustrious successors who have made Scotland religiously what it is, ever followed the example of the Apostles, who called upon men to repent and to believe in the Lord Jesus Christ. They spoke as men who had entered, not the academy, but the arena. They did not content themselves with a presentation of truth under general and impersonal aspects, talking about religion as they would of art or any branch of science; but they grappled with the consciences of men, so as to bring about entire and immediate surrender to God.

A writer of the present day refers in mournful terms to "the slow but sure development of the belief in the bankruptcy of nature which promises to become the gloomy faith of the nineteenth century." There is something to favour that pessimistic view if those who lead us in literature and philosophy cease to have the fear of God before their eyes, and regard morality as something that does not go further back than social expediency. What happened to ancient Rome may happen to us if the same forces are allowed to work. Nay, that cannot be: God is in His heaven. We need to pray for more faith. An accession of faith when it comes—and it will come—is sure to bring so much with it. The men and women who during the course of this century have left their mark upon our nation's history were all reared in an atmosphere of faith. Newman, George Eliot, Gladstone, Bright, Tennyson, and Browning were all, to a large extent, the offspring of the great Evangelical revival with which the century began.

It is only an age of faith that is creative, that can have genius, public spirit, and heroism as its natural fruit. When men have no vision of unseen realities, no apprehension of eternal truth, no intimate personal converse with the great Father above, who is the fount of thought and inspiration, life sinks down to a lower level, and the glories and joys of existence are so much less exalted. An age of unbelief produces acute critics, learned commentators, but the creative work, in which man shows himself indeed to be made in the image of God, is not possible where there is no faith.

Let all who have faith draw more closely together in these days. A British ambassador some years ago, in addressing an English congregation on the Continent, not belonging to his own Church, said, "At home we recognise and emphasise our differences; abroad we realise the identities." Why should our countrymen abroad have an advantage over us at home? Should we not, for the sake of our common Christianity and the world that needs it so much, and in the face of abounding religious indifference, draw nearer to the "identities" and therefore nearer to each other?

APPENDIX.

THE BRECBANNOCH.

(Page 11.)

"But there remains a most interesting traditional link with Columba in 'a very beautiful and very remarkable reliquary' that has been preserved time out of mind in Monymusk House, and that is evidently a small casket for containing some relics of a saint. Dr. Anderson makes an elaborate statement regarding it, and says that as far as he knows it is the only one of its kind and period now existing in Scotland—and that, if it is not the Brecbannoch of St. Columba, it is one of the strangest coincidences that a reliquary answering so closely to it should have been preserved at Monymusk. . . . This is a small wooden box hollowed out of the solid, and covered with plates of pale bronze and silver. It was originally jewelled, and is still enamelled, and the tracings of the characteristic Celtic spiral ornaments that were engraved on it, are still visible. At both ends it had a hooked plate with a hinge, and a strap might readily be inserted into the hook to let it be carried on one's breast, but one plate is now lost."—From *"Church and Priory of Monymusk," pp.* 3-4.

STATUTE ANENT PROCESSION ON SAINTS' DAYS.

(Pages 81-82.)

"22 May 1531.—Ordour of Candilmess Procession, and of Corpus Cristi.—The said day, it was statut and ordanit, be the prouest, bailyeis, and counsaile present for the tyme, conforme to the auld honorabil consuetudis and ryte of this burgh, and of the nobill burgh of Edinburgh, of the quhilk rite and consuetude the forsaid prouest hes gotten copy in write; that is to say, in the honor of God and the Blissit Vurgyne Marye, the craftissmene of this burgh, in thair best aray, keipe and decoire the procession on Corpus Cristi dais, and Candilmes day, als honorabillye as thai can, every craft with thair awin baner, with the armis of thair craft tharon; And they sall pass, ilk craft be thame self, tua and tua, in this ordour, that is to say, in the first, the fleschars; and, nixt thame, the barbouris; nixt thame, skynnaris and furroweris, togidder; nixt thame, the cordonars; nixt thame, tailyours; eftir thame, the vobstaris and valcaris, togidder; nixt thame the baxtaris; and last of all, nerest the sacrament, passis all hemmermen, that is to say, smythis, wrichtis, masonis, cuparis, sclateris, goldsmythis, and armouraris: And every ane of the said craftis, in the Candilmes procession, sall furneiss thair pageane, conforme to the auld statut maid in the year of God j^m v^c and x yeirs, quhilk statut was maid with the awiss of the haill counsaile, and approvit be the craftsmen of the towne, for the tyme, and thair successors, and oblist thame to the keping of the samyn, under the pain of xl shillings, and the bailyeis unlaw unforgiven, to be uptakin of thame that vas absent but one resonabill causs frae the said processiouns, or that makkis trubill or perturbation tharin, to the quhilk thai var oblist be thair hands uphaldin in jugement: And the prouest, bailyeis, and consale present for the tyme, ratifies and approvis this present statut, and the paines contenit tharin, to be kepit inviolablye, in all manere in tyme coming.

The crafts are chargit to furneish the paugeanys underwrittin:—

The flescharis, Sanct Bestien, and his Tormentouris;
The barbouris, Sanct Lowrie, and his Turmentouris;
[The] skynnaris, Sanct Stewin, and Tormentouris;
The cordinaris, Sanct Martyne;
The tailyeouris, The Coronatioun of our Lady;
[The] litstaris, Sanct Nicholass;
[The] wobstaris, walcaris, and bonet makaris, Sanct John;
[The] baxtaris, Saint Georg;
[The] wrichtes, messounis, slateris, and cuparis, The Resurrection.

The smyths and hemmermen to furneiss, The Bearmen of the Croce.

—*From Burgh Records of Aberdeen.*

QUAKER SETTLEMENT IN KINMUCK.

(Page 170.)

In the little graveyard adjoining the Quaker meeting-house at Kinmuck one of the rows of gravestones contains a record of the respective ages of the persons there interred, showing the longevity of the race—85 years, 80, 40, 72, 90, 79, 72, 93, 76, 84, 85, 60, 84.

A FAMOUS ABERDEEN SOCIETY.
(Pages 222 and 224.)

The "Philosophical Society in Aberdeen," as it called itself, but better known in popular phrase as the "Wise Club," came into existence in January, 1758. The members met once a fortnight in a tavern, at five o'clock. "Entertainment" was provided as a relief from the dissertations; but it was a distinct rule that "the members shall leave the meeting-room at ten, and the entertainment shall not exceed eighteenpence a head." A writer in *Macmillan's Magazine*, Vol. VIII., from whom we have obtained the above information, also gives us the transcript of one of the tavern bills for a sitting:—

		£	s.	d.
To One Bottle Port	. . .	0	2	0
To Punch	. . . . .	0	2	6
To Porter	. . . . .	0	0	8
To Pipes and Tobacco	. .	0	0	4
Entert.	. .	0	4	6
		0	10	0
Bill at J. Bean's.	.	0	0	6
		£0	10	6

11th March, 1772.

Almost the whole of Campbell's "Philosophy of Rhetoric" was submitted piecemeal to the criticism of the members. The following are some of the subjects they discussed:—"Is the human soul confined to any part of the human body, and, if so, to what part?" (Stewart)—"What is the foundation of moral obligation?" (Farquhar)—"Whether brutes have souls, and, if they have, wherein do they differ from human?" (Dr. Skene).

JACOBITISM IN CHURCH.

(Page 236.)

"I saw frequent example of the people's disaffection to the present Government in the above-mentioned church of Aberdeen, where there is an organ, the only one I know of, and the service is chanted as in our cathedrals. Being there one Sunday morning with another English gentleman, when the minister came to that part of the litany where the King is prayed for by name the people all rose up as one in contempt of it, and men and women set themselves about some trivial action, as taking snuff, &c., to show their dislike and signify to each other they were all of one mind; and when the responsal should have been pronounced, though they had been loud in all that preceded, to our amazement there was not one single voice to be heard but our own, so suddenly and entirely were we dropped."—*Burt's* "*Letters from the North of Scotland*," 1754.

Dr. Cunningham, in his "Church History of Scotland," quotes the remark of an "old Jacobite," which agrees with the above:—"Well do I remember the day on which the name of George was mentioned in the morning service for the first time—such blowing of noses, such significant hums, such half suppressed sighs, such smothered groans and universal confusion, can hardly be conceived."

INDEX.

Aberdeen, bishopric of, 53; foundations of friars in, 54; early importance of, 55; cathedral of, 33, 63; ecclesiastical establishments at Reformation, 78; ancient pageants, 81; visit of Margaret, queen of James IV., 83; donations towards repair of St. Nicholas Church, 84; population of at Reformation, 107; Covenanting struggle in, 146; famous "Doctors" of, 155; formation of Methodist Society in, 247, 253; Synod of—overture from, as to vagrant teachers, &c., 272; first Congregational church, 273; first Baptist church, 275; list of ministers who left charges at Disruption, 304; revival of 1858-60, 308; a famous society, 334.

Aberdour, tradition as to visit of Columba to, 15.

Aboyne Castle, incised stone at, 27.

Adamnan—Life of Columba, 2.

Anti-burghers, branch of the Secession Church, 206, 212.

Baptists, the, 274.

Barbour, Archdeacon, 57; references to, 59, 60; the "Brus," 60, 62.

Barclay, David, of Ury, 173.

Beattie, author of the "Minstrel," 217.

Bisset, Mr. John, minister of St. Nicholas, 210.

Boece, Hector, principal of King's College, 72.

Brecbannoch at Monymusk House, 10, 331.

Brown, Rev. William, Craigdam, 287.

Brown, Principal, 288.

Brown, Provost, 288.

Brownists, the, 266.

Burghers, branch of the Secession Church, 206, 212.
Burnett, Alexander G., of Kemnay, 315.

Campbell, Principal, 221; parentage, 221; minister at Banchory-Ternan, 222; at Aberdeen, 223; principal of Marischal College, 224; works of, 225; death, 231.
Candida Casa, foundation of, 18.
Cant, Andrew, 157; parentage, 158; minister at Alford, 159; at Pitsligo, 160; extract from sermon at Inverness, 162; minister at Aberdeen, 165; death, 168.
Celtic Church, nature of, 40.
Chalmers, John, minister of Keith, 126.
Christianity of the present day, 318.
Church dues, hardship of, 80.
Church life during seventeenth century, 188.
Columba, 1; parentage, 3; character, 4; leaves Ireland, 7; lands at Iona, 8; work there, 9, 11; travels northward to Inverness, 14; visits Aberdour and Old Deer, 14.
Congregationalism in the north, 273.
Cowie, George, of Huntly, 255; parentage, 256; ministry at Huntly, 258; deposed by Synod, 262; forms independent congregation, 262; death, 263.
Craig, John, minister, 103, 110; parentage, 110; studies abroad, 111; returns to Scotland, 112; ministry at Aberdeen, 113; chaplain to James VI., 113.
Craigdam, Secession church at, 209, 287.
Culdees in Scotland, 43.
Customs derived from old religion, 23.

Deer, Book of, 14, 15.
Dickson, David, commissioner to Aberdeen, 152.
Disruption of 1843, 296; causes leading up to, 297; list of Aberdeen ministers who left their charges, 304.
Drostan, early missionary, 1, 18; parentage, 24; labours at Deer, 26; retires to Glenesk, 26.
Druids, priests of native religion, 21.
Dunbar, Bishop, 73.

INDEX. 339

Elphinstone, Bishop, 65; education, 66; appointment to See of Aberdeen, 66; founder of King's College, 67; death, 71.
Episcopacy and Presbyterianism contrasted, 116.
Episcopacy, introduction of diocesan, 53.
Erskine, Ebenezer, 203.

Forbes, Dr. John, of Corse, 155.
Forbes, Bishop Patrick, 115; parentage, 123; letter to James VI., 125; enters the ministry, 126; ministry at Keith, 127 bishop, 127.
Fordoun, John of, 64; his "History," 64.
Fraser, Mr. Alexander, minister of Botriphnie, 193.

Gerard, Alexander, works of, 218.
Gordon, Duchess of, 31.
Gordon, John, of Parkhill, 315.
Grant, Hay Macdowall, of Arndilly, 315.

Haldane, James, 267; visit to Aberdeen, 270.
Haldane, Robert, 267.
Hamilton, Patrick, martyr, 97.
Henderson, Alexander, commissioner to Aberdeen, 150.
Heriot, Adam, first Protestant minister at Aberdeen, 109.
Hill, Rowland, journal of visit to Scotland, 255.

Independents, the, 264; origin of, 266.
Insch, monumental stone at, 75.
Inverness, visited by Columba, 14.
Iona, landing of Columba, 8; reference to by Dr. Johnson, 9.
Ireland, condition of during fifth century, 6.
Irvine, "devils" of, 153.

Jacobitism in church, 335.
Jaffray, Alexander, of Kingswells, 175; his "diary," 177; early life, 179; a commissioner to Charles II., 181; prisoner in England, 182; a member of Parliament, 185; death, 187.

Kidd, Dr., 227, 276; ministry at Gilcomston Chapel, 277.
Kinmuck, Quaker settlement at, 333.
Kintore, Earl of, 315.
Knox, services as a leader, 92.

Lollards, the, 90.
Luther's books forbidden, 91.
Lynturk, Secession church at, 209.

Machar, parentage of, 33; chooses site for church, 33.
Margaret, Queen, her influence on Scottish Church, 47.
Marshall, John, rector of Grammar School, 108.
Methodists, the, 245; various societies of, 252.
Missionaries, work of early, 28, 29, 30.
Moderates, the, 213.

North, Brownlow, 315.
Norsemen responsible for loss of records, 37.

Old Deer, tradition as to visit of Columba to, 15.
Oldmachar Cathedral, foundation of, 33, 63.

Parochial system, introduction of, 52.
Philosophical Society in Aberdeen, 334.
Pictland, evangelisation of, 1.
Picts, religion of the, 21.
Presbyterianism and Episcopacy contrasted, 116.
Priests, position of, 77.
Processions on saints' days, statute anent, 332.

Quakers in Aberdeen, 170; other settlements, 170, 333.

Radcliffe, Reginald, visit to Aberdeen, 309.
Reformation, the, 87; condition of Church at, 89, 90; authority of Scripture fundamental principle of, 94.
Reid, Professor of Moral Philosophy, 218.
Romans in Britain, 2.

Robertson, Patrick, of Craigdam. 287 ; parentage, 289 ; ministry, 290.
Rutherford, Samuel, 130 ; parentage, 131 ; banishment to Aberdeen, 132 ; his "letters," 133 ; treatment in Aberdeen, 139 ; returns to Anwoth, 142 ; declines professorship of divinity at Aberdeen, 142.

St. Bartholomew's Day, massacre of, 102.
St. Devenick, 34 ; churches of Nether Banchory and Methlick dedicated to him, 34.
St. Fergus, 34.
St. Ninian, labours in Galloway, 3.
St. Ternan, 34 ; church dedicated to, 34.
St. Wollok, 34 ; church of, at Glass, 34, 191.
Saints' days, statute anent processions on, 332.
Scotland, early condition of, 18 ; origin of name, 19.
Sculptured stones, value of as records, 39.
Seceders, the, 197.
Skinner, John, of Linshart, 232 ; parentage, 233 ; schoolmaster at Monymusk, 233 ; marriage, 234 ; settles at Longside, 234 ; apprehension and imprisonment, 237 ; works of, 242 ; death, 244.
Stone circles, purpose of, 22.

Turriff, "devils" of, 153.

Vitrified forts, purpose of, 20.

Wesley, John, visit to Aberdeen. 247, 249.
Whitburn, Anti-burgher Divinity Hall at, 290.
Wingate, Ninian, of Linlithgow, 88.
Witchcraft, suppression of, 192.

www.ingramcontent.com/pod-product-compliance
Lightning Source LLC
Chambersburg PA
CBHW031432230426
43668CB00007B/507